CW00482165

MODERN HUMANITIES RESEARCH
NEW TRANSLATION
VOLUME 11

GEORG KAISER
*AFTER EXPRESSIONISM*
*FIVE PLAYS*

TRANSLATED BY
FRED BRIDGHAM

# Georg Kaiser

## *After Expressionism*
## *Five Plays*

*Translated by*
Fred Bridgham

Modern Humanities Research Association
2016

*Published by*

*The Modern Humanities Research Association,*
*Salisbury House*
*Station Road*
*Cambridge CB1 2LA*
*United Kingdom*

*First published 2016*

*ISBN 978-1-78188-266-5*

*www.translations.mhra.org.uk*

# CONTENTS

# INTRODUCTION

Expressionist theatre rose to the challenge of a tumultuous decade, spanning the years of the Great War and its aftermath of humiliating defeat, failed revolution, crippling reparations, and ruinous hyperinflation (felt not least by the theatre-going middle classes). By the early years of the Weimar Republic, the radical innovations of this essentially German version of modernism had begun to pall. No later than 1925, after currency reform and a return to relative if still hectic normality, it had had its day. Audiences, and consequently theatres, turned away from its harrowing projections towards lighter, more escapist entertainment, above all 'boulevard' theatre and revues. An astonishing 900 or more new comedies were staged during the 'Golden Twenties' (a term more aptly applied to the short-lived period of stability 1925–28). For Alfred Kerr, breathing a sigh of relief — 'sic transit gloria expressionismi' —, it was the lusty naturalism of *Der fröhliche Weinberg* (*The Grapes of Mirth*, 1925) that marked the end of an era, while Berlin's other leading (and often more perceptive) critic, Herbert Ihering, agreed that Carl Zuckmayer's bucolic *Volksstück* had 'blown Expressionism off the stage in a gale of laughter'. In fact, another comedy, *Kolportage* (*Pulp Fiction*), had been the great hit of the previous season. Its author, Georg Kaiser (1878–1945), was Kerr's particular *bête noire*, but also clearly a man for all seasons, and *Kolportage*, as Kerr later conceded, 'his most entertaining play'. It was a sensational come-back for an author who had dominated the German stage between 1917 and 1920 with some half-dozen plays epitomizing Expressionist theatre. (A further dozen, mainly reworkings of earlier efforts, were also premièred in these years, though almost all fell flat.) To read the reviews today is to understand the depth of resistance to Expressionism, perhaps specifically to Kaiser, and calls for a backward glance.

### Kaiser 'at the Heart of Expressionist Theatre'[1]

Audiences had been alternately gripped and perplexed, sometimes exhilarated though increasingly exasperated, by the utopian visions and frenzied nightmares of the new style. Horrors that might have caused the primal scream in Edvard Munch's iconic painting vied with enactments of regeneration: the birth of the

---

[1] Thus John Willett in his superb account of *The Theatre of the Weimar Republic* (New York/ London: Holmes & Meier, 1988, p. 91), though he does not cover the Kaiser plays translated in the present volume. I am especially indebted to Peter Tyson's invaluable compilation, *The Reception of Georg Kaiser (1915–1945), Texts and Analysis* (2 vols, New York: Peter Lang, 1984).

'New Man', and the 'New Woman' too, typically demanding sacrifice in the service of Humanity at large. The episodic plots of these 'station-dramas' — like their immediate precursor, the autobiographical trilogy *To Damascus* of August Strindberg, whose plays enjoyed enormous popularity in Germany around 1913–16 — mirror the Stations of the Cross, often aptly, sometimes outrageously. Their feverish tempo, their exclamatory diction — an over-abbreviated, staccato *Telegrammstil* or 'telegraphese', relieved, or exacerbated, by ecstatic monologues — and their abandonment of psychological character development for stylized types ('the father' pitted against 'the son', the leader against the masses) or mere automata (soldiers or workers) required a depersonalized, puppet-like way of acting. This was in itself a sacrifice which many actors (veering between naturalism and rant, to the detriment of stylistic coherence) were reluctant, or unable, to make.

Kaiser's overnight success, *Die Bürger von Calais* (*The Burghers of Calais*), turns on the readiness of six volunteers to sacrifice themselves in order to save Calais during the Hundred Years' War, but whose lives are subsequently spared by the English king. Of understandably little appeal to German patriotic sentiment when published in 1914, the play's pacifist message on its 1917 première in Frankfurt am Main chimed powerfully with the war-weariness of a country growing sceptical of further military resistance. It certainly produced a New Man as protagonist, but his suicide, undertaken to purify the sacrificial resolve of the others and an undoubted *coup de théâtre*, still struck some as an unnecessarily abstruse complication after the clear-cut exposition for which Kaiser was famous. Indeed, recognition of Kaiser's mastery of structure and theatrical technique in general would be increasingly offset in these years by such critical comments as 'contrived', 'coldly over-intellectual', 'verbose', even 'obscure'. In 1919, it flopped in Berlin, when Ihering was reminded of *Parsifal*, its ponderous seriousness depriving it of the essential tempo which 'alone'[!] made Kaiser's plays palatable. In other words — and despite its enduring, soon even international, reputation — it was not Expressionistic enough.

The same cannot be said of *Von morgens bis mitternachts* (*From Morn to Midnight*), Kaiser's Expressionist masterpiece, written in 1912 though it too was first staged only in 1917, in Munich, subsequently providing a star role for Max Pallenberg in Vienna and Berlin and becoming a classic of Expressionist film with Ernst Deutsch. Its premise is one of the more intelligible, and for the Expressionist generation influential, tenets of Fichte's philosophy. Much simplified, this proposes that only under the impact of some blow or stimulus from without ('Anstoss') is the self awakened to a life of action ('Aufbruch') in accordance with man's *raison d'être*: 'Handeln! Handeln! Das ist es, wozu wir da sind' ('Action! Action! We are here to *do* things'). Kaiser's protagonist, a bank clerk, functions as a mere automaton until sparked into life on misunderstanding an exotic lady customer's touch as an erotic invitation, absconds with 60,000 marks in an attempt to buy 'fulfillment'. Instantly transformed from speechless drudge into hyper-articulate New Man, he nevertheless experiences only disillusionment in a breathless sequence of proto-cinematic scenes, notably a biting satire on the philistinism of his own family (a step down from the 'heroic life of the bourgeoisie' unmasked by Carl Sternheim's pioneering subversive comedies); a six-day bicycle race in which the crowd's soaring communal ecstasy at the ever higher prizes he offers reverts to conventional servility on the appearance of royalty; the exposure of sexual allure as a grotesque sham (if only he had met Wedekind's Lulu!); and the power of scattered banknotes to pervert a Salvation Army confessional into a frenzy of greed, opening his eyes to the futility of his quest. His diurnal progression, ending in Judas-like betrayal, suicide, and a whispered 'Ecce Homo', echoes medieval mystery and passion plays, but the effect on respectable though impoverished audiences, averse to wartime profiteering and the threat of financial anarchy, was rather one of blasphemous provocation. It cannot have helped Kaiser's reputation when performances in 1920/21 coincided with his imprisonment for embezzlement — he had pawned the contents of a rented flat on the not unreasonable assumption of future earnings as Germany's most performed dramatist. He declared his sentence a 'national misfortune', but might have avoided accusations of arrogance if, by way of vindication, he had simply declared, like Oscar Wilde, 'nothing but my genius'.

These two plays found some favour in the provinces but not in Berlin, where whistling and jangling of key-rings often accompanied Kaiser performances, until the central play of the *Gas* trilogy at the populist Volksbühne in 1919 captivated an audience currently living through its own (abortive) revolutionary moment and potential for change. The right play at the right time in the right house, *Gas* evoked recent memories of poison-gas production and subsequent strikes in German armaments' factories; it also anticipates and perhaps inspired Fritz Lang's futuristic film *Metropolis*. But the syndicalist experiment of the New Man millionaire-proprietor, his proposal for agricultural collectivism to replace technology after a warning explosion, is defeated by the workers' conditioning to mechanized monotony, capitalist pressure, the promise of power and the profit motive. The production of gas must continue, its explosive potential vividly realized in the nihilistic, apocalyptic ending of *Gas II*. A more topically all-embracing symbol than any Doll's House or Wild Duck, the gas of the title is the monopolistic, hence indispensible, driving force of the technological age. (For 'gas', post-Hiroshima, read 'atomic power', as in Piscator's 1958 update.) The striking sights and sounds of Expressionistic stage effects, here notably the novelty of colour symbolism, match the rising linguistic tempo of explosive abstract nouns without articles and impersonal infinitive verb-forms.

Several commentators also noted a similarity between the deadening effect of mechanistic mass production and that of Kaiser's own productions. In this — it might be thought, appropriate — correspondence of form and content, what was missing was a sense that genuine passions were involved, real flesh and blood. The severest critics suggested that Kaiser's own prolific output was opportunistic rather than a sincere commitment to change the world for the better. 'The most astonishing virtuoso of European drama' to some, and by common consent a master of the techniques of dramatic construction and dialogue, he is also repeatedly accused of cold aloofness, of simply playing off grandiose abstract ideas against one another, 'thought experiments' or 'mind games' which ultimately lack real depth and nuance for want of psychologically interesting characters who might breathe life into them. His form of Expressionism is relatively moderate when set against the more obviously felt passions and frequent grotesqueries of a Barlach or a Kokoschka, but equally, the alienation effect it had on audiences, unlike that of his respectful and admiring younger colleague Bertolt Brecht, was not necessarily intended.

### Pulp Fiction

Kaiser's very name may have sounded ominous in England, but he was the first German playwright to be accepted there after the War. While audiences were catching up on the latest offerings from the Continent (*From Morn to Midnight* was staged in 1920 by the Incorporated Stage Society London, *Gas I* in 1923 by the Birmingham Repertory Theatre), their author himself had moved on, picking up perhaps on an isolated prophetic response to his Expressionist period: if only Kaiser would try comedy, for here was a born comic writer. Indeed, several of his early plays satirically inverted and undermined heroic subjects (Judith and Holofernes, Tristan, Socrates) to comic effect, such Shavian de-idealising being often sexually charged, and as often on that score — as also for political, religious or moral reasons — subject to localized censorship. So a title explicitly promising mockery of some earlier or contemporary literary phenomenon was already intriguing. *Kolportage* is a term once used for the hawking of religious tracts (French/English: colportage), but which now signified, unambiguously, 'literary trash'. The immediately recognizable target of Kaiser's parody was Hedwig Courths-Mahler (1867–1950), erstwhile bible-reader herself (like Miss Grove in Kaiser's play), now *grande dame* of the sentimental *kitsch* market and author of some thirteen novels in 1924 alone (material for the burgeoning 'dream factory' of German film), her Berlin salon frequented by actors and other prominent figures, if not the literary avant-garde.

At the joint 1924 première of *Kolportage* in Frankfurt and Berlin, both directors understood the crucial importance of being earnest when playing parody — an art which Wilde's masterpiece was simultaneously demonstrating to German audiences under the title *Bunbury*. Kaiser's foundling, as the Prelude to *Kolportage* graphically dramatizes, is not left in a handbag but snatched from a pram, some twenty years before the main action begins. What ensues, however, can be — and was — enjoyed by many (like the 'groundlings' of Shakespeare's day) simply for its familiar ingredients: a wronged heiress and her revenge, a mistaken kidnapping, class conflict, inheritance intrigue, a suspenseful love interest, and a happy end. The beggar-woman's abducted son, now an aristocrat seemingly to the manor (and the manner) born, has also the makings of an up-to-date New Man when the younger generation finally escape a moribund social order for the land of opportunity — America. To the more sophisticated, the Scandinavian setting will have echoed Strindberg's attacks on the hypocrisy and corruption of the Swedish elite; and the heroine's wager — that environment trumps heredity — will have called to mind Naturalism's great and enduring debate in the tragi-comedies of Hauptmann or Sudermann's entertaining melodramas. And when they read (or saw projected) the play's motto: 'To promote child welfare and the contemporary theatre', watched the progression 'yesterday a ragamuffin — today a count — tomorrow an American', and heard proclaimed its concluding moral 'Just give us enough to eat and pamper us a bit — that's my recipe for paradise', seasoned theatre-goers will have appreciated Kaiser's dry take on theatre's new competitor, the silent cinema with its moralizing plots and banal interpolated commentaries. In fact, *Kolportage* was rapidly filmed, and would be again in 1935, as a talkie entitled *Familienparade* starring Curt Jürgens, but without acknowledgement of Kaiser, whose work had been banned in 1933.

The play was revived in a major new production, for Max Reinhardt's elegant new 'Komödie' theatre on Berlin's Kurfürstendamm in 1929. This time, the director went for all-out parody, underlined by Walter Goehr's catchy pastiche of 'The Carnival of Venice', *Il Trovatore* (when the babies are swapped), and military marches (at each mention of the foundling's commission in the King's Dragoons), performed by Sid Kay's Fellows jazz band. But hilarious as the production was adjudged to be, the constant use of film projections, the wittily allusive movable props, and the actors' 'a parte' asides to the audience were felt to over-egg the pudding — indeed, this 'Kaiser-Schmarrn' (in Austria, a Kaiserschmarrn is a sugared, cut-up pancake, while ein Schmarrn is simply tosh) should have been served up straight as the light and fluffy confection Kaiser intended. The actress in the Lady Bracknell role of Hereditary Countess was thought especially at fault, compared with her predecessors in the part, the great Adele Sandrock (known for her 'formidable dragon' characterizations, à la Edith Evans, in over 100 films), and Ilka Grüning (anticipating her American film career as the refugee wife of Ludwig Stossel in *Casablanca*: 'Liebchen, what watch?', 'Ten watch', 'Such watch?'). The point was well, if inadvertently, made by one provincial theatre director after seeing this production, who misguidedly cabled home — 'Ab morgen *Kolportage* ironisch spielen', 'Play *Kolportage* ironically from now on'.

## One Day in October

After this sparkling comedy, *Oktobertag* (*One Day in October*) was another huge success for Germany's now most-staged dramatist and an emerging golden generation of actors: first in Hamburg, directed by and starring Gustav Gründgens, then, in quick succession, Dresden, Berlin (at Max Reinhardt's Kammerspiele, with Albert Steinrück and Oskar Homolka), Düsseldorf, Munich, Gelsenkirchen and Frankfurt/M. In the same year, a New York production at the Forty-Ninth Street Theatre was entitled *The Phantom Lover*, apparently with Kaiser's approval, though *Transfigured Night* might have conveyed less melodramatically the triumph of Romantic 'inwardness' over sordid reality (in Dehmel's poem and Schönberg's setting, *Verklärte Nacht*, the lover nobly accepts another man's child). It also calls to mind the imaginative world of Heinrich von Kleist which exercised a lifelong hold on Kaiser, here Käthchen von Heilbronn's dream of her knight in shining armour, or the nocturnal substitution of maid for mistress and resultant birth in *Der Zweikampf*, or, perhaps most closely of all, the redeemed innocence of the Marquise von O....

The birth of a child is one of Kaiser's recurrent motifs, a natural if rather unexpected symbol at the end of *Gas I*, for instance, when the hoped-for New Man fails to materialize and the despairing protagonist's daughter vows 'I will bear him!' Subsequently (see especially *Agnete* below), this token of rejuvenation is not merely superimposed, but becomes an integral part of the plot. The natural father of the child in *Oktobertag* is a butcher's boy, and it is the world of the flesh in both senses which propels him from reluctant blackmailer (aspiring to a shop of his own), to aggrieved underdog (thwarted of his hush money), to jealous, avenging fury (in remembrance of his unforgettable night of passion). His rival's aloof military bearing and indignant rejection of alleged paternity undergoes a parallel transformation, resulting in a mystical, spiritual union and climactic avowal "I am the father of the child" — a dramatic *coup*, reviews confirm, as far removed from 'Kolportage' as from any melodramatic, Victorian curtain-call. The catalyst of these two intersecting trajectories maintains her serene (if almost literally 'blind') conviction that the lieutenant is the father of her child, recalling the 'encounters' about which he has remained in the dark: jeweller's shop = engagement ring; mass = marriage ceremony; opera = wedding banquet — on leaving which his accidental touch on her bare arm (the familiar 'Anstoss') is taken to seal a nocturnal rendezvous and consummation of the marriage (also in the dark — hence the mistaken identity). With its French setting, unity of time, place and action, small cast and female protagonist, *Oktobertag* is one of several such *pièces de chambre*, a love story (as Kaiser called it) in which heroic adherence to a higher 'inner reality' prevails over all worldly considerations. Each twist and turn of the dialogue gives rise to ever-heightened tension. Besides some isolated moral objections in the provinces, only the Nazi *Völkischer Beobachter*, true to form, wondered whether the lieutenant should not have accepted the blackmailer's pay-off rather than risk fifteen years' hard labour — the consequence of the play's drastic resolution being an understandable omission, however, given Kaiser's experience of incarceration.

### Clairvoyance

Much lighter fare, devoid of social critique while latching on to contemporary interest in the unconscious and an attendant fascination with the occult, is *Hellseherei* (*Clairvoyance*). This features the New Woman as vamp, from whose clutches Vera, the loving wife — by the end no longer quite so innocent — rescues her potentially wayward husband. 'He is the temple I pray in. The noisy street outside — it mustn't be allowed to intrude with its filth.' Kaiser's protagonists habitually seek refuge in an idealistic private world, but in this amiable social comedy we merely smile as the plot unfolds: Victor as would-be Master Builder tempted by the architectural-cum-erotic designs of his client, while playing Pygmalion as his wife's dress-designer; Vera's visit to a clairvoyant who finds her a psychic medium of rare ability, capable of locating her lost ring, but also distressed to visualise Victor's impending seduction (no blithe spirit, she); her suppression of the one — the ring must remain lost — lest the other — her husband's infidelity — be true; and after each logically compelling stage of the ensuing confusion, the (cinematic) happy end. Yet no single director and few if any of the actors involved in the seven simultaneous productions seem to have found the appropriate tone. The glamorous Art Deco setting is certainly up-to-date: an architect's fashionable home, its lack of 'seating arrangements' a standing joke; his aesthetic appreciation of fast cars, fast women and *haute couture* more highly developed than his morality; the fascination of the domestic triangle and witty repartee as topical as any would-be sophisticate in a provincial audience could wish. A public convenience — one recurring landmark in the tracing of the ring — elicited laughter as predictably as the erotic *frisson* when Vera outstrips her rival. And since clairvoyance itself was all the rage, *Hellseherei* could surely be played from start to finish as pure 'Kolportage', to the same acclaim that at least some première audiences registered.

But what if the clairvoyant is not a charlatan? Kaiser's probable model, one Erik Jan Hanussen, besides starring in revue at Berlin's Scala, could also boast of forensic success assisting the police[2] — a theme taken up in the *Dr Mabuse* films. The Nietzschean idea that strong minds might control more susceptible ones already obsessed Strindberg. True, Sneederhan's appearance is clearly caricature — he is generally played by the star actor like some fantastical figure out of E.T.A. Hoffmann, with the jerky movements of a sinister Caligari (long

---

[2] Ernst Schürer, *Georg Kaiser* (New York: Twayne, 1971, pp. 145, 237, n.20).

shabby coat and boots, lace gloves, full beard, glinting spectacles — all indeed prescribed by Kaiser). As one perceptive critic observed, clairvoyants are nowadays chauffeured, together with their secretaries, to the best hotels, and are expert manipulators of psychology, especially female psychology, not fanatical blackmailers defending their black art. But in spite of such Gothic exaggeration — a commonplace in contemporary film — Kaiser drew his character as at least in part a plausible visionary, and one 'willing to sacrifice himself … to his god' in defence of his 'new science … the radiant beginnings of a new dawn'. His counterpart, a *femme fatale* expert in her own black art of seduction, initially dismisses his 'quackery' as 'mumbo-jumbo … that should be banned', but comes to acknowledge him as her master. Above all, he is ultimately vindicated, and — puzzlingly for some, though he admits to no more than a fifty per cent success rate — without any 'rational' explanation. Clairvoyance, then, might best be understood here as a metaphor for insight into that higher reality which transcends the world of appearances — the idealistic side of Kaiser which balances, and perhaps outweighs, his predisposition to mockery and parody. In Sneederhan's words: 'You think the dark powers do not exist? They are life itself — what we call life is their shadowy reflection.'

After the Great War, many of the bereaved resorted to occult experiments in the hope of communicating with the dead. The legitimacy of such 'commerce' naturally divided opinion, perhaps especially when given comic treatment. With his ultra-modern 'sophistication' and reputation for witty if brittle comedies, Noël Coward invites comparison with Kaiser. Coward's output in the inter-war years was as uneven as Kaiser's, bringing him both notoriety with *The Vortex* (1924) and *Design for Living* (1932), and enduring fame with *Hay Fever* (1925) and *Private Lives* (1930), until he, too, turned to the occult in *Blithe Spirit* (1941), a wartime entertainment which, as pure comedy, demanded and received the full suspension of disbelief that seems to have eluded Kaiser. As in *Hellseherei*, a flamboyant psychic steals the show. Madame Arcati is a true believer, who, like Sneederhan, urges participants in her séance to 'put their backs' into it, and whose power to produce ghosts — adding a dead ex-wife to the current model in a strikingly novel version of the *ménage à trois* — is memorably vindicated. Kaiser's charming play also awaits resurrection and vindication.

### Agnete

In 1933 Kaiser rejected an offer to work for the Ministry of Propaganda, and after collaborating with Kurt Weill on *Der Silbersee* was accused of 'Kultur-bolschewismus'. The ensuing scandal provided the Nazis with a pretext for banning performances of his work, leading to his expulsion from the Prussian Academy of the Arts and the burning of his books. Until 1938, he remained in 'internal exile', though at the height of his powers.

*Agnete* was written in 1935. As in *Oktobertag*, a unio mystica is celebrated — choir, candles, marriage, wedding feast, wedding night, consummation — all experienced this time by a delirious soldier in a remote field hospital. The other celebrant is his dead fiancée's sister, who has made this life-saving mission to soften the blow, and who willingly accepts the consequences of mistaken identity. Heinrich's post-war return from Russian captivity threatens to destroy the tranquil family refuge Agnete has provided for her child (an uncanny anticipation of the fate of so many soldiers returning home from Russia after 1945, often long after, and of the 'Heimkehrer' literature that common dilemma inspired). Each character struggles with the conflicting claims of compassion and truth, concealment and exposure. Though seemingly incompatible, their motives are compelling and the stakes very high, their individual, almost Wagnerian, recapitulations of Agnete's labour of love shifting the focus of the moral dilemma from Agnete herself, to her husband Stefan, to Stefan's protective mother, to his friend Heinrich — the father of her child. Each turn of the screw inexorably leads to an *Oedipus*-like unveiling, until the moment Agnete and Heinrich declare themselves, and beyond that to a searing denouement and resolution of heroic self-sacrifice. The language is at times heightened, visionary, ecstatic, culminating in Agnete's epiphany: 'I have given birth to this child, this son!' Here it feels entirely appropriate, as does the choice of this play, its first performance, by the Nationaltheater in Mannheim, to mark the birth of the Federal Republic of Germany in 1949.

*Agnete* provided Kaiser with an ideal vehicle to convey his recurrent themes and their dramatic realisation to maximum effect, again with a minimal cast and adherence to the 'three unities'. Once more, a woman bears another man's child in mysterious circumstances, and is forgiven. Here, the child's presence restores both men to Life from present sterility, confusion and aimlessness. Elements which elsewhere belong to 'Kolportage' — a projected kidnapping of the child, a duel on the town ramparts since 'only a sword could cut the knot', escape to an exotic island (as in *Oktobertag*, or Kaiser's extraordinary 1932 novel, *Es ist genug*) — are seamlessly incorporated before being rejected, without affecting the tone of tense anxiety as we wait for the truth to out. The figure of Stefan, the intellectual, is certainly in part a self-portrait of Kaiser himself, who shared with Shelley an unwavering belief in the *Dichter* as 'unacknowledged legislator of the world'.

### The Gordian Egg

When prohibition of his work became financially as well as morally intolerable, Kaiser chose Swiss exile in 1938, since Austria was no longer an option after the *Anschluss*. Though he had no very high regard for Swiss theatrical life, the Zurich Schauspielhaus was prepared to stage two of his new plays, both bitterly antiwar — *Der Soldat Tanaka* and *Zweimal Amphitryon*. (Over the next decade it also launched Brecht's *Mother Courage, Galileo, The Good Woman of Sezuan* and *Puntila*). Of Kaiser's last two comedies, one, *Klawitter*, written in 1940 though, like *Agnete*, first staged only in 1949, is more a tragi-comedy, full of bitter recrimination at the Nazi appropriation of culture. A successful dramatist, Ernst Hoff, dispossessed of the serious hope of further performance his name suggests, is driven to submit a new play under a randomly chosen assumed name, Klawitter, and when the play is a hit, to find through the directory a real Klawitter to act as author. This turns out to be a wretched cinema projectionist, and the film rights promise such wealth that he need write no more. But the unscrupulous Klawitter is no better than his new Nazi patron, and the impoverished Hoff, driven to protest openly, faces not only loss of identity, but of life itself. 'After *Klawitter*', Kaiser wrote, 'which satisfies me technically and morally more than any of my other plays, I shall write no more'.[3]

The other, altogether lighter, comedy, *Das gordische Ei*, is very much a companion piece. An affectionate — and, it would seem, wryly self-critical — homage to his own trade, a 'pure' comedy elevated above mere politics.[4] The curtains part as the great author, Abel Oberon, surreptitiously enters his own darkened house though the French windows. Let the play commence! But what we see is a play about a play, one that Oberon has not written, though his famous name as king of theatrical fairyland has ensured that *The Gordian Egg* has been an unprecedented success. Banished from London's social whirl to produce the hit which might recoup his publisher's outlay, he has not only experienced writer's block, but, like his Biblical namesake, had his very identity usurped.

The mystery slowly unravels: the play is the collaborative work of two mere students, who when tracked down to their garret defend their one-off *jeu d'esprit*, and their totally unmercenary motives in writing it, against contemporary authors, not least Oberon himself: 'Naturally we had noticed that you weren't too particular any more about what you were offering the public'. Since Oberon, in his weaker moments, fears his own work is indeed stale and passé; since he admits to being 'in awe of my own name sometimes ... merely the guardian of the name, to protect it from abuse'; and since, after all, the play's the thing — hailed by his unwitting publisher as the crowning achievement of his now complete *Collected Works* — why not go along with the sham, and play host to this theatrical

---

3 See Brian Kenworthy, *Georg Kaiser* (Oxford: Basil Blackwell, 1957, p. 171). In fact, there were seven more plays still to come.

4 Walther Huder suggests in a programme note to the Marburg première of *Das gordische Ei* on 21.11.1958 that Kaiser may have broken off finishing it — the last few scenes were completed by another hand (itself an ironic, if fortuitous, reflection of the plot) — in favour of *Klawitter's* explicit political ramifications. Huder later argued that Kaiser had certainly completed the play, though some pages were, and are, still missing — Georg Kaiser, *Werke*, Vol. VI, ed. by W. Huder (Frankfurt/M: Ullstein/Propyläen, 1972, p. 841).

'cuckoo's egg'? That would solve the conflict of interest at a stroke — just as Alexander cut the Gordian knot — though at the expense of the truth.

This extreme form of unravelling the knot, its *dénouement*, in fact occurs as an image in all five of these plays. At the climax of *Kolportage*, 'all will be revealed, one way or the other — whether the Gordian knot turns into a nosegay or a noose!' In *Oktobertag*, the lovers are warned they will always be yoked together with their blackmailer 'unless you cut loose' by paying hush-money, though it is the lieutenant's sword which more literally cuts through the problem. Turned on its head, no such uncompromising resolution is available to the would-be adulterers in *Hellseherei*: 'Like the Gordian knot that is cut through in the legend? Those times are past. No such flamboyance allowed these days'; instead, as befits comedy, the dragon lady is dispatched by cunning rather than force. Nor is it true that 'only a sword could cut the knot' in *Agnete*, since a duel for the child is not how the rivalry is finally resolved.

And so, our final play's title also incorporates an alternative approach — a compromise, as befits both comedy and its collaborative origins. Just as Columbus solved the problem of making an egg stand upright by tapping one end rather than slicing it through, so logic and rational self-interest, we suspect, shall override severance of the play from its putative author, and the cuckoo's egg, already successfully hatched, shall continue to flourish. In one review, even Oberon's fiercest critic has ostensibly had a change of heart (as had Alfred Kerr over *Kolportage*) and celebrated 'the light touch … the gaiety which *The Gordian Egg* radiates … sunshine in the soul, a heart-warming affirmation of life'. It is a world — a plot — and players — which Wodehouse would have recognised. The happy end of two young couples united can safely be left to the imagination.

# Pulp Fiction

## (*Kolportage*, 1924)

### Comedy with a prologue and three acts which take place twenty years later

Written in support of child welfare and
the contemporary theatre

# CHARACTERS

Count James Stjernenhö
Karin, formerly Countess Stjernenhö, née Bratt
Erik, their son
Hereditary Countess Stjernenhö
Miss Grove, her companion
Baron Barrenkrona
Alice, his daughter
Knut Bratt
Mrs Appeblom
Acke, her son
Lindström
Johannson, porter
Footman

# PROLOGUE

*Extremely elegant boudoir, bright sunlight illuminating the cloud-patterned, cream-coloured roller blinds on the rear windows. One door to left, two doors to right.*
*Knut Bratt sitting in an armchair, left. He is a substantial figure, extravagantly dressed, suggestive of an American millionaire on his travels.*
*Karin, leaning against the fireplace on the right, soignée in a flowing gossamer-silk gown.*

KNUT BRATT *shaking his head.*   Pure fiction, my dear niece, pure fiction!

KARIN   It sounds like some trashy novel about the count and the commoner, with me as the main character standing before you, tearfully lamenting her fate.

KNUT BRATT   Tell me more. *Taking out his pipe.* May I?

KARIN   Oh, how remiss of me. Please do. There's some punch too.

KNUT BRATT   Splendid.

KARIN   I'm in a muddle about what happened. It was all too much, overwhelming! — Just picture it: a girl like me — secure, happy upbringing — indulged and idolized by a loving father, the apple of his eye — the sole object of all his goodness and affection after Mama's death.

KNUT BRATT *sighing.*   Poor Anne! She left him much too soon.

KARIN   How spoilt I was from the day I was born! Reared in a grand chateau — servants galore dancing to my every whim — every conceivable luxury taken for granted — limousine trips to the Riviera or Paris as often as other people go for a walk in the woods —

KNUT BRATT   He lost no time in letting you see the world.

KARIN   No sacrifice was too great for him, if it made me happy. It was like a fairy-tale, and just as every proper fairy-tale has to have its Prince Charming, so

Papa conjured one up for me, and I duly became engaged, here, and not long after, in an ivy-clad castle, Countess Stjernenhö!

KNUT BRATT   Your noble husband overlooked your lack of noble birth and saw the charms of youth!

KARIN   That's where you're wrong, Uncle! Papa's money made the marriage socially acceptable. Without the immense wealth that Papa had accumulated from his timber business, the noble eyes of the Count would never have deigned to look on me. The huge fortune to which I would one day be the sole heir lured his lordship, who happened to be in dire financial straits. The marriage, he hoped, would get him out of the red and placate his creditors, who were after him like hounds after a fox. And I was blind, didn't see what he was after.

KNUT BRATT   You've suffered many cruel disappointments.

KARIN   The fairy-tale was short-lived and I was in for a rude awakening. Papa's death — a bolt from the blue — threw a garish light on the true situation, as even I could finally see all too clearly.

KNUT BRATT   Maybe he should have been more careful in his choice of husband for you.

KARIN   I don't blame Papa at all. It is perfectly understandable and only too human to be dazzled by the lustre of linking up with the noble house of Stjernenhö — after all, they are descended from Gustav Vasa and rank among the top families in Sweden. They provide the king with his counsellors. Papa worked his way up from the humblest beginnings and in his own eyes always remained plain Lars Bratt from Malmö, who had once stoked the stove and wiped the dust from the desks in the log cabin that was his office.

KNUT BRATT   Yes — my brother and I once didn't have a penny to our name.

KARIN   When the news came through that Papa had been killed in the far north by a tree-trunk — you know he took charge himself of felling every tree he bought — I collapsed on the carpet, unconscious — but as I fell — and my eyes filled with tears, and the pattern on the carpet became blurred — I saw something — something so terrible that the memory of it is still like a whiplash: —— my husband was laughing!

KNUT BRATT   Lars died like a hero on the battlefield — in the midst of the trees he had bought.

KARIN   I was in a fever for weeks. One morning — the first time I felt my strength beginning to return, though I still had to take things very easy — the room was full of people. Papa's last will and testament was read out: everything had been left to our little Erik as sole heir. No laughter from the Count this time! — He cursed — I could hear it distinctly. Even the lawyer looked up. — That showed what kind of man I had married, the father of my child! The mask was off, and his true character was borne out in what followed — beyond the wildest imaginings of some penny dreadful!

KNUT BRATT   —— And when will Erik come into his vast inheritance?

KARIN   At the end of his twenty-first year — so, in twenty years' time. The interest has to be spent on his education — and the interest alone from Papa's fortune amounts to — well, enough ten times over to provide in addition for a Count weighed down with debts.

KNUT BRATT   What are you getting at?

KARIN   Listen, I'll tell what happened. My marriage now became a living hell. I could not forget the laughter, and the curse — the castle seemed to echo nothing but the blasphemies the Count had hurled after my father in his grave — every eruption of his rage at having been excluded from the inheritance became more and more unbridled, and only added to my repugnance for him — he hurled it in my face that he had only sold himself for my money — I bore it all for Erik's sake — in my anguish I found consolation in my child, and I vowed to suffer and endure it — until ——

KNUT BRATT   What happened?

KARIN   — until I had clear, tangible proof of his infidelity. At that point I took Erik one night and decamped from Stjernenhö Castle — and initiated divorce proceedings.

KNUT BRATT   —— And how did the case turn out?

KARIN   The court granted the decree — I kept the child, the Count's claim was rejected. I returned to Papa's chateau with Erik and set up home again here as before. That's the story of my marriage, which, from the outset, was a sensation without precedent in Sweden —

KNUT BRATT *raising his punchglass.*   — and is now a closed chapter in your young life.

KARIN  Wrong again, Uncle! Now begins the martyrdom of a mother unparalleled anywhere in the world. Don't forget Erik's whereabouts — here, as heir to an enormous fortune — and over there the Count, his father, up to his eyes in debt. It was inevitable there would be a struggle for the child — given what we now know of the Count — and that's what has happened.

KNUT BRATT  He popped up again?

KARIN  He sent people to negotiate. Peacefully at first — by powers of persuasion. I stood firm — and again later, when the language became more threatening. Finally they quite openly mounted a systematic smear campaign against me to the effect that I wasn't worthy to bring up a child of such noble birth.

KNUT BRATT  Whoops!

KARIN  They even attacked Papa after he was dead. Allegedly not all the business he transacted was above-board — witnesses were bribed to give false testimony — and finally all these fabrications were presented as evidence that the daughter of a racketeer should not have custody of the son of a Count.

KNUT BRATT  What a bunch of hypocrites! Despising poor Lars just because he grafted away all his life —

KARIN  Don't get worked up — not yet!

KNUT BRATT  What was the court's ruling?

KARIN  It awarded me custody a second time.

KNUT BRATT  There is justice after all!

KARIN  But it couldn't protect the child.

KNUT BRATT  Against what?

KARIN  Abduction. One day the child was seized from its pram — and if its nanny hadn't shouted like mad and alerted the passers-by to what was happening — that would have been the last I'd seen of Erik: for once the Count had him in the castle, it would have been beyond any means in my power to get him back.

KNUT BRATT   I would have crossed the ocean to come to your help —

KARIN   I wouldn't have summoned you and you couldn't have changed my mind. I would have resigned myself to my fate — for Erik's sake: for when parents fight, it's the child that suffers most — it's condemned to instability from the start and never knows a sense of security again.

KNUT BRATT   Such magnanimity!

KARIN *drawing herself up.*   *If* the abduction had been successful. But as it hasn't been yet, I'll go on defending myself against my enemies like a tigress.

KNUT BRATT   Do you think the villains will have another shot at it?

KARIN   At any moment. The Count needs Erik as a guarantor for his borrowing — and not to become the laughing stock of the Stjernenhös — they would want him expelled from the family if his mésalliance with a timber princess didn't at least bring him in a fortune. Everything depends on Erik — Erik is the sole object of his pursuit — and he won't rest until he's achieved his goal.

KNUT BRATT   —— And how are you protecting yourself against this threat of abduction?

KARIN   How can I protect myself? By surrounding myself with detectives?

KNUT BRATT   You wouldn't do that?

KARIN   I'd feel like a prisoner of those protecting me.

KNUT BRATT   Weren't those men hiding among the trees along the driveway your detectives?

KARIN *shocked.*   You saw strangers near the villa?

KNUT BRATT   When you're from the Wild West and as eagle-eyed as I am, I could see at once they were watching me when I drove past. They were even quite open about it, staring right into the car.

KARIN *horrified.*   To see if Erik was in it!

KNUT BRATT *paces up and down — then stops, facing Karin.*   So does life here hold any attraction for you?

KARIN   I'd as soon drown myself — and Erik.

KNUT BRATT   Come with me — across the ocean — to Kansas. What a country! Nothing but forest and more forest, and I'm a timber merchant there like my brother, your papa. It'll seem like home to you. And no Swedish robber baron will lay his hands on Erik — my cowboys will guarantee his safety.

KARIN   No, uncle.

KNUT BRATT   It sounds wilder than it is — Kansas! On my timber ranch life is more tranquil than here in the big city — and when we want we can fit out a nice comfortable white yacht and sail the seven seas, just as I am doing right now in *Butterfly.* No fixed itinerary — not registered in any one harbour — we simply set off — and end up who knows where months later. It was on a whim I landed on your coast — car on board — and off to see my niece, and find her embroiled in a nasty business that only speedy departure overseas can extricate her from — and no risk involved. Come with me. I'll give you half an hour — you'll find all you need on board — and over there a new world spread out at your feet, and Erik's. *Exit rear right.*

KARIN *hand on chin, deep in thought — goes to window — half draws up the blind and looks out. Gradually something absorbs her attention and she reflects.*   Happy mother! Even if you go begging from door to door in rags — you still have your child safe in your arms and are not afraid of someone stealing it. I envy you from the bottom of my heart. You've no idea how dismal it can be behind the gleaming windows of the rich. —— No, Johannsson shouldn't give her any alms — she has a greater fortune wrapped in that bundle of rags than I possess. *She lifts the telephone receiver — is about to phone — then pauses.* —— Now she is thrusting her child at him, begging him, beseeching him — old Johannsson is trembling with pity and sympathy — reaches into his pocket — to give her money for the child's sake —— *Aroused, with altered voice, aloud.* Woman, wretched as you are, you are going to help me and give me in my mansion a gift beyond rubies. *Telephones.* Johannsson — bring the beggar-woman to me. — *She waits — excitedly watching the door.*

*A knock front right.*

KARIN   Come in!

*The old white-haired porter Johannsson opens the door.*

JOHANNSSON   The beggar-woman.

KARIN   Send her in.

JOHANNSSON *turning.*   Please go in.

*The beggar-woman enters: she is young, wretchedly dressed — her bedraggled hair falling over her face; in one arm she carries her child in a dirty bundle of rags.*

KARIN   Thank you, Johannsson.

*Exit Johannsson.*

BEGGAR-WOMAN *looks around in astonishment, smirks admiringly.*

KARIN   Come closer.

BEGGAR-WOMAN *doesn't move.*   Nice — nice.

KARIN   Show me your child.

BEGGAR-WOMAN *as before.*   Nice — nice.

KARIN   Unwrap your child. Here, on the table. It's of the greatest importance for me to see your child. Please be quick.

BEGGAR-WOMAN *runs to the table — puts down her bundle and opens it.*

KARIN *taken aback.*   Naked under the rags?

BEGGAR-WOMAN *half-cunning, half-submissive.*   You give him a shirt.

KARIN *inspects the child closely.*   Blue eyes — blond hair — like all children born in Sweden. Almost a cliché.

BEGGAR-WOMAN   Give him an old shirt.

KARIN *draws herself up.*   He shall have it all: silk shirts — pants — caps — coats — if you so desire.

BEGGAR-WOMAN   Don't I just!

KARIN   We'll see! — Who is the father?

BEGGAR-WOMAN *bursting with indignation.*   That scoundrel — the trickster — drunkard — ruffian — but they've got him again — and they won't let him out so quickly this time!

KARIN *uncertain.*   Where — have they got him?

BEGGAR-WOMAN   Where he belongs — the good-for-nothing — in jail.

KARIN   In —??

BEGGAR-WOMAN   It was the last time we tried to pull a stunt: — I had just got out a couple of weeks earlier —

KARIN   You mean you were serving time too??

BEGGAR-WOMAN   Where it's nice and warm and you get regular meals and are never hungry? You'd be out of your mind not to get wise to that.

KARIN   So you actually try to get yourself arrested so that ——??

BEGGAR-WOMAN *sings.*   A place where, truth to tell, — is as nice as it could be — a nice warm cosy cell — is just the place for me.

KARIN   How shocking! Have you no shame?

BEGGAR-WOMAN   Feel shame and you go hungry — on the fiddle you can grow fat. *Stroking her child.* He'll be the same. Quick on the uptake. A chip off the old block. Born under the open sky — what larks! — *She giggles to herself.*

KARIN   You 've no home for yourself or your child?

BEGGAR-WOMAN   In the summer the open air, in the winter, the nick — ideal lodgings!

KARIN   And what about the child?

BEGGAR-WOMAN   He goes into a home — and if you've ever been in a home, you learn all the tricks. He'll be well-prepared!

KARIN *resolutely.*    Give me your child. I'll place him with a good family — and will take care of you too, if you're agreed.

BEGGAR-WOMAN *astonished.*    Where am I here?

KARIN    You're with a mother who also has a child — one that sleeps in a silk cot. It's not right for your child to grow up as a beggar in rags. I'll see to it your child is taken care of — as if it were my own. — Agreed?

BEGGAR-WOMAN    I certainly am!

KARIN    And you won't take fright when you see the child being handed over under somewhat — unusual — circumstances?

BEGGAR-WOMAN    However — wherever — once I'm rid of the little bundle, I won't be complaining.

KARIN    Wait here. *Exit left quickly — returns with sponge, scent and baby linen.* Now let's wash the little chap.

BEGGAR-WOMAN    Nice smell!

KARIN    We want him swathed in fragrance.

BEGGAR-WOMAN    Can I try some?

KARIN *gives her the flask.*

BEGGAR-WOMAN *dabs some on — then surreptitiously drinks it.*

KARIN *busy dressing the child.*

BEGGAR-WOMAN    Is that a shirt?

KARIN    Yes, a silk one — monogram this way up — that's right.

BEGGAR-WOMAN    It's like gossamer.

KARIN    The finest there is, light as a feather — as befits a young count.

BEGGAR-WOMAN    Is that what he's going to be?

KARIN   Do you swear absolute silence?

BEGGAR-WOMAN   Not a peep.

KARIN   Your child will be raised by Count Stjernenhö in Stjernenhö Castle. It may be a godsend for him, provided you don't breathe a word.

BEGGAR-WOMAN   I'll leave well alone — with the father and mother he has, he's not going to set the world alight.

KARIN   You can see that?

BEGGAR-WOMAN   Clear as day.

KARIN   If you keep your word, I'll arrange for you to receive a monthly allowance, enough to relieve you from all poverty. *She quickly writes a note.*

BEGGAR-WOMAN *takes it — reads.*   Sweet Jesus!

KARIN   But if you break your word, the bank immediately cuts off the payments and you'll be as poor as before — and the Count will be out for revenge as long as you live.

BEGGAR-WOMAN   I'd sooner die on the spot.

KARIN   In twenty years' time you are to go to Stjernenhö Castle and enquire after your son, who will have come of age. Will you do that?

BEGGAR-WOMAN   If they let me in through the back entrance.

KARIN   I'll take care of that. *Exit left — returns with a pram.*

BEGGAR-WOMAN *claps her hands.*   Let the show begin!

KARIN   And this locket goes around the child's neck. *She unclasps it from her own neck.*

BEGGAR-WOMAN   Twinkling like gold stars.

KARIN *lays the child in the pram.*   Now the dear little chap can sleep on in his silk cot — hushabye baby — how soft it is —— So, now we're ready. *She goes to telephone — telephones.* Johannsson — I need you. *To beggar-woman in surprise.* Why are you shaking your head?

BEGGAR-WOMAN   To think a wretch like me gave birth to something like that!

*Enter Johannsson.*

KARIN   Johannsson, it's the nanny's day off — the weather's nice: take the pram down to the front of the park. Put it next to the railing where it will get the most sun.

JOHANNSSON   Should I stay with the pram?

KARIN   No. The child is fast asleep. You can go back to the window in your lodge.

JOHANNSSON *exit with pram front right.*

BEGGAR-WOMAN   Can I be off?

KARIN   Certainly not — you must stay! *Goes to window — looks out.* There he goes with the pram — along the gravel path — *not* behind the rhododendrons! — right up close to the railing, where it can be seen from outside — Now he's going back to his porter's lodge — now — now — now — Here they come — they're at the railing — one of them is up and over — his hands are in the pram — he's got hold of the child — lifts it out — reaches it over the railing — climbs after it — and they're gone — disappeared over the road and swallowed up in the forest. *Breathes out — turns to beggar-woman.* What are you laughing for?

BEGGAR-WOMAN *splitting her sides.*   Those idiots, ninnies: all that for the brat of a jailbird and his floozy — running like greyhounds as if they had the Emperor of China by the scruff of the neck until they're worn to a frazzle, and no one's chasing them. What suckers!

KARIN   Quiet! — Here's Johannsson.

*Johannsson in the doorway — trembling, out of breath.*

KARIN   What is it, Johannsson?

JOHANNSSON   The pram —— the pram ——

KARIN    Johannsson!

JOHANNSSON    The pram —— the pram ——

KARIN    — is empty?!

JOHANNSSON    Only the pillows left — the child gone — before my very eyes — I was too late getting there — my knees, my knees! — only the pillows left!

KARIN *feigns distress, then draws herself up.*    Abducted before your very eyes — Johannsson!

JOHANNSSON    Before my very eyes!

KARIN    Johannsson, we are not alone — in our own distress we must not forget the needs of others: fetch a loaf from the pantry for this poor woman!

JOHANNSSON *exit left.*

BEGGAR-WOMAN *waving the note.*    I can pay for that now.

KARIN    You wrap your shawl around the loaf and carry it like a child in your arms. Johannsson saw you come with your child, he might be puzzled otherwise.

*Enter Johannson with loaf.*

JOHANNSSON    The police should be informed.

BEGGAR-WOMAN    God forbid —

KARIN *makes her a sign. To Johannsson.*    The woman is right, Johannson. The stronger side has won. I admit defeat. The child must have the father who wants him.

BEGGAR-WOMAN *giggles.*    And how!

KARIN    My nerves can't take any more. I'm leaving for America this very day. In the New World I will learn to forget. You don't need to pack anything. My uncle has all I need on his yacht. Farewell, Johannsson. We will meet again in twenty years!

JOHANNSSON *kisses her hand — in a voice choked with tears.* You'll scarcely see me again then.

KARIN In the meantime look after the chateau — and post a letter for me that I will give you at the gate.

JOHANNSSON *exit.*

KARIN Now quickly wrap up the loaf.

BEGGAR-WOMAN At least it doesn't kick and get hungry. A loaf of bread getting hungry — that's a laugh!

KARIN Now trudge out of the house and past the porter's lodge looking as dejected as when you came in.

BEGGAR-WOMAN That'll be hard now — but we've pulled off more shady stunts in the past. Once you've been in the poorhouse —

KARIN That's enough of that. Off you go.

BEGGAR-WOMAN *exit.*

KARIN *at writing desk — writes — reads it through.* Count Stjernenhö! I accept that the child you forcibly abducted today is better off in your castle than in the arms of the mother you snatched it from. Turn it into a worthy member of the society you claim as of right to represent. *She gives a short laugh.* Now the signature — and off to the right address. *She seals the letter — jumps up — flings open the door rear right and calls out.* Uncle! — Uncle! — Nodded off? Wake up! I've got a surprise for you. Come quickly! *Exit left.*

*Knut Bratt enters right — rubs his eyes.*

KARIN *returns, dressed ready to leave, with her child in one arm, her uncle's overcoat in the other.* Here! — we're coming with you — Erik and me. On the *Butterfly* — off to the timber ranch — off to America!

KNUT BRATT *gives a loud cheer.* Prepare yourself, Kansas, in your best bib and tucker for the finest pearl of the Old World. *He puts on his voluminous overcoat — takes a cap from the pocket and puts it on.*

KARIN *And* her child.

KNUT BRATT　Who, as of today, is my sole heir — to a thousand square miles of thousand-year-old primordial forest.

KARIN　All aboard, Uncle — and button your heir up under your coat in case he catches cold and brings a permanent case of Swedish sniffles with him. *She hands over little Erik.*

KNUT BRATT *takes him.*　Do you think I'm afraid of your brigands out there? I'll carry him in front of me like a flowering pot plant.

KARIN　You will not — for I forbid it.

KNUT BRATT　I bow before such implacable, sparkling eyes. *He buttons Erik under his coat and goes to door front right.*

KARIN *into telephone.*　Johannsson — Mr Bratt's car!

# ACT ONE

~

*Large high-ceilinged hall in Stjernenhö Castle. On the walls knightly armour, ancestral portraits. Heavy armchairs. On the right, a staircase to the gallery above running round the hall. Doors right and left. To the rear, a wide French window leads on to the terrace. Beyond, a park with trees throwing shadows — shots can be heard from time to time.*

*From left, a young footman in colourful livery — hesitantly admitting Hereditary Countess Stjernenhö and Miss Grove. The Hereditary Countess is an imposing, white-haired lady with a walking-stick; her dress is ornately old-fashioned, including lace mantilla and plumed hat. Miss Grove is a gaunt figure dressed all in black, with a flat straw hat; she is carrying a book with gilt edging under her arm.*

FOOTMAN    Who shall I say —— ?

HEREDITARY COUNTESS    No — I repeat. You are to announce no one. Simply: there is someone to see the Count. So, now run off and fetch him here. Off you go, young man. Or haven't they taught you how to obey yet at Stjernenhö Castle?

FOOTMAN *exit to rear.*

HEREDITARY COUNTESS *sits down.*    Come, Miss Grove, let us be quite cool and formal at this meeting. You stand behind my chair and put on that supercilious look — he'll quake at the sight!

MISS GROVE    Count Stjernenhö has offended against the privileges of his birth.

HEREDITARY COUNTESS    I'm going to take him seriously to task about it once more —

MISS GROVE    And then what?

HEREDITARY COUNTESS    Then I shall decide whether or not to let bygones be bygones and let grass grow over the whole story.

MISS GROVE   It would need to be stronger and thicker grass than grows in England!

HEREDITARY COUNTESS   Perhaps our Swedish grass is more suitable, dear Miss Grove. — *Looks around.* Back in Stjernenhö Castle after twenty years! As if it were yesterday when I withdrew from the field — at the hands of the commoner! It was here in this hall that he told me of his marriage plans. I thought he had gone mad!

MISS GROVE   Not all the millions of that timber Croesus could wash out the stain of her lowly birth.

HEREDITARY COUNTESS   He almost missed out on those, too. That would have capped it all.

MISS GROVE   Does one even mention such a person, notably one who has disappeared?

HEREDITARY COUNTESS   That was her one redeeming feature: to disappear without trace, without either sight or sound of her.

MISS GROVE   Requiescat!

HEREDITARY COUNTESS   For me she never existed. —— *Looks around again.* Yes, there they all are, proud forebears of a noble dynasty that kept its blood pure through all the centuries.

MISS GROVE   I look up in deep devotion.

HEREDITARY COUNTESS   That one is Gustav, bearded like the Pard — son of Vasa and founder of Stjernenhö Castle. Then Philipp, commander-in-chief in a hundred battles and the King's favourite and champion — how they gaze down on every side as if they were guarding the hall against any descendant unworthy of them. They would surely turn their faces to the wall if a child grew up here who brought discredit on them.

MISS GROVE   Is young Count Erik without blemish?

HEREDITARY COUNTESS   By reputation, absolutely. He is said to be a most agreeable young man, charming and irreproachable.

MISS GROVE   That may be just empty talk.

HEREDITARY COUNTESS    That's precisely why I've come to Stjernenhö, to see for myself.

MISS GROVE    The bastard child of a timber merchant's daughter who has disappeared!

HEREDITARY COUNTESS    The current heir to the House of Stjernenhö, if he passes muster in my eyes!

*Count Stjernenhö appears on the terrace — peers cautiously through the French window — then throws open the door.*

COUNT *surprised and delighted.*    Aunt Julia ——?!

HEREDITARY COUNTESS *by way of introduction, aloof.*    Miss Grove, my Bible reader.

COUNT    I must be dreaming ——!

HEREDITARY COUNTESS    I believe I've always inhabited this world, and commanded its respect. *She proffers her hand to be kissed.*

COUNT *falls to his knees and kisses it repeatedly.*    O forgive me — will you forgive and forget?

*The footman has appeared again to the rear, and looks on in astonishment.*

HEREDITARY COUNTESS *withdrawing her hand.*    That depends on what I have yet to find out. — *To Miss Grove.* Dear Miss Grove, please prepare everything in my room for our devotions.

COUNT    So you'll be staying in Stjernenhö Castle again?

HEREDITARY COUNTESS *to the footman.*    Prepare the green suite.

COUNT    Of course, the green suite! *To the footman.* The Hereditary Countess will be occupying the green suite — she must have flowers — yellow carnations!

*Miss Grove follows the footman up the staircase, exit above.*

HEREDITARY COUNTESS    You have forgotten nothing.

COUNT   And half a lump of sugar in your tea.

HEREDITARY COUNTESS   Yes, my dear, I don't like innovations — yellow carnations and half a lump of sugar — no innovations — they always turn out for the worse.

COUNT *on a stool, facing her.*   Your opening shot has pierced my heart.

HEREDITARY COUNTESS   So be it. If you challenge, you must expect resistance. That is the chivalric code.

COUNT   My defiance has cost me dear.

HEREDITARY COUNTESS   It's not evident to look at you. You've preserved yourself tolerably well — a few grey hairs at the temples.

COUNT   And your hair has turned white as snow.

HEREDITARY COUNTESS   No wonder after twenty years — when one's dear nephew has kindled a certain agitation.

COUNT   I deeply repent it, and will make a full confession.

HEREDITARY COUNTESS   Do you think the story of your marriage still holds any secrets for me?

COUNT   You are right, I was dragged through all the papers.

HEREDITARY COUNTESS   It was certainly quite amusing for their readers — the family felt somewhat differently.

COUNT   Aunt Jutta — I *had* to marry — or put a pistol to my head! — Is something bothering you?

HEREDITARY COUNTESS   Is someone practising pistol shooting?

COUNT   Only at clay-pigeons. Erik and —— *He stops.* But the sound of it disturbs you?

HEREDITARY COUNTESS   It reminds me of my late husband, the Lord Chamberlain, who died in a duel. Every time I hear shots I can see it again with frightening clarity: how they carried him into the house with his brains blown out — and made me a widow.

COUNT *jumps up.* I'll forbid any more shooting at once. *Exit through French window on to terrace, claps his hands and fends off a stream of protests from below.* Please forgive them their sport.

HEREDITARY COUNTESS *becoming agitated.* Don't you see, James — in our circles one dies for one's principles — that's why I couldn't understand how you could sell yourself for money.

COUNT I was young, I wanted to live life to the full —

HEREDITARY COUNTESS We all do — and that goes for us more than other mortals. But that's why we owe it to life to be ready for the ultimate sacrifice.

COUNT I came to realize that in a roundabout way —

HEREDITARY COUNTESS But, for a Stjernenhö, tradition has marked out the proper path in advance.

COUNT Nevertheless, I believe there are good grounds to vindicate me —

HEREDITARY COUNTESS You were lucky, James — and I am pleased you were lucky.

COUNT Lucky? In what way?

HEREDITARY COUNTESS The scandal of your marriage was short-lived — and the one who caused the scandal left the country — Have you never heard from her again?

COUNT Neither directly nor indirectly. Allegedly she found refuge with an uncle in America — perhaps she's dead.

HEREDITARY COUNTESS Nor have I heard anything about her.

COUNT Did you try and find out?

HEREDITARY COUNTESS One safeguards oneself against being taken unawares.

COUNT So — dead then?

HEREDITARY COUNTESS   Conclusively so.

COUNT *presses her hand.*   Thank you.

HEREDITARY COUNTESS   James — how could you marry that woman? You needed money — and she was pretty —

COUNT   I was blind!

HEREDITARY COUNTESS   I understand everything — and accept it in retrospect — a slight weakness of character if the girl is pretty and rich —

COUNT   With no faults?

HEREDITARY COUNTESS   The deficiency of her birth — but all that is blotted out by a single stigma which cannot be erased: how could she give up the child that she had fought over in court, and not enquire about it once in twenty years?

COUNT   Now my eyes are opened.

HEREDITARY COUNTESS   There is an instinct — the maternal instinct — which is present in both great and small, in the highest and the lowest in the land —: offend against that and you are no longer a member of the human race — just as that woman has obliterated every trace of herself and her name. — That gives me the right to denigrate her name in this hall, where respect for the law of inheritance is as sacred as the Holy Gospels.

COUNT   You know that I abducted the child?

HEREDITARY COUNTESS   Everything. The fact that she didn't create an outcry — or run to the court that she had previously manipulated so skilfully — that she didn't say a word that might upset the indolence and creature comforts the lower orders enjoy, and then calmly took off into another world —

COUNT   No, Aunt.

HEREDITARY COUNTESS   Do you deny it?

COUNT   If you permit. It won't have been indolence that kept her silent after the abduction — it will have been a sense of shame that was uppermost —

HEREDITARY COUNTESS *laughs.*   In little Miss Timber?!

COUNT   — shame at the prospect of raising a Count Stjernenhö.

HEREDITARY COUNTESS   There can be no excuse for a mother to let her nearest and dearest be snatched away. Not in the eyes of God — or of the Law, as Erik acknowledged when there had been no sight of his mother for ten years.

COUNT   And made over to me all rights over his person and his fortune.

HEREDITARY COUNTESS   —— And how have you managed that?

COUNT   Young Count Stjernenhö has been raised as befits his station.

HEREDITARY COUNTESS *looks around.*   Have you been doing restoration work?

COUNT   There were cracks and holes in all the walls of the castle.

HEREDITARY COUNTESS   Good for you. But it will have cost a lot?

COUNT   Of course.

HEREDITARY COUNTESS   And you didn't put any restrictions on your spending on yourself?

COUNT   You only live once, Aunt.

HEREDITARY COUNTESS   Your philosophy from when you were a child.

COUNT   As approved by nature, which made me that way.

HEREDITARY COUNTESS   You are an incorrigible reprobate and one shouldn't cross your threshold again.

COUNT   But you have?

HEREDITARY COUNTESS   Not on your account. You no longer interest me greatly.

COUNT   Some better reason, then?

HEREDITARY COUNTESS   My visit concerns young Erik.

COUNT   Certainly the greater attraction.

HEREDITARY COUNTESS    A real Stjernenhö, I'm told in Stockholm.

COUNT    Before whom I am the palest imitation.

HEREDITARY COUNTESS    Does he bear any resemblance to you?

COUNT *indicating the ancestral portraits.*    There's rather something of that lot in him. As if the whole lineage combined to produce in him the finest bloom of our race.

HEREDITARY COUNTESS    He enjoyed a good education?

COUNT    So gifted his tutors were in raptures.

HEREDITARY COUNTESS    And is now the finished article?

COUNT    A perfect young count from top to toe.

HEREDITARY COUNTESS    God has had mercy on our family and used the power of blood to correct your indiscretion. Let His goodness be a warning against further experiments. Praise be to God in the highest for this son and heir.

COUNT    Would you like to see Erik?

HEREDITARY COUNTESS    I can see through people, you know, James.

COUNT    Examine him as thoroughly as you like.

HEREDITARY COUNTESS    If he passes with top marks, I have a surprise in store for him tomorrow on his twenty-first birthday for which he will be exceedingly grateful.

COUNT    I'm all agog!

HEREDITARY COUNTESS    I am the bearer of a commission for him to join the King's Dragoons, which His Majesty graciously granted me in person at a royal reception when I depicted my great-nephew's noble bearing, which was enthusiastically confirmed by all present.

COUNT    What a bolt from the blue — that will remove the last scruples — *He breaks off.*

HEREDITARY COUNTESS    Whose scruples?

COUNT    Let it be a surprise that Erik has in store for you tomorrow! — I'll fetch him now. *He steps out on to the terrace — calls.* Erik! — Can you come? — No, alone.

HEREDITARY COUNTESS *powders her face — strikes a pose.*

*Erik appears outside — in white sporting attire.*

COUNT *leads him in.*    Greet Hereditary Countess Stjernenhö — your great-aunt, as you will know from the many times I've talked of her.

ERIK *glances at him questioningly — then quickly goes to the Hereditary Countess and kisses her hand.*

HEREDITARY COUNTESS *smiling.*    It was tactful of you not to give your father away — of course he has never once mentioned me.

COUNT    At all events, you will never forget Aunt Jutta from this day forth.

ERIK    Your will shall be my pleasure.

HEREDITARY COUNTESS    Little flatterer — you make an old woman blush.

ERIK *to Count.*    May I not speak frankly before Her Illustrious Ladyship, the Hereditary Countess?

HEREDITARY COUNTESS    Even better! You know your Almanac de Gotha like the Earl Marshal. Have you been immersing yourself in it?

ERIK    My tutors provided me with instruction in our family history when I showed an interest in it.

HEREDITARY COUNTESS    And it fell on fertile ground?

ERIK    I am familiar with the rights and responsibilities of my birth.

HEREDITARY COUNTESS    Which are?

ERIK    Your question is one I myself chose as the dissertation topic for my final examination, Your Ladyship. I compared the population of a country with a theatre audience. In the boxes are the real families — as I call the noble families whose lineage can be traced through generations. They take only slight interest in the story being presented on the stage. Their duty is to be omnipresent — their right: never to become too involved.

HEREDITARY COUNTESS    Nicely observed.

ERIK    The stalls and circle are taken up by contemporary families — the bourgeoisie, where parents and children maintain a certain coherence but who have no links with the distant past or the future. It is their right to applaud vigorously but to refrain from all criticism.

HEREDITARY COUNTESS    Excellent detail.

ERIK    The gallery is packed with a random mix of undistinguished families from all corners. They live neither for yesterday nor tomorrow, and here the very word 'family' is a paradox. Their duty is to have no rights — and their right is to acknowledge no duty. The bourgeoisie can hardly avoid contact with these creatures — the nobility runs no danger of becoming contaminated since its highly-bred instinct immediately senses the inferior product and is consequently able to steer well clear of it.

HEREDITARY COUNTESS *rises, her eyes shining — goes to Erik — kisses him on the forehead and both cheeks.*    You have composed the catechism of mankind, it should be hanging in every castle — *glancing at the Count* — then no one would ever go astray! — Yes, you are the real thing — a genuine Stjernenhö.

ERIK    Your Ladyship is too indulgent.

HEREDITARY COUNTESS    Let me offer my congratulations without further ado, along with the most important birthday present I had intended to keep for tomorrow: the King wants you to join his Dragoons. *She fishes out a letter and hands it to Erik.*

ERIK    Incredible! *He opens it — reads.*

COUNT *peers over his shoulder and reads as well.*    Black on white! — Let me have it — just till tomorrow. *He takes it from him and puts it in his pocket.*

HEREDITARY COUNTESS *to Erik.*    Are you pleased with me?

ERIK    Your Ladyship has —

HEREDITARY COUNTESS   You can be less formal with your old great-aunt Jutta and give her a kiss on the lips.

ERIK *does so.*

*Miss Grove descends — watch in hand; at the sight of the Hereditary Countess and Erik she stops short half-way down the staircase, rooted to the spot.*

HEREDITARY COUNTESS *notices her.*   Yes, Miss Grove, we are reconciled: the intermediary has more than proven his worth and brought peace between me and him. *She holds out her hand to the Count.*

COUNT *kisses it.*   What bountiful generosity —

HEREDITARY COUNTESS   You need never have forfeited my blessing — I'm coming, Miss Grove, don't be angry — the Bible has survived two thousand years — it will survive a quarter-hour delay in our devotions — Give me your arm, James. The occasion calls for a special text — the story of the Prodigal Son, who was lost and is found. *Exit on the Count's arm up staircase — followed by Miss Grove; the three disappear above.*

*Alice appears behind the French window — peers into the hall — enters.*

ALICE   When can we start shooting again?

ERIK   I forgot to ask Papa for permission. I'll ask him now. *Makes for staircase.*

ALICE   Now my Papa has fallen asleep. At the first bang he would fall out of his chair.

ERIK   Then we'd better have a pause.

ALICE *sitting down in one of the ancestral chairs.*   Do you always ask your Papa first?

ERIK   Ask him what?

ALICE   If you may breathe — if you may eat — if you — and so on.

ERIK   It was the shooting he expressly forbade, and he hasn't said we can yet.

ALICE   I hope he doesn't forget — before I leave.

ERIK   It will be the first thing I —

ALICE   Otherwise you'll choke on the secret you were dying to tell me when you'd hit six targets in a row.

ERIK   I'd already got five!

ALICE   I'll do you a favour and let you off the sixth. Come on, what is it I should know?

ERIK *embarrassed, laughs.*

ALICE   Was it only a joke?

ERIK   It could be fun — but — perhaps you'll laugh.

ALICE   But if it's a joke you should laugh.

ERIK   You see — you already think it's a joke.

ALICE   But I haven't heard it yet.

ERIK   Will you be serious?

ALICE   Deadly serious.

ERIK   No, you mustn't be that either.

ALICE   Then we'll split the difference — half sad, half funny.

ERIK   All right — half and half — but they have to coincide — my funny half with your funny half —

ALICE   — and my sad half with your sad half. It's a deal.

ERIK *tentatively.*   Baroness Alice ——

ALICE *looks him full in the face.*   Count Erik?

ERIK   If you look at me like that ——

ALICE *continues looking him up at him.*   Well, forbid it then.

ERIK   If only I could pluck up courage — with six shots.

ALICE   I don't have to let you off the sixth —

ERIK   I would have hit it anyway.

ALICE   The bullet is —

ERIK   Still in the gun —

ALICE   Already in my heart.

ERIK *gazes down at her.*

ALICE *slowly raises both arms towards him.*

ERIK *leans towards her.*

ALICE *pulls him to her.*

ERIK *returns her kisses — silence.*

*Almost simultaneously the Count appears above and Baron Barrenkrona below through the French window.*

BARON *looks at the pair kissing.*

COUNT *does so too.*

BARON *coughs.*

COUNT *coughs.*

BARON *coughs more loudly.*

COUNT *coughs more loudly.*

*Alice and Erik are startled.*

ALICE *flies into the arms of Baron.*   Papa!

ERIK *flies into the arms of Count.*   Papa!

*Baron and Count look at one another over their children's heads.*

COUNT *smiling.*   We are presented with a fait accompli, Baron.

BARON *quietly.*   Wait for me in the pavilion, my dear Alice.

COUNT   In my room, Erik.

*Exit Alice through French window — Erik to the right.*
*Baron goes to an armchair — looks enquiringly at Count; Count invites him to sit; both sit.*

BARON   —— I won't deny I let things take their course — the first thing was to make sure the young people were fond of each other.

COUNT   As we've just seen, there are no doubts on that score.

BARON   That side of things is resolved —

COUNT   The arguments seemed convincing.

BARON   But whether I should now condone my daughter's role —

COUNT   Speak your mind frankly.

BARON   I will then. I have no objections to Erik himself — his whole bearing is exemplary, I could not wish for a better son-in-law —

COUNT   — Very flattering for Erik.

BARON   — if only the standing of both his parents had been socially acceptable. And with Erik that is not the case. Do I take too many liberties in making myself clear, as you suggested?

COUNT   On his mother's side he is indeed of inferior social standing.

BARON   Half nobility, then, on the one hand — and on the other, Baroness Barrenkrona. I don't need to give you a lecture on the genealogy of the Barrenkronas. Feudal nobility — spotless lineage. Both their reputations and their estates. Not the slightest deviation from the legitimate line of provenance.

COUNT   Their enormous fortune made it that much easier for the Barrenkronas to remain irreproachable.

BARON   In no circumstances would they have contemplated such a *faux pas*. Strong blood does not mix with weak.

COUNT   Alas, your reproaches come too late for me.

BARON   I'm sorry. — But if I may —?

COUNT   Please do, put your cards on the table.

BARON   I find it difficult to consent to a union of the House of Stjernenhö and the House of Barrenkrona. The children have spoken. This fact has to be taken into account.

COUNT   Let us regard it as never having happened.

BARON   You are very courageous, Count, discarding your best trick.

COUNT   I was braver when I abducted little Erik from the hands of his mother in disregard of the court's judgement.

BARON   Can that permit us to disregard his origins?

COUNT   It can completely eclipse them.

BARON   I can't deny that I like the young man — but my love for Alice, for whom I want nothing but the best, has somewhat prejudiced me.

COUNT   Then we should call on someone who can give an impartial decision — I suggest Hereditary Countess Stjernenhö.

BARON   Your courage has grown to recklessness — since the Hereditary Countess is your bitterest enemy, and would not set foot in Stjernenhö Castle.

COUNT   The Hereditary Countess arrived an hour ago and is at her devotions in her room.

BARON   I'm amazed, Count — you're trying to bluff me. There's too much at stake for you not to try every ruse. You're short of money again — my fortune, which will all go to Alice — is what you need, to —

*Enter footman with bouquet.*

COUNT *to footman.*   Who are the yellow carnations for?

FOOTMAN   For Her Ladyship, the Hereditary Countess Stjernenhö. *Ascends staircase — exit.*

COUNT   She's come for Erik's twenty-first birthday.

BARON   Did you manage to placate her?

COUNT   Through the good offices of Erik — whom she worships after talking to him for ten minutes.

BARON   As you see, I breathe a sigh of relief. You have successfully negotiated the first obstacle which would have wrecked our children's hopes — if this family feud had not been resolved.

COUNT   And the second obstacle?

BARON   What the world thinks, whenever we are in its gaze. I'm sorry, Count, but you shocked society and shouldn't be surprised if its reaction is somewhat frosty. Count Erik could not expect to be favourably received at Court — if received at all. I don't want to expose my daughter — a Baroness Barrenkrona by birth and accustomed as of right to the greatest respect — to any sort of embarrassment.

COUNT   I can only concur, Baron Barrenkrona.

BARON *rising.*   Then that would seem to mark the end of our discussion —

COUNT   — to be continued perchance, by Lieutenant Erik of the Royal Dragoons.

BARON   Very droll, but —

COUNT   — worthy of even your commendation when it comes from the King's own mouth.

*He hands him the commission.*

BARON *reads — draws himself to attention.* I am at Count Erik Stjernenhö's disposal, should he consider himself insulted by my derogatory remarks, which you will please convey to him. I should be honoured if he demands satisfaction.

COUNT *pats his shoulder.* I think we'll leave the fighting to the children since they have given us a little prelude with their amorous wranglings.

BARON You have my word.

COUNT I'll convey it to Erik.

BARON I'll send Alice to him. *Exit to rear.*

*Enter left a footman, approaches the Count and whispers in his ear.*

COUNT Let him wait!

FOOTMAN *taken aback.* Is the Count at home?

COUNT Of course. Offer him a cigar.

FOOTMAN *exit left.*

COUNT *opens door on right.* Erik, please come in.

*Erik enters.*

COUNT *gestures towards an armchair for Erik — and sits himself.* You will marry Alice — I've arranged it.

ERIK *astonished.* You?

COUNT Are you surprised?

ERIK I — I love Alice.

COUNT As well you might, and you have a right to.

ERIK I don't understand, Papa.

COUNT There were certain irregularities that needed smoothing over — concerning the House of Barrenkrona and your birth.

ERIK    What do you mean?

COUNT    Certain reservations —— 

ERIK    What are you getting at, Papa?

COUNT    —— which the Baron raised concerning equality of birth.

ERIK *jumps up.*    Where is the Baron? I demand immediate —

COUNT    Sit down. There is some justification — and in any case, he has retracted.

ERIK *sits down.*    It's getting more and more embarrassing!

COUNT    I had to embarrass you some day, I'm afraid, but then it will be disposed of, once and for all. — On your father's side, you are a Stjernenhö —

ERIK    And my mother?

COUNT    Bourgeois!

ERIK    Papa!

COUNT    I wish I could undo what is done —

ERIK *buries his head in his hands, sobs convulsively.*

COUNT    Who she was — can be of as little concern to you today as it was to me ever to talk of her to you.

ERIK    —— Is she dead?

COUNT    For me, since twenty years ago. — You spent just one year of your life with her — and obliterated all trace of her over the next twenty with me. Proof of that is assent to your engagement and the King's commission.

ERIK    Papa —— you —— it's inconceivable —— !

COUNT    Money, Erik, money played a part. I enjoyed life — and incurred debts. That spoilt the fun. I had to get money, otherwise Stjernenhö Castle would have collapsed round my ears. As it is, I restored it and managed to give you an upbringing fitting to your station.

ERIK   But for money ——!

COUNT   For — your money, Erik! — Your grandfather had left it all to you —

ERIK   Don't say — my grandfather!

COUNT   So I stand before you today in your debt — and can't pay.

ERIK   You don't owe me any of that money, Papa!

COUNT   It's all gone, down to the last penny.

ERIK   Then I'm grateful that you got rid of that money. I would have found it intolerable, touching it — and thrown it out of the window.

COUNT   Aren't you curious to know how that capital was acquired and spent even before you take possession of it tomorrow?

ERIK *stands.*   If I'm not needed here for anything else ——

COUNT   Only to sign the document in which you renounce your grandfather's legacy. *He takes a piece of paper from his pocket and hands him a fountain-pen.*

ERIK *signing.*   My first — and last — contact with that clan! *He strides off through French window.*

COUNT *folds the piece of paper — puts it in his pocket — rings.*

*Enter footman from left.*

COUNT   Mr Lindström!

*Footman beckons — admits Mr Lindström — exit.*

COUNT   Today already? Tomorrow is the day it's due.

LINDSTRÖM   The sum in question is such a large one that I wanted to make sure —

COUNT    What does the whole caboodle amount to?

LINDSTRÖM    Your son's inheritance!

COUNT    In round figures — in the region of...?

LINDSTRÖM    If I were to calculate it at the full interest rate —

COUNT    At the extortionate Christian rate!

LINDSTRÖM    I slept every night with the risk hanging over me.

COUNT    So you slept badly for twenty years?

LINDSTRÖM    My hair's gone grey and I've turned into an old man!

COUNT    We all have to slog away to provide for our old age.

LINDSTRÖM    I agreed back then for the first time to provide you with a loan —

COUNT    Was that meant to be enough to get by on?

LINDSTRÖM    — and since then I haven't had a moment's peace until you'd raised money against every last penny of the inheritance.

COUNT    At any rate, you'll feel good at having served loyally and earned your percentage.

LINDSTRÖM    And what's going to happen tomorrow?

COUNT    Nothing!

LINDSTRÖM    Why ——?!

COUNT    Because I've taken care of everything today! *Gives him the piece of paper.*

LINDSTRÖM *reads — gurgles with pleasure.* Count — Erik — has been — accepted at Court!

COUNT    He'll especially enjoy hearing that from you! Drink yourself silly tomorrow, Lindström!

LINDSTRÖM    Champagne! — to Count Erik's health!

COUNT    And the health of his fiancée, Baroness Alice Barrenkrona!

LINDSTRÖM    The daughter of the *crème de la crème* of Sweden?!

COUNT    It's all settled.

LINDSTRÖM    May I provide you with an advance?

COUNT    Thank you, but no — we are now in the black for keeps. *He bundles Lindström off, left. Exit Lindström.*

*Enter Hereditary Countess above — very agitated.*

HEREDITARY COUNTESS    James — James! — have you seen — Baroness Alice! — and Erik! — and Baron Barrenkrona! — the most embarrassing situation for two young people to be caught in — and her papa stands there on the lawn congratulating them! — James — I only caught a glance through the blinds and there they were, in flagranti ——!

COUNT    Since you've already committed an indiscretion —

HEREDITARY COUNTESS    In cases like this, always!

COUNT *goes to French window, calls out.*    Aunt Jutta would like to see the newly engaged couple and the father of the bride-to-be.

*Enter Miss Grove above — walking slowly.*

HEREDITARY COUNTESS *to her.*    Miss Grove — now you can witness what you scoffed at when I dreamt of turtle doves the night before we left for Stjernenhö Castle.

*Enter Baron, followed by Alice and Erik.*
*Baron goes straight to Hereditary Countess and kisses her hand.*

HEREDITARY COUNTESS    My dear baron, what star has brought us together here!

BARON    Destiny has united two young stars.

HEREDITARY COUNTESS *turning to Miss Grove.* How poetic, Miss Grove! *Introduces Miss Grove.* This is Miss Grove, my Bible reader.

ALICE *kisses the Hereditary Countess's hand.* Your Ladyship!

HEREDITARY COUNTESS You have found yourself a true *preux chevalier — To Erik.* — and I have no doubt that you will hold fast to your good fortune. Now let Aunt Jutta see you kiss.

*Alice and Erik kiss.*

HEREDITARY COUNTESS Baron, let us seal the union of our two houses.

COUNT *aside to Hereditary Countess.* Now I should kiss Miss Grove or I'll be left out.

HEREDITARY COUNTESS *gives him a light slap on the cheek.* Formality is a joke for you. Let James celebrate in his own way. *Sits in an armchair.* I'm content. The Barrenkronas and the Stjernenhös under one banner — that guarantees — *Glances at James.* — that we are now immune to further aberrations and confusions — *Looks at Erik.* — here among our own kind in the private boxes reserved for the real families.

*Enter footman left, presents the Count with a visiting card.*

COUNT *takes it — reads —— looks up ——— reads it again.* Karin Bratt.

*Baron and Hereditary Countess look at each other.*

ERIK ———— Who is Karin Bratt?

HEREDITARY COUNTESS *rises.* I suggest we get some fresh air in the park — while James clears the air in here once and for all. *Takes Baron's arm, exeunt to rear — letting Erik and Alice go first.*

COUNT *signals to footman to show visitor in.*

*Exit footman.*
*Enter Karin Bratt: she is twenty years older, little changed in appearance.*

KARIN ———— We haven't seen each other for a long time.

COUNT   I am not aware of any connection that justifies the We.

KARIN   There is one, an unbreakable one.

COUNT   Namely?

KARIN   The child.

COUNT   You have come for Erik's twenty-first birthday?

KARIN   Erik is twenty-one tomorrow.

COUNT   Amazing that you haven't forgotten.

KARIN   I was reminded of it constantly, tangibly.

COUNT   Are you pinning any hopes on this day?

KARIN   I'm not sure myself.

COUNT   Then I can save you from troubling yourself in vain: Karin Bratt has no further business in Stjernenhö Castle.

KARIN   Not even the inheritance of Erik Bratt?

COUNT   There was only ever one Count Erik Stjernenhö, who comes of age tomorrow and disposes of his inheritance as he thinks fit.

KARIN   So the poor boy holds you in such affection?

COUNT   Count Erik Stjernenhö will not countenance any such dishonourable description.

KARIN   You're too eager to stand up for other people's children.

COUNT   You have lost the right to call yourself this child's mother.

KARIN   When did I claim it?

COUNT   When you went to court.

KARIN   Never!

COUNT    Is this some cheap trick?

KARIN    I'll enlighten you, Count Stjernenhö. It's high time, if we are to prevent a misfortune. The boy might not be able to find his way back.

COUNT    To you?

KARIN    To his mother!

*Enter Erik Bratt: tall, American-looking, dressed entirely in leather.*

ERIK BRATT    You left the folder in the car, the one that was apparently so important, you said.

KARIN    Yes, there are documents in it. Thanks.

ERIK BRATT *notices the Count.*    Who is that?

COUNT *red with rage, to Karin.*    I am not disposed to make the acquaintance of your chauffeur, with whom you seem so familiar — Mrs Bratt! *Storms off through French window.*

*Erik Bratt, amused, looks at his mother questioningly.*

# ACT TWO

~

*The same hall.*
*Karin and Erik sitting in armchairs, facing each other — both still in coat and hat;*
*Erik Bratt playing with his leather driving cap — Karin with a fixed look.*

ERIK BRATT *after a pause.*    What are we waiting for, Ma?

KARIN    I was — just remembering things, Erik.

ERIK BRATT    Kansas?

KARIN    No — here.

ERIK BRATT    Have you been before, in this fairy-tale castle?

KARIN    With you — Erik!

ERIK BRATT    No!

KARIN    Once upon a time — that's how all stories should start here.

ERIK BRATT    Something romantic, then?

KARIN    Uncle Knut gave it a better name: pulp fiction.

ERIK BRATT    Let's hear it then, Ma.

KARIN    You spent the first weeks of your life here.

ERIK BRATT    Where?

KARIN    Here!

ERIK BRATT    I protest — belatedly.

KARIN    You were certainly too young to do so then — and I protested for you.

ERIK BRATT   Vehemently enough?

KARIN   Under cover of darkness, I fled out of the reach of your father with you in my arms.

ERIK BRATT   Hold on a minute, Ma.

KARIN   Go on, ask me about your father for the first time, and I'll give you the full story.

ERIK BRATT   Do I have to be interested in that?

KARIN   I've never forced you to.

ERIK BRATT   Dear old Uncle Knut was all I needed.

KARIN    — But today you must show more interest in someone else.

ERIK BRATT *with comic seriousness.*   Who is my Pa? Where is my Pa? How is my Pa?

KARIN   Not so fast, not so emotional, Erik.

ERIK BRATT   Come on, Ma!

KARIN   Your father was a nobleman with debts.

ERIK BRATT   Had his firm gone bankrupt?

KARIN   There was no firm — it was his blue-blooded family.

ERIK BRATT   How did that incur debts?

KARIN   Through loans.

ERIK BRATT   With what security?

KARIN   His illustrious name.

ERIK BRATT   And how were they meant to be paid back?

KARIN   By manoeuvres — like marriage.

ERIK BRATT   With you?

KARIN *smiling.*   Simple!

ERIK BRATT   And he wasn't a shining light, either?

KARIN   How do you make that out?

ERIK BRATT   You taking off under cover of darkness, with me under wraps!

KARIN   That's true. He could marry me all right — I used to be pretty — and my fortune didn't necessarily stop him from seeing that. But he didn't see me at all — he only took the little commoner as the key to your grandfather's millions.

ERIK BRATT   But you presumably went along with that?

KARIN   By marrying him? I saw your grandfather happy — and that made my mind up. I trusted him implicitly — and went along with his plans without question. I was a child that hadn't learnt to think for itself. After all, marrying a Count Stjernenhö — I was as impressed by that as everyone else.

ERIK BRATT   So that's my Pa. What's he called?

KARIN   Yes, your Pa, Erik — Count James Stjernenhö.

ERIK BRATT   My name is Bratt.

KARIN   You'll soon find out! — This is where the marriage took place.

ERIK BRATT   In this — chamber of antiquities?

KARIN *looking around.*   It looked more dilapidated then — he's done it up.

ERIK BRATT   For the wedding ceremony?

KARIN   No, he must have done it recently. — Everything happened as it had to happen: one day my eyes were opened, when your grandfather had his accident up there in the forest, and died —

ERIK BRATT   Uncle Knut called it a lumberjack's honourable death.

KARIN   — and his great fortune was bequeathed to you.

ERIK BRATT   Now I understand the reason for this mysterious trip: tomorrow I come of age and shall come into my inheritance. I'm ready, Ma!

KARIN   I was thinking less of you —

ERIK BRATT   It's nice to inherit. That's only human.

KARIN   But your father went empty-handed, and I was on the receiving end of his disappointment.

ERIK BRATT   Seriously, Ma?

KARIN   So seriously that the court granted the divorce — and left you to me.

ERIK BRATT *slowly.*   You're right — I couldn't help you yet, then.

KARIN   No, I had to resort to someone weaker to rescue me from persecution — someone picked up off the street.

ERIK BRATT   I'm getting interested, Ma.

KARIN   The money went with you — me he discarded with contempt — you he had to get his hands on. Then he would have the interest and later the capital. Where the child is, the money is. He tried to abduct you. The first time it went wrong — the second time even more so. But he got the child!

ERIK BRATT   That's a contradiction. The second attempt failed too, yet —

KARIN   His stalkers found a child — the one I had switched — in the pram I arranged to be left at the front of the park.

ERIK BRATT *looks at her — roars with laughter.*   Why didn't you tell us that in Kansas and have us in stitches? The tables would have cracked up laughing — Uncle Knut would have shot out of his grave like a rocket and exploded!

KARIN   Uncle Knut laughed just like you when I told him on the *Butterfly* how I had taken advantage of his visit: he had to carry you out of the house and into the car under his big coat, so no one would know there were two Eriks.

ERIK BRATT *laughing.*   And never once mentioned it while he was alive!

KARIN   I made him solemnly swear not to.

ERIK BRATT    After six grogs!

KARIN    We took it very seriously — we stayed in the harbour another two days — Uncle Knut arranged my passport — no mention of you — and we landed inconspicuously on the other side: a replacement had been well and truly installed here, and you were safe from any further inquiries.

ERIK BRATT *stands and kisses her on the mouth.*    That's to show my gratitude for allowing me to be with you.

KARIN    You were a constant joy —— but I'm rather worried about the other Erik.

ERIK BRATT *looks at her quizzically. Then in amusement.*    Ah yes — I left my double behind. Did you make sure he was worthy of me?

KARIN    No, Erik — I can't say I did. He was a little ragamuffin and his mother — a streetwalker with her lover in gaol — presented him to me. She was only too happy to be rid of him, and laughed herself silly at the abduction we both witnessed.

ERIK BRATT *left speechless — laughs, splutters.*    And that's what has grown up here?! — amid the ancestors and the knights in shining armour?!

KARIN *sternly.*    That was the intention — and how it was reared here, that will determine what I decide to do — when I see the result.

ERIK BRATT    And what happened to the streetwalking mother?

KARIN    I know nothing. Nothing, Erik. Not even her name. I instructed my bank to pay her an allowance — to the person who presented my authorization — and that was the last I saw of her.

ERIK BRATT    And she was never to say a word?

KARIN    Until twenty years later, when she should come to Stjernenhö Castle — that's today, for that day in the harbour we celebrated your first birthday after my escape.

ERIK BRATT    That could well be a charming reunion — for all concerned!

KARIN   Today the clock strikes twelve and all will be revealed, one way or the other — whether the Gordian knot turns into a nosegay or a noose!

ERIK BRATT *jumps up — seizes the bell on the table — rings loudly.*

KARIN   What are you doing?

ERIK BRATT   Give me your coat — hat!

*Enter footman from left.*

ERIK BRATT *to footman.*   Please take our coats — we're staying. *He brings Karin's things and drapes them over his arm — then his own leather coat and cap.* And please come straight back.

*Exit footman.*

KARIN   But we haven't been invited.

ERIK BRATT   They've taken such extraordinary care of me for twenty years that I must surely have the freedom of the house. I invite you.

KARIN   Why do you want the footman again?

*Enter footman.*

ERIK   Now show me the castle.

FOOTMAN *intimidated.*   Has Mr Lindström sent you?

ERIK *hesitates briefly.*   As you say — Mr Lindström. Let's go — first the ground floor. *To Karin.* Please ring if you need me. *Exit right, with the over-zealous footman.*

*Enter from rear Baron Barrenkrona — as if looking for Karin — then approaches her, keeping his distance.*

BARON   Mrs Bratt?

KARIN *does not respond.*

BARON   I have been intrusted with the task of —

KARIN *without looking up.*    Are you the caretaker?

BARON *clears his throat in embarrassment — bows briefly.*    Baron Barrenkrona.

KARIN *surprised.*    In Stjernenhö Castle?

BARON    Finding me here is — a striking illustration of the *entente cordiale* — absolutely cordiale! — between the houses of Stjernenhö and Barrenkrona.

KARIN    To my surprise —

BARON    Which you didn't hide, but which is a matter of indifference.

KARIN    Nevertheless, I am burning with curiosity.

BARON    The point is: a complete restoration of strained relations has been established —

KARIN    How?

BARON    That is immaterial. The important thing at this moment is solely to correct the misapprehension which seems to have led to your presence here.

KARIN    Namely?

BARON    That, being on the other side of the ocean, you remained in ignorance of the fact that, by a retroactive judgement of the court, Erik has become a member of the noble house of Stjernenhö.

KARIN *stares at him.*

BARON    I assume my word as a gentleman is sufficient, and that it is unnecessary to produce the document.

KARIN *remains speechless.*

BARON    That would appear to conclude my mission — Mrs Bratt! *Makes to leave.*

KARIN    No — wait. I've just had a shock. Who has become a member of which family?

BARON   There is only one legitimate Count Erik Stjernenhö.

KARIN   But that must be —— rescinded immediately!

BARON   I fear it is probably too late for you to trouble the authorities today — Count Erik comes of age tomorrow.

KARIN   Then I must speak to the boy — here — now!

BARON   What boy?

KARIN   I won't call him by name. The young man who was brought up here.

BARON   Your way of speaking of Erik —

KARIN   I'm not talking about Erik! Sent me the boy — immediately!

BARON *somewhat puzzled.*   You insist in a manner —

KARIN   Which necessity dictates!

BARON *collecting himself.*   Mrs Bratt — you force me to be more direct: as soon as I have left you are expected to disappear from here, and not be seen again in future.

KARIN   That's all complete nonsense. I'm staying until the boy comes and I have made the situation clear to him.

BARON   The situation is perfectly clear, Count Erik —

KARIN *gives a ringing laugh.*   Count Erik!

BARON   For my part, I fail to see the comic side of the situation.

KARIN *laughs unrestrainedly.*   I really must see your Count Erik!

BARON   You 'll wait a long time —

KARIN   It will be worth it, though.

BARON *exit to rear, more or less speechless.*

*Enter Erik Bratt from right.*

ERIK BRATT *shuddering.* From one catacomb to the next — like some death cult — hideous, Ma — *Stops short on hearing her laughter.* Ma?

KARIN Erik — you've been —

ERIK BRATT *looking down at himself.* Have I caught a spider's web?

KARIN — enobled — you're a Stjernenhö!

ERIK BRATT Thanks, but no thanks.

KARIN Your protest is in vain — the court has made you Count Stjernenhö.

ERIK BRATT That's crazy.

KARIN Or else designated the false Erik a count in your place.

ERIK BRATT Then it must be the other one.

KARIN Who was merely deputizing for you temporarily, Erik.

ERIK BRATT What are you getting at?

KARIN Wouldn't you like to be a Swedish count?

ERIK BRATT *laughs.* I'll tell you when I've finished inspecting my ancestral home! *Goes to right — enter footman.* The upper floor — after you! *Follows footman up staircase — exit right.*

*Enter Erik quickly from rear — a tennis-racket under his arm.*

ERIK *stands before Karin.* Here I am. — Will that be all?

KARIN *quite amazed.* So that's you? — Fantastic! — Turn round: — I must see you from all sides!

ERIK I —

KARIN Don't speak yet! I have to get over my surprise — Am I dreaming? — is such a thing possible?

ERIK   I set no great store by conversation, since I have to get back to an unfinished tennis match. I'm leading by two sets.

KARIN   It's enough to make you believe in miracles — can it be true?

ERIK   After fulfilling your wish, I take my leave of you once and for all! *Bows — makes to leave.*

KARIN   Let me at least say something, young man. I've come across the ocean in order to meet you. Don't spoil our rendezvous.

ERIK   At least I am grateful you don't use the familiar form of address.

KARIN   I have no right to do so — I never had.

ERIK   You yourself draw the dividing line so clearly between the Stjernenhö dynasty — and the Bratt family?

KARIN   In your case, there is a veritable chasm!

ERIK   Then your arrival for my birthday is all the more astonishing.

KARIN   I'm not sure if tomorrow is your birthday.

ERIK   As you've forgotten that as well, I'm amazed —

KARIN   I have thought about you constantly. I've occupied myself with you more than you can know. It was half the content of my life. The experiment that began quite by chance evolved into one of universal human significance.

ERIK   —— You already baffled my father-in-law —

KARIN *with a start.*   Your father-in-law?

ERIK   — Baron Barrenkrona — with some unintelligible rigmarole —

KARIN   You have a fiancée here ? — Is it —?

ERIK   My engagement to Baroness Alice will be announced tomorrow.

KARIN *slumps back.*   Boy, oh boy!

ERIK    As you see, this union with the oldest noble dynasty will finally cancel out the inequality of my birth.

KARIN *groans, smiles.*    As a Bratt — yes!

ERIK    As a Bratt.

KARIN    Which you never were!

ERIK    It is erased from my memory.

KARIN *sitting up.*    Come and sit down. Give me ten minutes. You'll thank me for it later. I don't want to shock you — only to ask you something.

ERIK *sits reluctantly.*

KARIN    Do you love your fiancée?

ERIK *simply.*    I love Alice.

KARIN    Does Alice love you?

ERIK *simply.*    She loves me.

KARIN    Who is it she loves? Count Stjernenhö — or the person sitting before me?

ERIK    We love each other, each loves — the other.

KARIN    How nicely you put it. — I do believe: with this declaration you are immune from any disappointment. If you're quite steadfast in your resolve. All depends on that, of course. — Now can I ask you to return to the park — and not to play tennis: but to take your fiancée for a quiet walk through the park and once again make sure of her love for you — and for yourself alone.

ERIK *rises — forgets his tennis-racket — exit to rear.*

*Enter Erik Bratt from above — descends in leaps and bounds.*

KARIN *goes to meet him at the bottom of the staircase.*    Erik —

ERIK BRATT    Hallo?

KARIN — You are engaged!

ERIK BRATT Who to?

KARIN To Baroness Alice Barrenkrona.

ERIK BRATT *sinks into an armchair.* What is that supposed to mean?

KARIN Baroness — Alice — Barrenkrona.

ERIK BRATT Am I meant to remember that?

KARIN For the moment the other Erik will register it for you.

ERIK BRATT Did you see him?

KARIN You won't have an easy time with him.

ERIK BRATT Can't he go on deputizing for me?

KARIN That won't work —

ERIK BRATT Do you expect me to make use of my rights here?

KARIN If your fiancée is pretty?

ERIK BRATT Give me a kiss, Ma — *Warbles.* In Kansas lives a maiden fair —!

*Enter footman from above.*

ERIK BRATT Are there even more dusty corners?

FOOTMAN You might like to inspect the cavaliers' house.

ERIK BRATT More horseplay, Ma — but then back to the Wild West and four weeks under the open sky with no roof over our head! *Exit left with footman.*

*Enter Count from rear.*

COUNT Both Baron Barrenkrona and Erik emerge from their conversations with you visibly — perhaps I exaggerate — dumbfounded. I also see that you have discarded your coat and hat in the meantime and made yourself at home. Please drop all pretence and tell me what it is you want.

KARIN   I now want — to thank you, James.

COUNT   What for?

KARIN   For saving me — and that's no exaggeration — from something I dreaded.

COUNT   Concerning?

KARIN   Your young charge.

COUNT   What were you afraid of?

KARIN   Since I was only ever something to invest in —

COUNT   That lies too far in the past to be of further interest.

KARIN   Should we not revisit it once more?

COUNT   Was there any point which remains unclear?

KARIN   The most essential one.

COUNT   Namely?

KARIN   The disappearance of the mother.

COUNT   On that subject, here is what you yourself wrote. *He takes out the letter and reads aloud.* Count Stjernenhö! I accept that the child you forcibly abducted today is better off in your castle than in the arms of the mother you snatched it from. Turn it into a worthy member of the society you claim to represent as of right. *Looking up.* Or did you not write this letter?

KARIN   With my own hand.

COUNT   That's why it was the decisive argument for the court. Quite apart from your renunciation it endorses my — abduction.

KARIN   Granted. — But you never had any doubts?

COUNT   With this piece of paper, and your disappearance for twenty years, and never the slightest suspicion of any protest on your part, however futile.

KARIN   Will the day not come when a mother shows concern for her child?

COUNT   You've provided proof to the contrary for too long to be convincing.

KARIN   I lived only for my son.

COUNT   In your wildest imagination.

KARIN   No — literally.

COUNT   Unfortunately your presence here was observed by no one.

KARIN   In order to be with my son?

COUNT   Yes — literally.

KARIN   Then I must clarify my statement more fully — I arrived with Erik today.

COUNT *laughing.*   Where from?

KARIN   From Kansas.

COUNT   From the moon!

KARIN   No — let's stay on the earth. I never parted from Erik for a single day — and have just accompanied him over the ocean.

COUNT   Let's give Erik the pleasure of telling us about his wonderful adventures.

KARIN   Let me get Erik.

COUNT   I'll get him.

KARIN   Erik is not in the park.

COUNT   Erik is in the park.

KARIN    Not my Erik.

COUNT    My Erik —

KARIN    — is not Erik!

COUNT *struck dumb.*

KARIN    No — Erik is still Erik Bratt. He never shed his skin and became a count. Plain, straightforward Erik Bratt — whom you've already addressed as my chauffeur. — Incidentally, that would never have offended me: since I was once led astray by a Count Stjernenhö, why not also by a smart chauffeur?

COUNT    Who is this — Erik?

KARIN    Which one?

COUNT    My one!

KARIN    You raided a pram — and what the thieves got, they carried off to you in the castle.

COUNT    You switched children!

KARIN    Yes!

COUNT    What a piece of villainy!

KARIN    Preemptive retaliation for your attack. First you stole — a failure, then I deceived you — a success. C'est la guerre!

COUNT    You should have informed me, after wreaking your revenge —

KARIN    No. My son would never have been safe from your attempts to hunt him down. You needed Erik.

COUNT    That's true — I needed Erik ————

KARIN    So I left you undisturbed with your prey — and today I am happy I didn't spoil your pleasure in bringing the boy up. You've turned him into a charming young man in both mind and body — apart from the odd affectation.

COUNT    Who have I squandered myself on?

KARIN    The family tree goes no further back than the road outside, which both mother and father were well acquainted with. At the time, papa was in prison —

COUNT    Scoundrel —!

KARIN    — and mama was sleeping around in haystacks.

COUNT    Deserves strangling —!

KARIN    The little waif was in a bundle of rags —

COUNT    Despicable —!

KARIN    — I peeled off what he had been wrapped in — washed him clean and sprinkled on some scent — attached a locket around his little neck and bedded him down in lace pillows. Old Johannsson had to push the pram down to the front of the park and witness the abduction with his own eyes. — Like some trashy novel, James — but that's life!

COUNT    —————— You must disappear immediately. With Erik. I'll pay for the trip back. Second class? — First class?

KARIN    Do you want to continue with the deception?

COUNT    Whatever happens. It's too late for revelations — Erik — the false Erik — is engaged — has a commission in the King's Dragoons —

KARIN    But all that doesn't have to change.

COUNT    If he is no longer Count Stjernenhö?

KARIN    He can still be a beloved fiancé and a good soldier.

COUNT    You must live on the moon!

KARIN    You're prepared to commit any deception?

COUNT    Did I ever deceive anyone?

KARIN    Yes — me.

COUNT   You exaggerate.

KARIN   Because love has no exchange rate that you can put a figure on? But you calculated it exactly when you married my money — that's not love. You stole my feelings by all the means that you and your kind are familiar with. You made a whore of me, and you were no more than the pimp. I had to provide money — then you took me. Exactly the same as the street-walker whose child you now have in your house. *That* child belongs to you — not *mine*! And woe betide you if you hadn't fed it with milk and honey — I would have such revenge that you wouldn't have drawn breath for the rest of your life.

*Enter Hereditary Countess from rear.*

HEREDITARY COUNTESS   I've ordered tea here in the hall in ten minutes, *en petit comité*. I assume it will be just us again in ten minutes. *To Karin*. Madame is still here?

COUNT *going to her — trying to mollify her.*   Aunt Jutta —

HEREDITARY COUNTESS   'Your Ladyship' when strangers are present, my dear James. *To Karin again*. Baron Barrenkrona has shunned you — Count Erik presented himself — James devoted some of his precious time to you — now I will grant you ten minutes — *To Count*. The table set for six persons — Miss Grove will participate. Ring for the lackey.

COUNT *rings quickly — and continues ringing.*

HEREDITARY COUNTESS   Enough, James — he's not deaf! *To Karin*. How can I get you back into the fresh air? Are you in financial difficulties? *To James*. What's keeping the lackey? We've another task in hand for him.

KARIN   The lackey is showing Erik the castle and the cavaliers' house.

HEREDITARY COUNTESS   Count Erik is walking in the park with Baroness Alice.

KARIN   But then the lackey would have appeared after all that furious ringing.

HEREDITARY COUNTESS   What nonsense to talk of a lackey.

KARIN   You started it.

HEREDITARY COUNTESS   And for you — for you, above all — I am 'Your Ladyship'.

KARIN   What nonsense to talk of titles.

HEREDITARY COUNTESS   Are you a more important personage?

KARIN   I would hardly have come so far if I wasn't convinced of it.

HEREDITARY COUNTESS   The occasion being?

COUNT *rings again like mad.*

HEREDITARY COUNTESS   That's tactless, James, I deplore ringing —

COUNT   And shooting, Aunt Jutta — if someone were to blow his brains out — as I am about to do!

HEREDITARY COUNTESS *to Karin.*   What have you done to him?

KARIN   I've merely cleared up a misunderstanding after twenty years: that Erik Bratt has never been in Stjernenhö Castle after escaping with me.

COUNT   I opened my arms to the offspring of a crook and his paramour! — Embarrassing, Aunt Jutta — for the whole family.

HEREDITARY COUNTESS *recovers her poise.*   Count Erik is no fake. My judgement is infallible. You are a liar, madame.

KARIN *takes her folder.*   You want to see proof —

HEREDITARY COUNTESS   That's immaterial — all fake. Keep it. — Do you know the mother who provided the child?

KARIN   Yes.

HEREDITARY COUNTESS   Her name?

KARIN   I don't know her name.

HEREDITARY COUNTESS   Where does she live?

KARIN   I don't know.

HEREDITARY COUNTESS   Did you see her often?

KARIN   Just once — for ten minutes.

HEREDITARY COUNTESS   And she made a present of her child without further ado, and disappeared?

KARIN   It was as quick as that.

HEREDITARY COUNTESS   And no more was heard of the mother?

KARIN   I heard no more.

HEREDITARY COUNTESS   Did you say where the child would be taken?

KARIN   To Stjernenhö Castle.

HEREDITARY COUNTESS   James — did the woman appear here?

COUNT   Heavens above!

HEREDITARY COUNTESS   Now you dare accuse a mother of having no concern for her child for twenty years?! Because you didn't?! Was it that gave you the idea of creating havoc here? I will defend all true mothers against your barbaric onslaught ——

KARIN *rings the bell.*

HEREDITARY COUNTESS   You have the audacity to —

KARIN   I want to send for Erik.

HEREDITARY COUNTESS   The handsome chauffeur? The American? This is a real American plot and no mistake, but our police will sort it out.

*Enter Erik Bratt from left.*

ERIK BRATT   Ma — the one good thing: the garage. I've put our car away.

HEREDITARY COUNTESS   You won't be needing it when you're in custody. James — inform the police.

*Enter from rear Baron, Alice, Erik, Miss Grove.*

HEREDITARY COUNTESS   Too early for tea. It took more than ten minutes. But happily with the result that two confidence tricksters have been exposed — who wanted to turn you, Erik, into a foundling, and the chauffeur into Count Stjernenhö!

*Enter footman from left.*

HEREDITARY COUNTESS   Ah, the lackey. Go for the police — we need them.

FOOTMAN *doesn't move.*

HEREDITARY COUNTESS   First you don't hear the bell, now — James, is the man really deaf?

COUNT   What is it?

FOOTMAN   A woman at the door.

COUNT   Name?

FOOTMAN   She calls herself Mrs Appeblom — says she is expected today at Stjernenhö Castle.

COUNT   By whom?

KARIN   By everyone here!

COUNT *after a pause.*   Show her in.

FOOTMAN *exit.*

*Silence — until Mrs Appeblom arrives: of ample proportions, she is dressed in an overly ornate, provincial fashion.*

MRS APPEBLOM *curtseys several times to all present — then looks from one to the other — approaches Karin.*   You are the lady! The spitting image of twenty years ago. Almost younger — perhaps her daughter?

KARIN *amazed.*   Are you ——?

MRS APPEBLOM   The same — and yet not the same.

KARIN   You're —

MRS APPEBLOM   — double the size — treble. I wasn't as active as I used to be. Perhaps all too active!

KARIN   I would never have guessed!

MRS APPEBLOM   That's flattering — but I think I've been worthy of your trust.

KARIN   Yes — that you would keep your promise —?

MRS APPEBLOM   And one day not appear too out of place here.

KARIN *more composed.*   How have things gone for you?

MRS APPEBLOM   Not easy — but not too difficult either, like the cards life deals you. At first it was hard to keep on the straight and narrow. I was often blown off course. I was still hot-blooded — but I prefer not to dwell on such lapses. Then the allowance I collected every month had its effect. Going to the bank on a certain day each month brought order into my life. The bank became my church and the cashier my pastor. It was the period that marked the death of my husband, who passed away in prison. So I didn't need to take anyone else into account and was able to settle down as a respectable person. I also entered into a second marriage — and he established himself in the dried fish business. But it was neither dried cod nor my personality that attracted him — all he had his eye on was my allowance which he wanted to diddle me out of. I soon became wise to that — so I drew the logical conclusion which had far-reaching consequences: forcible ejection — literally — out through the shop door — in front of all the customers who cheered me on. I ask you: is a scoundrel a scoundrel or is he a gentleman?

KARIN *shakes her head.*

MRS APPEBLOM   Not in a million years, according to the Roman calendar. I don't know what tribe he came from, the rogue who only wanted my money when he married me. But it would be an insult to the heathen or the Mohammedans to think he was one of them. What dregs — scum — trash — ugh!

KARIN *nods.*

MRS APPEBLOM   Forgive me for getting carried away. But a human being who has kept her humanity — anyway, enough of that. I'd sooner talk about dried cod. Business flourished — I kept an eye on the deliveries and became the terror of the dealers. I'd had enough of scoundrels, from now on things ran according to the book. Profit and loss. In my own best interests. As my bank balance shows. Didn't touch the allowance any more. It was savings and it accumulated interest — as someone will discover one day. And the dried-fish business — I've feathered a nice little nest for him with that, too. The respect and love of my child will gladden my declining years.

KARIN *gives her her hand.*   You've turned your talents to good account, Mrs Appeblom, as the Bible says. I wouldn't have believed that our brief acquaintance twenty years ago could have borne such rich fruit.

MRS APPEBLOM   You come to understand the debt you owe a child that has grown up in a castle. Children can educate their parents as well — and I have always kept in my mind's eye the day I would be reunited with my Acke! — Now who is my Acke, that I left in your pram twenty years ago, so that he would be brought to Stjernenhö Castle?

KARIN   False Erik, whom you call Acke — who twenty years ago instead of the real Erik — *Pointing to Erik Bratt.* — was abducted by Count James Stjernenhö's henchmen and grew up here without being identified until today — *Points to Erik.* — is standing there!

MRS APPEBLOM *stares at him — makes to raise her arms towards him, lets them fall again as if paralysed — can only breathe.* Acke ————

*General amazement; gradually all draw back from Erik, who now stands isolated in the centre. —*
*Erik Bratt has gone over to Karin and puts an arm round her shoulder.*

ERIK *looks around — turns — storms off to rear.*

KARIN   Mrs Appeblom — go after your son, he could do himself a mischief.

MRS APPEBLOM *emits a little cry, follows Erik, exit rear.*

HEREDITARY COUNTESS *sternly.*    Baron Barrenkrona — your arm! Miss Grove, accompany us with Baroness Alice. *Disdainfully — already going towards staircase.* Acke —! *Exeunt all four above.*

COUNT *goes to Erik Bratt.*    Please let me have a bullet from your Browning in my brains — I'm too cowardly to do it!

# ACT THREE

~

*The same hall.*
*Erik Bratt sits behind a large newspaper — smoking a cigar and listening to a*
*portable gramophone in a leather case.*
*Enter Baron from above — slowly descends staircase — tries to catch Erik Bratt's*
*attention by clearing his throat — finally sits down in an armchair.*
*Erik Bratt reads and smokes.*

BARON  —— If I may interrupt your reading?

ERIK BRATT  Well noticed! I almost didn't hear the end and the needle would
have scratched the record. You have to go sparingly with the parts when you're
on your travels and can't pop into the nearest shop for a replacement in the
middle of the ocean. Without my gramophone I'd bore holes staring at the
horizon. *He has rewound the gramophone and is about to take up his paper
again.*

BARON  I'm afraid I rather neglected the formalities — other things seemed
more pressing at the time — I am Baron Barrenkrona — Alice's father.

ERIK BRATT *adjusting the gramophone.*  Too slow.

BARON  I am momentarily unable to find my bearings in the labyrinth of
connections between you and the House of Stjernenhö and, last but not least, my
family. Permit me to say a few words to draw these threads together — and
propose an arrangement. Perhaps the clarification will also suggest ways to you
which might lead to an appropriate solution to the satisfaction of all concerned.

ERIK BRATT *adjusting again.*  Faster!

BARON  The duplicity by which a child grew up here under false pretences has
naturally caused the greatest consternation among all parties. I cannot imagine
how a more sensational *éclat* could have been produced. I refrain from broaching
the subject of guilt. With a *fait accompli* of such magnitude, a rectification of the
damage caused is its own justification. May I count on your agreement?

Erik Bratt *yet again occupied with the gramophone.* The sea obviously didn't agree with the mechanism — it's jerking and stuttering like an asthmatic.

Baron Any more profound interest in calling yourself Erik Bratt is surely not possible. You bear an everyday name no more durable than the day itself. It can scarcely have got under your skin — you could change it like a suit of clothes. A simple operation which would pass off painlessly and pleasantly enough.

Erik Bratt Now it's working. Do you know this? No? It's a negro song — fiddle, trumpet, human voice all booming away. You should hear the uproar it creates over there — it gets you up and tap-dancing fit to crack the planks under your feet. Nothing but cowboys in a fug of tobacco smoke down on the ranch — pandemonium, like all hell had broken loose!

Baron Very uncomplicated — hence an environment that makes no demands. So I anticipate no complaints on your part and can breath a sigh of relief.

Erik Bratt Still much too much of a whisper. That gives no real sense of the scandal!

Baron The disgrace is unimaginable: Count Erik Stjernenhö — lieutenant in the Royal Dragoons — fiancé of Baroness Alice Barrenkrona: a common guttersnipe! Unbridled laughter is the only possible response to the whole affair!

Erik Bratt *adjusting.* Louder!

Baron And so this pseudo-count sinks without trace below our field of vision. An empty space yawns — which must be filled as rapidly as possible. The true Count Erik must appear — the true Stjernenhö — the true lieutenant — the true fiancé!

Erik Bratt Much louder!

Baron There are no special difficulties: the false Erik — this so-called Acke — has been little seen in public — Count James had good reason to keep the object of his abduction well under wraps in Stjernenhö Castle — the court passed judgement sight unseen, and anyway, that judgement becomes inoperative with the coming of age tomorrow. — Alice's consent is unnecessary — I'll vouch for that. A Barrenkrona corrects any *faux pas* punctiliously!

Erik Bratt Now we hear the full orchestra!

BARON   To summarize: this Appeblom disappears — at our expense, of course — to America, whither other superfluous persons have already betaken themselves —

ERIK BRATT *jumps up — dances, sings.*   In Kansas I've a maiden fair ——

BARON *abruptly.*   Can't you turn that thing off for five minutes?

ERIK BRATT *at the gramophone.*   Much — much louder!

BARON   Your curious failure to see the seriousness of the situation —

ERIK BRATT *dancing — singing.*   I've got one in Orinoco —

BARON   You avoid answering in a somewhat original manner —

ERIK BRATT   And in Missouri one loves me too ——

BARON   You show hardly the slightest interest in the fate of two noble houses —

ERIK BRATT   But in Ohio I know them all —

BARON   I understand — Mr Bratt! — please don't trouble yourself with further refusals. Much obliged! *Exit up staircase.*

ERIK BRATT *throws himself into an armchair — the gramophone runs down.*

*Alice was already visible above earlier: she was listening — and hid as the Baron departed; now she rushes down the stairs.*

ALICE *face to face with Erik Bratt.*   Papa insulted me! I've no intention of marrying a complete stranger! Not even the Emperor of China, if I wasn't in love!

ERIK BRATT *has got up.*   I've no intention of stealing you away from Acke.

ALICE   I don't know — who I love — but it's definitely not you!

ERIK BRATT   You have a somewhat original manner of addressing a complete stranger —

ALICE   I heard it all — in spite of your gramophone and Indian dance.

ERIK BRATT  Didn't I extricate myself from that predicament rather tactfully?

ALICE  Tact won't get us any further. It's always tact — tact — tact, until you run out of breath — *Already tearful.* — and you're dying of ——

ERIK BRATT  Love.

ALICE *stamps her foot.*  I'm not in love! — I don't want to be in love! — I want —

ERIK BRATT  To correct the *faux pas* punctiliously.

ALICE *after a pause.*  How do you get to America?

ERIK BRATT  By ship.

ALICE  Does it cost a lot?

ERIK BRATT  Depends what demands you make.

ALICE  I make none!

ERIK BRATT  Then it's cheap.

ALICE  And when you get there?

ERIK BRATT  Depends on your abilities.

ALICE  He's none.

ERIK BRATT  Who?

ALICE  Acke.

ERIK BRATT  Is he going as well?

ALICE  Of course.

ERIK BRATT  Your papa will hang himself.

ALICE  Can you play patience after you're dead.

ERIK BRATT  Hardly.

ALICE　Then he'll get over it. Everyone can live if he wants to. I want to — I demand to live — and I'll fight like a tiger to hang on to my life!

ERIK BRATT　Then I congratulate you and Acke.

ALICE　That means nothing. You're an American — it's your duty to help others. How will you help Acke and me?

ERIK BRATT　There are certain difficulties —

ALICE　Huge ones, I hope, otherwise it's not worth the effort.

ERIK BRATT　　— which Acke could make!

ALICE　Never!

ERIK BRATT　It's not so easy marrying a baroness if you're a proletarian.

ALICE　The opposite is true!

ERIK BRATT　You don't usually want to start with people who are already the finished article. It's a bad deal.

ALICE　Will you tell him that?

ERIK BRATT　You tell Acke — and if you find favour in his eyes, I'm willing to play the ferryman.

ALICE　Have you got money?

ERIK BRATT　Tomorrow I will renounce my inheritance from my grandfather and make it over to Acke. He deserves to be rewarded in some way for having had to live here.

ALICE　Is it a deal?

ERIK BRATT　Shake! *They shake hands.*

ALICE *exit to rear.*

ERIK BRATT *follows her with his eyes.*

*Enter Count from right.*

COUNT   I tried.

ERIK BRATT *turns round.*   What?

COUNT   You probably have to be born to it — I've no talent whatsoever for suicide.

ERIK BRATT   You've shrouded yourself with an air of tragedy.

COUNT   With every justification.

ERIK BRATT   Semicolon. Your son has returned —

COUNT *quickly.*   Can I take it that you are my son?

ERIK BRATT   I'm the real thing.

COUNT   I'll remind you of that.

ERIK BRATT   The fact that you are my father is not something that comes off in the wash.

COUNT *looks at him.*

ERIK BRATT *indicates the armchairs. Both sit down.*

COUNT   The details are more or less sorted — to adopt a purely business tone.

ERIK BRATT   That's the first friendly word I've heard in this gathering of the clans!

COUNT   Without for my part wanting to allot any exaggerated importance to financial affairs.

ERIK BRATT   So that's — what concerns you at this time of reunion?

COUNT   That's why I needed your Browning — to put that calculation to the test.

ERIK BRATT   I'm an excellent calculator — only I use my head — not a pistol.

COUNT    —— Has your mother told you about an inheritance you come into when you come of age?

ERIK BRATT    That's what our trip has been all about. Tomorrow I am twenty-one and inherit my grandfather Lars Bratt's estate.

COUNT    You won't forget that I was labouring under a misapprehension, raising this Acke instead of you?

ERIK BRATT    I declare myself retrospectively in agreement with my stand-in.

COUNT *quickly*.    So you also recognize the costs involved in caring for him?

ERIK BRATT    Covered by the interest which was decreed solely for that purpose.

COUNT    It's all spent —

ERIK BRATT    Which I find astonishing, since Ma told me the amount involved —

COUNT    It was a question of moulding a Count Stjernenhö —

ERIK BRATT    It would have been enough to fund a home for a hundred foundlings. You used it up on one — and a proletarian child to boot.

COUNT    I didn't know that.

ERIK BRATT    Does that make your extravagance any better?

COUNT    — We're lingering over the interest —

ERIK BRATT *dismissively*.    Liquidated!

COUNT    The question of the capital will provide more than enough food for thought.

ERIK BRATT    How is it invested?

COUNT    According to your overseas criteria probably wrongly — but here we are convinced correctly.

ERIK BRATT    Money is international: the investment criterion is everywhere the same: profitability.

COUNT    As we see it, this — profitability — is expressed in a succinct axiom: a life-style befitting one's social standing.

ERIK BRATT    If you've got money, spend it!

COUNT    It was my duty to live an exemplary life, as every Count Stjernenhö has done for generations.

ERIK BRATT    Do I deny you the right to do what you want with your money?

COUNT    It wasn't my money — that I spent.

ERIK BRATT    Whoever lent you it can be of little interest to me.

COUNT    No. But signed statements were called for, and I pledged what was at hand as security.

ERIK BRATT *shrugs his shoulders.*

COUNT    Your inheritance.

ERIK BRATT *stares at him.*

COUNT    —— I will not attempt to defend my actions. The divide between us is too deep to cross. The attempt would be in vain. Let me give you the facts: Stjernenhö Castle had become badly delapidated — the ancestral home of the Stjernenhös — and restoration was urgently needed, otherwise the roof would have fallen on our heads. Now it will last for centuries to come — a sanctuary for the dynasty, past and future.

ERIK BRATT *rousing himself.*    Both the interest and the capital — you could have built a town for that — instead of this desolate pile!

COUNT    You overlook the occupants. I revived the old festive splendour of Stjernenhö Castle. We were on people's lips again — talk of our glory even reached the King — and that bore fruit: members of the family who had distanced themselves from me returned — the Regiment of Dragoons opened its doors — the most distinguished baroness gave her hand to a Stjernenhö. — But all that is surpassed by the effect of living in Stjernenhö Castle, and what it brought to fruition in that simple Acke Appeblom: an hour ago, every inch the gentleman, he signed the deed which handed over his supposed inheritance to my creditors.

ERIK BRATT *reaches in his pocket — takes out his Browning — pushes it over the table — takes it back again — puts it away.*   It would be a pity to waste the bullet.

COUNT   When I asked you to render me that service, you hesitated. Now let me remind you of your own words: prove you are my son.

ERIK BRATT *looks at him — breaks out in unbridled laughter.*   That's my Pa! — and that's what Ma married! — a shabby little swindler, who'll resort to anything to get what he wants. Bone-idle, barefaced — and cowardly as a coyote!

COUNT *obsequiously.*   Have your say —

ERIK BRATT   You build yourself a house so rotten in its foundations that — even the wood panelling creaks. You steal the money for it from your own son — and afterwards beg for a letter of indulgence! — Enough, Pa — I've made my inheritance over to Acke —

COUNT *joyfully.*   And the deed is valid?

ERIK BRATT   If Acke Appeblom makes over to Count Stjernenhö once again what only now belongs to him!

COUNT   Where is Acke?

ERIK BRATT   Provided he's not dead —

COUNT   Acke has to live until he's paid me compensation! Otherwise Lindström will strangle me!

ERIK BRATT   The same Lindström whose name opens all doors as if by magic?

COUNT   That scoundrel of a profiteer — extortion!

ERIK BRATT   You're no better, Pa — only more dangerous.

*Enter Acke from rear.*

ACKE *going up to Erik Bratt.*   Mr Bratt — my fiancée has informed me of your gift. I accept it and thank you.

ERIK BRATT *shakes his hand.*   I think you may need it.

ACKE   You shall control how it should be spent over in America.

ERIK BRATT   I shall always be at your disposal as a friend.

ACKE   That's even more important than working capital.

COUNT *almost angry.*   What more do you want. Haven't you got a dried-fish shop?

ACKE *sharply.*   Orders should be directed to Mrs Antje Appeblom.

COUNT   One moment, young man —

ACKE   Are our scores not settled?

COUNT   You signed a deed which is invalid.

ACKE   You induced me to make gifts which were not at my disposal to make.

COUNT   But now they are at your disposal.

ACKE   With which to determine my future and Alice's.

COUNT   I incurred expenses —

ACKE   Did I force you to incur expenses on my behalf?

COUNT   Here you grew up into what you now are. I am the broker of your good fortune. One pays one's debts!

ACKE *looks at Erik Bratt questioningly.*

ERIK BRATT   Let my father take you to court.

ACKE *to Count.*   I await your action. *Exit rear.*

COUNT *looks stonily at Erik Bratt.*

*Enter Hereditary Countess above — swishes down the staircase.*

HEREDITARY COUNTESS *below.*    Alice has disappeared from her room! The child was in my care — the Baron is asleep, exhausted — Alice won't survive the shock! — Yes, James, won't you search?

COUNT    I'll — search —— *He staggers off, right.*

HEREDITARY COUNTESS *to Erik Bratt.*    Perhaps you too could be minded to search for the Baroness!

ERIK BRATT    That won't be necessary, since Alice is — with her Acke.

HEREDITARY COUNTESS    —— Alice?? —— Acke??

ERIK BRATT    I thought they were engaged?

HEREDITARY COUNTESS    To this —— Appeblom??

ERIK BRATT    The name has changed somewhat, but it's the same person.

HEREDITARY COUNTESS    If only my knees hadn't given way ——

ERIK BRATT *pushes an armchair towards her.*    Best not disturb the pair.

HEREDITARY COUNTESS *groaning.*    Why weren't the police summoned ——!

ERIK BRATT    Best not give Count James too great a shock.

HEREDITARY COUNTESS    His fate is wretched enough. But that's the result when one ignores one's obligations.

ERIK BRATT    The Count has certainly seen to that.

HEREDITARY COUNTESS    It began with a marriage —

ERIK BRATT    And will end with a marriage. Guilt and atonement balanced out.

HEREDITARY COUNTESS    We haven't reached that point yet. No, my dear boy. Obedience is what is needed. The first *mésalliance* was mere child's play compared with this affront.

ERIK BRATT    I find that my Pa made an extraordinarily good marriage.

HEREDITARY COUNTESS   Has he recognized you?

ERIK BRATT   If Mr Appeblom settles Pa's debts, I would have no objection. Otherwise he seems to me to be too pathetic a figure.

HEREDITARY COUNTESS *already confused.*   But Erik inherits tomorrow?

ERIK BRATT   Erik is a busted flush — a burst bubble.

HEREDITARY COUNTESS   Are you now — the heir?

ERIK BRATT   There's nothing left to inherit. The Count has already run through it all.

HEREDITARY COUNTESS   The hall is beginning to sway ——!

ERIK BRATT   It's creaking in every joint, Aunt Jutta.

HEREDITARY COUNTESS   Dust swirling before my eyes ——!

ERIK BRATT   A whole world crashing down in rubble — but let's save what scant residue there is.

HEREDITARY COUNTESS   You can save whatever can be saved: the Stjernenhö name — the lieutenant — the —

ERIK BRATT   That's too heavy a burden.

HEREDITARY COUNTESS   This Acke — don't you at least want to —?

ERIK BRATT    — marry him off, with your help.

HEREDITARY COUNTESS   With my ——??

ERIK BRATT   I'll pay your nephew's debts — if you talk the Baron into agreeing to the marriage — without conditions.

HEREDITARY COUNTESS   Have you so much money?

ERIK BRATT *writes a note.*   For Count James — after your discussion with Baron Barrenkrona.

HEREDITARY COUNTESS *takes the note with trembling hands — rises — slowly goes up staircase — exit above.*

*Enter Karin left — her hair ruffled by the wind.*

ERIK BRATT    Getting some fresh air, Ma?

KARIN    Boy, what you could make of this wasteland. No one lifts a finger here. There was money enough.

ERIK BRATT    But it's all been renovated.

KARIN    Acres upon acres could have been reclaimed and cultivated. With villages and settlements. Now it's all heathland running wild instead of fields and meadows.

ERIK BRATT    But there is something flourishing here.

KARIN    Apart from gorse and wild lettuce?

ERIK BRATT    Two people: Acke and Alice.

KARIN    Are they staying together?

ERIK BRATT    All arranged, Ma.

KARIN    And the Baron?

ERIK BRATT    Thrown in the sponge.

KARIN    What about a dowry?

ERIK BRATT    They don't need one.

KARIN    Then what will —?

ERIK BRATT *looks at her — wants to say more — kisses her on the mouth.*    Acke will inherit tomorrow in my place.

KARIN    You couldn't find a better heir than — this son of the proletariat!

*Enter Mrs Appeblom from rear.*

MRS APPEBLOM    He's decided on America and left me sitting on the dried fish. The firm of Appeblom & Son is not to be. The nicely feathered nest stays empty, and the bird flies up and away.

KARIN    Don't blame him —

MRS APPEBLOM    For finding it too constricting here with me? I didn't bring him into the world only to drill him to do whatever I want. My tears are tears of joy if he can do more than me. And Acke can: yesterday a ragamuffin — today a count — tomorrow an American. That's a potential you either have, or you don't.

KARIN    You're right, Mrs Appeblom, and your son is no exception.

MRS APPEBLOM    Then the world can start afresh — but this time the good Lord shouldn't make a mess of it, this time we take control of it ourselves. Give us something to eat and pamper us a bit — that's Mother Appeblom's recipe for paradise — no charge!

*Enter Acke and Alice from rear.*

ALICE *to Mrs Appeblom.*    Can you put us up tonight?

ACKE    Alice is leaving this house with me right away.

MRS APPEBLOM    There's always room for my children.

ALICE *to Karin.*    May we use your car?

KARIN    There's room for five.

ACKE    Who are — the five of us?

ERIK BRATT    And on *Butterfly* we can dance.

ALICE    What is the *Butterfly*?

ERIK BRATT    It used to be Uncle Knut's white yacht — inherited by me along with half of Kansas.

ACKE *rings the bell.*

*Enter footman from left.*

ACKE   Please bring our things — for Miss Alice and me.

KARIN   You'll find all you need on board — just as I did when I decamped twenty years ago.

*Enter Hereditary Countess, Baron and Miss Grove from above.*

HEREDITARY COUNTESS *below, to Baron.*   I still need to talk to James. *To Miss Grove in an undertone.* Take care of the Baron. *Exit right.*

BARON *sees the others.*

*Miss Grove stands stiffly, reading in a small book.*

BARON *goes towards Alice.*   Her Ladyship has informed me of your resolve. She says it is unshakable. Far be it from me to attempt to influence your decision — I've never done that. I've always wanted the best for you — I defer to your choice.

ALICE *calmly.*   Thank you, Papa.

BARON   It would go against my principles to give my blessing to your union. The affair lies beyond my grasp. Please let it remain so. We now part company and I hereby declare you disinherited. *To Miss Grove.* Is tea served?

ALICE *aloud to Mrs Appeblom.*   Shall we go, mother?

*Enter Hereditary Countess and Count from right; Count beaming.*

HEREDITARY COUNTESS   My dear Baron — *She presses his hand. To Count, who is making joyful gestures towards Erik Bratt.* Control yourself, James. Ring for tea, James.

COUNT *rings.*

*Enter footman from left — carrying coats.*

HEREDITARY COUNTESS *grasping the situation.*   You are leaving? *To Karin.* Decamping — *Glancing at Alice and Acke.* — with entourage?

MRS APPEBLOM *almost embarrassed.*   The children simply want to be with their mother.

KARIN *to Hereditary Countess.* A disarming argument. What has a mother a greater right to than her own child? I should repeat your own words, which were intended to sound to my ears like the last trump — but I'll make it simpler: whoever is of service to their child, is a true mother. Mrs Appeblom kept quiet for twenty years in order not to embarrass Acke — I hid for twenty years, in order to keep Erik. That is surely the true nobility of the blood, something which manifests itself day in, day out. *To Count.* Your assistance, James, was exceptional. Even though you totally confounded both yourself and your kind. *Looking at Acke.* But this result erases any shadow of a doubt. Thank you, James, you've done a good deed for mankind. Where there's a will, there's a way. How does Mrs Appeblom put it —: give us something to eat and pamper us a bit — that's paradise on earth.

*Short silence.*

ERIK BRATT *claps his hands.* Off to Mother Appeblom's!

*Alice and Acke already in coats.*
*Footman brings coats for Karin and Erik Bratt.*

COUNT *spotting the gramophone on the table.* The music box!

ERIK BRATT You can have that as well, Pa, in case you feel like tap-dancing — which I hope you will. *Everyone looks at each other in silence for a moment — then the five leave.*

*The others look blank.*
*Footman pushes in tea-trolley with a posy of yellow carnations in the middle.*
*The four sit down.*

HEREDITARY COUNTESS ———— Curious how this Acke illustrated the catechism of all noble families. There must be something of a count in every proletarian — and something of a proletarian in every count. But I'm too old to resign myself to such Bolshevism.

BARON ———— The yellow carnations.

COUNT And half a sugar-lump in your tea! *He puts it into the Hereditary Countess's cup.*

# One Day in October

*(Oktobertag, 1927)*

# CHARACTERS

M. Coste
Catherine, his niece
Lieutenant Jean-Marc Marrien
Mme. Jattefaux, housekeeper
Leguerche, butcher's boy
A Servant

*The entire action of this love story takes place in the spacious drawing-room of M. Coste's villa. In a semicircle: to the rear, a tall French window leading on to a terrace overlooking a park below; to the right, two doors; to the left, one door.*

# ACT ONE

*Enter Servant, left, crosses to right and knocks on downstage door.*

SERVANT *opens door.*   Madame Jattefaux has arrived and would like to know when you wish to see her. — At once? — I'll inform her. *Shuts door, exit left.*

*Servant returns with Mme. Jattefaux, knocks again and opens door, downstage right.*

SERVANT   Madame Jattefaux. *Shuts door, exit left.*

*Mme. Jattefaux looks apprehensively at door, right.*
*Enter Coste, goes quickly to Mme. Jattefaux and greets her with a handshake. He beckons her to sit and does so himself.*

COSTE   —— Did you have a pleasant journey? Did I give you all the right connections when I wrote?

JATTEFAUX   I would have sent a wire if I hadn't been able to come in time.

COSTE   I know I can always depend on you, Madame Jattefaux.

JATTEFAUX   One does what one has to do.

COSTE *shakes his head.*   As to that, opinions may differ. We had no agreement that you would stand by me in a situation as embarrassing as this.

JATTEFAUX   It is an all too human predicament, and it is our duty to meet it as best we can.

COSTE   Does that mean you can condone what has happened?

JATTEFAUX   I do not want to condemn anyone, Monsieur Coste, not before the mystery has been cleared up.

COSTE   But what's not clear about it? Catherine has named the father — Lieutenant Jean-Marc Marrien — and such a person actually exists — in Paris. Fifth regiment of the line. Here's his address. *Hands her a piece of paper.* Isn't that all real enough?

JATTEFAUX   That is certainly the first thing that needs explaining.

COSTE   The only thing, Madame Jattefaux. I reject any attempt to gloss things over or find some excuse — from any quarter.
—— Was your sister very inconvenienced at taking Catherine in during her confinement without it coming to public notice?

JATTEFAUX   My sister leads a very secluded life. Besides, Catherine was supposedly a relative whose husband was away on a trip to the colonies.

COSTE   Did she divulge his name to your sister?

JATTEFAUX   She did.

COSTE   But not to you?

JATTEFAUX   To me too — but without her realizing it.

COSTE   How was that?

JATTEFAUX   When she was having the baby. She seemed to feel no pain, only bliss, while she was in labour, even more so at the birth itself. At that moment an almost beatific smile spread over her face, her lips parted in a whisper, but what she said was quite distinct: Lieutenant Jean-Marc Marrien — our child! — I noted down the name and sent it to you.

COSTE   A note which has served its purpose admirably. It wasn't difficult to find an officer of that name, though it was a great surprise to find him in one of the best regiments in France. Not only that, but the son of one of the foremost families in the land. I had imagined him some sort of debauched scoundrel. But for her confession I would never have believed that someone of his social standing, and an officer to boot, could have allowed himself such licence and run from the consequences. And with my niece, too, a Coste — a name that deserves the utmost respect.
—— And Catherine is unaware that we now know who the father of her child is?

JATTEFAUX    I never mentioned it.

COSTE    I still think that is best — at least until Lieutenant Marrien confronts her.

JATTEFAUX    Is he coming here?

COSTE    After repeated demands — it was only after I threatened to notify his regiment that he agreed. He should have arrived almost at the same time as you. That's why I worked out exactly when you and Catherine would get here. The only reason I want to see Catherine here at all is to give her child a father. They can get married quietly in Paris. Not in my house!

JATTEFAUX    —— Perhaps Catherine should be spared all this, Monsieur Coste.

COSTE    Did either of them spare me the shame of it? Or is that what they were doing when the lieutenant kept his existence covered up and his paramour sworn to secrecy? What's your verdict, Madame Jattefaux?

*Jattefaux remains silent.*

COSTE    You can't answer, can you — and neither can I. What an out-and-out blackguard! Just imagine the sort of person this Lieutenant Marrien must be: sweet-talks a defenceless, love-sick girl into giving herself to him, then forcibly swears her to silence when she gets pregnant. Doesn't he deserve to be horsewhipped?

JATTEFAUX    The reason Catherine said nothing is because she didn't want to — neither before the birth of the child nor after. She never seemed oppressed by any secret. For the whole period of her pregnancy she was blithely happy.

COSTE    Then why did she remain silent when I questioned her? She clammed up like some wayward child caught in the act. All she did was smile — and that made me even angrier. What's behind her stubbornness?

JATTEFAUX    You will find out presently, Monsieur Coste, when Lieutenant Marrien and Catherine meet. — And you will also find out where they met before.

COSTE    That's a mystery I've given up trying to solve, Madame Jattefaux.

JATTEFAUX   It occupies my every waking moment. I wouldn't dare sit here before you, Monsieur Coste, if I could recall a single lapse of attentiveness. It would have been the death of me! I'm speaking in earnest, Monsieur Coste, like I would before God's Judgement seat. I watched Catherine's every step — followed her like her own shadow. I was proud when you entrusted your niece to my care — it was a heartfelt pleasure to devote myself to such a wonderfully sweet creature. I couldn't have taken better care of her if she had been my own daughter. I've been trying to think of any time I might have been off my guard. Where could she have met someone without my seeing him too? And struck up a friendship unbeknownst to me? When did I ever let her out of my sight long enough for her to — let it happen? How is it possible?

COSTE   You are not to blame, Madame Jattefaux. After the sacrifices you and your sister made for me, how could I harbour the slightest doubts. But for you, the stain would have blackened my doorstep and tainted the whole house. As it is, no one is aware of my niece's folly. I have you to thank for that. *He rises and kisses her hand.* I am greatly in your debt — how can I ever repay you?

JATTEFAUX   I beg you never to lose your confidence in me, Monsieur Coste.

COSTE   What could possibly shake it?

JATTEFAUX   What you are about to hear Catherine say in the presence of Lieutenant Marrien.

*Enter Servant, left, with a visiting-card on a salver.*
*Coste takes it — reads it — nods. Exit Servant.*

COSTE *to Mme Jattefaux.*   Please stay with Catherine until I call. *Brandishing the visiting-card.* Not a word about the visitor!

*Exit Jattefaux, upstage right.*
*Coste crushes the card in his fist — drops it.*
*Servant shows Lieutenant Marrien in.*
*Exit Servant.*
*Marrien eyes Coste coolly — bows briefly.*

COSTE *barely reciprocates.*   —— You delayed responding to the invitations I sent you in Paris. You were not in Paris?

MARRIEN   I received your letters in Paris.

COSTE   And paid them such little attention that you neglected to answer them.

MARRIEN   I thought I might spare myself the trouble.

COSTE   But then you changed your mind?

MARRIEN   When the last communication contained a threat.

COSTE   That caused you some distress?

MARRIEN   No.

COSTE   Yet you have come.

MARRIEN   After showing your letters to others and, by chance, being apprised of who had sent them. I was told that the name of Coste was among the most respected in France. I could no longer assume it was a case of personal abuse, but that some serious matter must have occasioned the letters.

COSTE   You had never heard of the name of Coste before?

MARRIEN   Not that I recall.

COSTE *heatedly.*   Do you mean to say you did not know with whom you —! *He breaks off.*

*Marrien waits.*

COSTE *quietly.*   It will soon be clear to what extent you are telling the truth —

MARRIEN   By what right —?

COSTE   — as soon as a certain affair is settled in the only way such affairs can be settled. When do you propose to marry?

*Marrien stares at Coste blankly.*

COSTE   Perhaps you are not adequately informed about the most recent events — after you broke off relations with my niece when the consequences became apparent. Catherine gave birth to a child a short time ago in the home of my housekeeper's sister in a remote town in the provinces, declaring the father of the child to be Lieutenant Jean-Marc Marrien. Since further enquiry ascertained that there was only one Lieutenant Jean-Marc Marrien in the whole wide world, there can be no doubt that it is the father of Catherine's child who is standing before me now.

MARRIEN *falteringly.*    I —— do not know your niece ——

COSTE    You did not know Catherine was my niece? She did not mention the name Coste? Out of regard for me? It was just some girl called Catherine who lay in your arms?

MARRIEN    I do not know of any Catherine ——

COSTE    So she didn't reveal her first name either? What name did she use when she was with you?

*Marrien shrugs.*

COSTE    Please don't hide behind meaningless gestures. Think hard, Lieutenant Marrien. You are trying to make it look like the sort of adventure one has with someone picked up from the street and no questions asked. It is my niece you made advances to — fully knowing who she was, just as Catherine knows your name and rank. I won't stand for your insulting my niece by branding her a whore!

MARRIEN *collecting himself.*    Where are we supposed to have met?

COSTE    Here, in town. Where else? Catherine never left the town all that year.

MARRIEN    I have never set foot in this town.

COSTE    You must be mistaken.

MARRIEN    That is to say, I set foot in it —

COSTE    Aha!

MARRIEN    — today, for the first — and last — time, to clear my name of an allegation I find incomprehensible. I am in no way linked to the events you describe. There is some misunderstanding which it is your duty, and yours alone, to remove.

COSTE    And I call on you, Lieutenant Marrien, to be of assistance. You deny all knowledge of my niece. Why then does Catherine know you?

MARRIEN   I don't understand your niece.

COSTE   Was she under some compulsion to keep silent? She did maintain her silence — and only fail to the once — in extremis — at the moment her child was born. A woman does not lie at such a time. And the name she uttered — involuntarily — was the name you bear. You alone, Lieutenant Jean-Marc Marrien. You are Lieutenant Jean-Marc Marrien?

MARRIEN   I am not the father of the child of your niece, Catherine Coste.

*Coste rings a bell.*
*Enter Servant, left.*

COSTE   Madame Jattefaux!

*Servant goes towards door, upstage right.*

COSTE *calls after him.*   And only Madame Jattefaux!

*Exit Servant, upstage right.*
*Enter Mme. Jattefaux.*

COSTE *makes an introductory gesture.*   Madame Jattefaux — my housekeeper and Catherine's governess. Please tell Lieutenant Marrien what occurred in your sister's house. I was not present myself — I rely on the testimony of witnesses whose trustworthiness is absolute. As is their conviction of what they heard — which is of vital importance. Did Catherine say anything during the birth?

JATTEFAUX   Very little.

COSTE   Perhaps her voice was drowned out by her — groans?

JATTEFAUX   She didn't utter a sound.

COSTE   Except for certain words?

JATTEFAUX   Which she said quite clearly.

COSTE   And those words were?

JATTEFAUX   Lieutenant Jean-Marc Marrien — our child!

COSTE    Which you heard distinctly?

JATTEFAUX    As did my sister.

COSTE *softly*.    Lieutenant Jean-Marc Marrien denies being the father.

*Jattefaux stares at Marrien in amazement.*
*Marrien remains motionless.*

COSTE *after a pause*.    Lieutenant Marrien has never seen Catherine. In spite of that she calls out his name — his full name. It has become an urgent necessity for Catherine now to answer our questions. If necessary, she may have to apologize to Lieutenant Marrien. *To Mme. Jattefaux.* Please fetch Catherine.

*Exit Mme. Jattefaux, upstage right.*

COSTE *to Marrien*.    My niece might be startled by your presence. If you would wait in my room — you'll find reading material to amuse yourself with. *He shows Marrien into room, downstage right.*

*Marrien leaves.*
*Coste paces up and down — stops.*
*Catherine enters — followed by Mme. Jattefaux, who quickly and silently leaves. Catherine slowly, without hesitating, approaches Coste. Smiling throughout, she looks him straight in the eye.*
*Coste looks at her thoughtfully — proffers his hand.*

CATHERINE    My hands have got caught up in the shawl. There, my left one is free. Do you want the other one?

COSTE    Whichever you wish.

CATHERINE    It really doesn't matter which?

COSTE    As I said.

CATHERINE    Ah, it has come free. Now I can give you the right one.

COSTE *takes her hand*.    I take it as a sign of your good will in returning to my house.

CATHERINE   Have I not always been obedient — whether you send me away or summon me back?

COSTE *pulls up a chair for her.*   Please sit down.

*Catherine sits.*

COSTE *also sits.*   Are you — very tired after your journey?

CATHERINE   Nothing tires me.

COSTE   You've recovered from the stress of what you've gone through? Madame Jattefaux wrote to me about it.

CATHERINE   It wasn't at all stressful.

COSTE   That's how giving birth is usually described.

CATHERINE   But wrongly.

COSTE   Perhaps it is not always so — at least, not in your case. From what you say, you are fully recuperated and in the best of health, and that reassures me. It means our talk will not be affected by your condition and you won't find it unduly taxing to hear what I have to say. Would you care for some refreshment?

CATHERINE   Thank you, no.

COSTE   I'm anxious to avoid any interruption later.

CATHERINE   I won't cause any.

COSTE   I could remind you that you have already been the cause of a disturbance, to put it mildly, not to say an upheaval. But I won't rake up the past. Nor need you concern yourself with what I might or might not know about what happened. I am quite resolved, however belatedly, to acknowledge your right to determine your own actions. You are a free agent — let no one set himself up as a judge over others. Be assured that there will be no more accusations.

CATHERINE   Have you ever reproached me?

COSTE *gazes at her.* No, Catherine, not if you cannot recall me doing so. Let us bury the past. It is no longer yourself and your secret liaisons at issue —— it is the child!

CATHERINE Yes.

COSTE When it was born — with its birth — it lay claim to become legitimate. It is a claim that cannot be ignored. It would be tantamount to murder to deny him the most natural of rights — the right to bear his father's name. Whatever reasons you had not to respond to my earlier probing, I will not pursue. It would be a gross trespass on your innermost being to do so — forgive me if I ever did — but for the child's sake alone, who needs my help, I ask you to enlighten me now. Who is the father?

*Catherine shakes her head — remains silent.*

COSTE A word will suffice. As a mother you bear an awesome responsibility. Don't let the child suffer for the sake of your secret, however confidential. I do not know what it is, nor do I want to. But the child must have that name.

*Catherine as before.*

COSTE *pauses, then in a brisk tone.* In that case I must inform you that I know the name: Lieutenant Jean-Marc Marrien.

CATHERINE *calmly as before.* Then why did you ask me?

COSTE *taken aback.* So it is true —— that Lieutenant Marrien ——?

CATHERINE You said you knew it was.

COSTE Then your confession still holds — it was Lieutenant Marrien?

CATHERINE Did he not tell you himself?

COSTE Catherine — you must try to recall everything you said. Or perhaps you can't recall since you were barely conscious — and that's what loosened your tongue. When the baby was being born. Madame Jattefaux and her sister heard you. You spoke his name — you, and no one else!

CATHERINE I spoke his name — when our child was born.

COSTE   And now I want you to repeat it. In full consciousness. Now that you can hear what you say. Think carefully! A man's honour and his whole future depend upon it. Is Lieutenant Marrien the father of your child.

CATHERINE   Yes.

COSTE   Lieutenant Marrien denies it.

*Catherine nods and smiles.*

COSTE   Does his denial not bother you? You seem to have expected it. Why should one party deny it after the other has confessed?

CATHERINE   He won't want to tell you, just as I didn't.

COSTE   In that case, it is chance that I must thank, chance that made you speak out involuntarily — for the child's sake — the child whose birth extracted the revelation. Otherwise the truth would never have come to light?

CATHERINE   It would have, some day.

COSTE   Was there an understanding between you as to how long you would maintain silence?

CATHERINE   Until I had given birth to our child.

COSTE   But now he has learnt of that — and still he refuses to acknowledge the child.

CATHERINE   He still doesn't know.

COSTE   What?

CATHERINE   That he is the child's father.

COSTE   —— It is hard for me to follow your train of thought and form a clear picture of your relationship when every step is shrouded in mystery. But one cannot evade the consequences. The fact is, the child exists. That is my only consideration if I am to find the right solution. Now please leave me alone for a moment. *Rises, goes to door upstage right, opens it.* Madame Jattefaux!

*Enter Mme. Jattefaux.*

COSTE     Catherine is to remain close by —

*Catherine has risen. Goes to door, upstage right, in measured steps. Exit.*

COSTE *closes door behind her. To Mme. Jattefaux.*     How would you assess Catherine's character? Does she tell lies? Have you ever found her out?

JATTEFAUX     Catherine is truthful in every word she utters.

COSTE     There was never any indication of a character defect that might show up later?

JATTEFAUX     I would have noticed if there had been.

COSTE     You are totally convinced you can believe everything she says?

JATTEFAUX     Absolutely.

COSTE     She has said again that Lieutenant Marrien is the child's father.

JATTEFAUX     Then it must be true, Monsieur Coste.

COSTE     I'm becoming convinced of that too, when I think of how she reacted. She didn't turn a hair when I mentioned his name. No trace of a blush or sign of anger when I told her Lieutenant Marrien had challenged her account. No one could smile like that who feared being exposed. Catherine is too clear in her own mind that —— *Breaks off, stops to think.*

JATTEFAUX     Clear that ——?

COSTE     — that Lieutenant Marrien —— *again falls silent.*

JATTEFAUX     What does she expect Lieutenant Marrien to do?

COSTE *collects his thoughts.*     Lieutenant Marrien shall not be permitted to discard this affair as if it were simply a glove.

*He makes a sign for Mme Jattefaux to withdraw.*
*Exit Mme. Jattefaux.*

COSTE *goes to door, downstage right — opens it.*     Lieutenant Marrien — let us conclude matters. *Enter Marrien.* I do not know by what ways and means you encountered my niece. Nor am I disposed to enquire any further. I shrink from the details. The time and place of the assignation are immaterial. It took place —

*Marrien starts.*

COSTE   Please don't interrupt. Your position has become untenable. Retreat no less so. For you everything is at stake. Catherine has a child, born before you were legally united. If that were to become public knowledge, it would ruin your career. You would have to disappear from Paris. Quit your regiment. You now try to stop the truth becoming known because you see these consequences clearly enough.

MARRIEN   It would be the consquences, if —

COSTE   Even if you resist marriage. I would immediately go to the commander of your regiment and inform him. You would be promptly cashiered. No position would be open to you, even in the most remote colonies. Do you realize what that means, Lieutenant Marrien?

MARRIEN   Your threats are a matter of complete indifference to me. I have never had occasion to make your niece's acquaintance.

COSTE   And I have never had occasion to expose my niece, who grew up under my watchful eye, as a liar.

MARRIEN   She persists in her charge against me?

COSTE   She is unshakably convinced that you are merely waiting — as a matter of course — for news of the birth, before appearing.

MARRIEN   She overestimates my interest in things which — happened in a world I find impenetrable.

COSTE   Is that your final word, a contemptuous denial?

MARRIEN   I do not know your niece and can do no more than deduce her character from your description. Someone intent on making an absolute stranger the father of her child by spinning a tissue of lies — is either ridiculous, or else —

COSTE   Or else what?

MARRIEN   Since it is a woman who accuses me, I can say no more.

COSTE *ironically.*   Do you feel insulted, Lieutenant? Shall I give you satisfaction?

MARRIEN   My interest in this matter scarcely extends that far. Your niece's audacity in wanting to appropriate my name to cover up some disreputable entanglement on her part —

COSTE   Appropriate your name!

MARRIEN   — is infamous, and deserves to be punished. And by you, Monsieur Coste, in my presence. That is the satisfaction you owe me. As an officer I am duty bound to punish any insult to the uniform. Your niece has made the most impudent attack on me, accusing me of dishonourable conduct. Please now reprimand her as requested — I'm waiting.

COSTE *goes to door, upstage right — opens it.*   Madame Jattefaux — please tell Catherine to come. *He takes up position with his back to French window.*

*Enter Catherine.*
*Catherine sees Marrien.*
*Marrien looks at Catherine.*
*Both remain looking at one another for some time.*

COSTE *finally, with a loud voice.*   Who is it, Catherine?

CATHERINE *turns to Coste — smiling.*   Who?

COSTE   Do I have to introduce him to you, Catherine?

CATHERINE *as before.*   Who?

COSTE   My guest here.

CATHERINE   Is this your visitor — Lieutenant Marrien?

COSTE *takes a few steps forward — fixes his gaze on Marrien.*   You heard correctly, Lieutenant Marrien.

MARRIEN   There is nothing —

COSTE *to Catherine.*   This is not the first time you have seen Lieutenant Marrien?

CATHERINE   His coming today means he wants me to reveal our secret.

COSTE *to Marrien.*   Don't you want to anticipate what she has to say? I must warn you, Lieutenant Marrien, this is your last chance!

MARRIEN   I have no secret to hide ——

COSTE *to Catherine.*   Why do you think Lieutenant Marrien has come here today?

CATHERINE   Because I have come.

COSTE   Was that pre-arranged?

CATHERINE   What is destined to happen does not need to be pre-arranged.

COSTE   What was it happened without pre-arrangement?

CATHERINE   This — and the other thing.

COSTE   You deny it was pre-arranged. And it wasn't a coincidence either. Indeed, I had to put the greatest pressure on Lieutenant Marrien to get him to come. I demanded his presence to extract from him a declaration which he is not yet prepared to make. Will you ask him, Catherine, if this is the first time he has seen you?

*Catherine turns her head towards Marrien — smiles.*

COSTE   A question she does not want to put into words, Lieutenant Marrien, but that should make it twice as difficult for you to withhold the truth.

MARRIEN *to Catherine, without emotion.*   Today, in this room, is the first time that I have seen you.

*Catherine continues to look at him and smile.*

MARRIEN   I am not mistaken.

*Catherine as before.*

MARRIEN    It is you who must be mistaken. I live in Paris, where you have not been for the past year — I have never set foot in this town.

*Catherine slowly shakes her head.*

COSTE    You are being contradicted, Lieutenant Marrien. Think hard! You must remember. *To Catherine.* Was Lieutenant Marrien never in this town before?

*Catherine looks again at Marrien.*

MARRIEN    Never.

COSTE *to Catherine.*    Is that not right?

CATHERINE    You were, on the fourteenth of October.

COSTE    What's the significance of that day?

CATHERINE    That's when Lieutenant Marrien stopped here.

COSTE *to Marrien.*    Where were you on the fourteenth of October?

CATHERINE *to Marrien.*    Here.

MARRIEN *ponders.*    On the fourteenth of October —— the middle of October last year —— I had orders —— to take some documents —— to the south. —— On the way back I had to change trains at midday —— to catch the Paris express —— which only left at midnight. —— That was in ———— *Looks up.* Was it here that I waited for the train?

CATHERINE    You were here from midday to night-time.

COSTE    You are exposed by your own words, Lieutenant Marrien. It has been established that you stopped off here. How did you spend your time here, Lieutenant Marrien?

MARRIEN    For me it was a town like any other one passes through. Did I even leave the station?

CATHERINE    At midday you inspected the display in a jeweller's window.

MARRIEN    You were watching me?

CATHERINE    In the afternoon, in church, you knelt before the crucifix.

MARRIEN    You saw me again in church?

CATHERINE    In the evening you were at the opera, in a box.

MARRIEN    And you discovered me at the opera, too?

CATHERINE *very shyly*.    And at night ——

MARRIEN    At night I caught my train.

CATHERINE *shakes her head*.    That night you did not leave ——

MARRIEN    Where else am I supposed to have been?

*Catherine looks at him.*

COSTE    You did not leave the town that night, Lieutenant Marrien.

MARRIEN    I had to be in Paris the next morning — to report for duty. I now recall that I left before the end of the opera so as not to miss my train. It caused some disturbance in the box, but I did catch my train on time. It cannot be the case that I spent the night anywhere else than on the Paris express. *To Catherine.* Even you will have to admit you are mistaken if I supply the evidence from the regimental records that I did indeed report for duty early the next morning. *To Coste.* Even better, if you were to accompany me to Paris to see for yourself and be convinced. I spent an afternoon and an evening here. — I was observed, but myself saw no one. — That night — and this is the crucial point — I slept in my compartment on the train.

COSTE *to Catherine*.    Lieutenant Marrien offers to provide demonstrable proof. What can you provide to counter that?

CATHERINE *in a whisper*.    Our child.

COSTE    Your assertion would not stand up against arguments that carry total conviction. Lieutenant Marrien was on the train the night you say you spent with him. Was it Lieutenant Marrien who was with you that night?

CATHERINE    Lieutenant Jean-Marc Marrien.

MARRIEN    When was it we arranged this rendezvous? In front of the jeweller's? In church? At the opera?

CATHERINE    In front of the jeweller's — in church — at the opera.

MARRIEN    Three times! — And I don't know of a single one!

CATHERINE    You do know.

MARRIEN *simply.*    How could I have forgotten?

COSTE    I shall accompany you to Paris, Lieutenant Marrien, if learn I must that only the dead letter of reports can convey the truth, not the spoken word of the living. Whom am I to believe? The depravity of it! A child is born, yet over its cradle they wrangle about who the father is.

*Enter Mme Jattefaux, upstage right.*

JATTEFAUX *to Coste.*    Monsieur Coste, the butcher's boy, Leguerche, would like to speak to you on a very urgent matter.

COSTE    Who?

JATTEFAUX    The butcher's boy, Leguerche, who delivers our meat.

COSTE    You're in charge of the housekeeping, Madame Jattefaux. I don't order the meat.

JATTEFAUX    He says it's a private matter.

COSTE    Send him away.

JATTEFAUX    He won't be put off. He absolutely insists on seeing you.

COSTE    A butcher's boy?

JATTEFAUX    Leguerche.

COSTE    Very well, send him in.

# ACT TWO

~

*Coste and Leguerche, sitting in armchairs*

COSTE    Do please begin, Monsieur Leguerche.

*Leguerche maintains an embarrassed silence while clasping and turning his stiff-brimmed hat.*

COSTE    I've agreed to see you in private, as you wished. As you see, we are alone.

*Leguerche as before.*

COSTE    I've done all I can to allow you to speak freely. Since you remain silent, I can only assume you are still thinking over what it is you want to tell me. If so, please come back later. *He rises.*

LEGUERCHE *remains seated.*    It's hard to know where to begin.

COSTE    What is it all about?

LEGUERCHE    A lot of things.

COSTE    Things that we need to discuss?

LEGUERCHE    First — there's Juliette.

COSTE    Who is Juliette?

LEGUERCHE    Well — we're engaged — *He falters.*

COSTE    That must be very interesting — for you —

LEGUERCHE *quickly.*    Don't you remember Juliette?

*Coste shakes his head.*

LEGUERCHE   She was in service — as a chambermaid in your house — then she left.

COSTE   Was there any special reason for her leaving?

LEGUERCHE   That's what I'm getting at. — Juliette gave up her job — to devote her time to her observations — which she naturally carried out with proper discretion.

COSTE   And who was the object of her — observations?

LEGUERCHE   The young lady.

COSTE   Which young lady?

LEGUERCHE   Mademoiselle Catherine.

COSTE   And why did your fiancée, a maid in this house until she left, continue to keep watch on my niece? *Sits down again.*

LEGUERCHE   Even before that, Monsieur Coste, she had already noticed certain things about Mademoiselle Catherine. A woman soon knows when something odd is going on. They seem to sense it and they don't miss a thing. It's remarkable. I say that about women in general, Monsieur Coste, for in Mademoiselle Catherine's case, it wasn't hard to discover what was going on. On the contrary, Monsieur Coste.

COSTE *with forced coolness.*   I'm listening.

LEGUERCHE   Mademoiselle Catherine had to rush off somewhere — destination unknown. After all, it was top secret.

COSTE   You think so?

LEGUERCHE   Sure of it. Juliette turned herself into a proper little detective. She actually found out at the station where they were heading. How do you think she managed that?

COSTE   How?

LEGUERCHE   She went in the same train. She got three days' leave from Madame Jattefaux, saying she was going to visit her mother in Normandy. In fact, she followed the two ladies south, not that they had any idea they were being followed. She followed them like their shadow when they changed onto the branch line, then she followed their car in another car. That's how careful Juliette was. The girl's got real talent, more than most of her sex.

COSTE    And how else did she use her remarkable talent?

LEGUERCHE    She found out where Mademoiselle Catherine was to stay — with Madame Jattefaux's sister. That was enough to be going on with. Then she returned here — kept on at her job for a while — gave notice, so she could return for a longer period to where Mademoiselle Catherine was staying. There was a reason for that.

COSTE    Go on, I won't interrupt.

LEGUERCHE *looks up with a frank expression.*    It's hard to put it all together in a way that doesn't give offence. The words that spring to mind don't come out right. A butcher's boy like me is more at home with knives and a cleaver.

COSTE    The way you described your Juliette's activities was perfectly clear.

LEGUERCHE    Juliette would know how to put it much better. But is there any point in bringing her here? After all, I'm the one who's most involved.

COSTE    Juliette stayed away for a longer period —

LEGUERCHE    — to make sure the birth had taken place, which it had.

COSTE    Who gave birth?

LEGUERCHE    Mademoiselle Catherine.

COSTE    And your Juliette caught the same train back as the two ladies, so she could inform you, Monsieur Leguerche, of their exact arrival time, and you wouldn't lose a moment telling me what she had discovered.

LEGUERCHE *eagerly.*    Juliette sent me a telegram on the way back, so I could get properly dressed for the occasion and appear here immediately after Mademoiselle Catherine.

COSTE *after a pause.*    And what is the purpose of your visit, Monsieur Leguerche — properly dressed for the occasion?

LEGUERCHE   To come to an agreement.

COSTE   About what?

LEGUERCHE   Where money is no object, it can settle anything.

COSTE   What should I pay for?

LEGUERCHE   For a promise that it will go no further.

COSTE   What you, with your fiancée's assistance, discovered by spying on my niece.

LEGUERCHE   If you want to put it that way —

COSTE   Permit me to employ a more explicit term to characterize your conduct. You are committing an act of blackmail by suggesting that I buy your silence to prevent things you believe to be highly sensitive becoming public knowledge. Your action was fully premeditated. You are a blackmailer, and the police shall eliminate the threat from you and your kind. I am not afraid of you, Monsieur Leguerche — I shall now summon the police.

LEGUERCHE *stunned.*   Must I marry Catherine then?

*Coste looks at him in amazement.*

LEGUERCHE   Summon the police — and call me a blackmailer — and have me thrown in jail — for what? Because Mademoiselle Catherine dragged me into her room one night and slept with me? I never pursued Mademoiselle Catherine — I didn't force myself on her — I didn't enter the house that night with any such intent. Mademoiselle Catherine offered herself to me — she begged me to stay with her. I couldn't make a fuss without publicly destroying her reputation. And for that I'm branded a scoundrel to be handed over to the police?

COSTE *leaning back in his armchair, tonelessly.*   What did you say?

LEGUERCHE   The truth, Monsieur Coste — nothing but the truth. Come what may, Leguerche always tells the truth. I've never been in trouble with the police. I'm as honest as they come. But I'm in a compromising situation. Would you want a butcher's boy as your son-in-law? Of course not — and that's fine by me. The child needs a father — and I'm its natural father, but I've no desire to be its legal father. Your class and mine don't mix. It was Heaven's decree that

Mademoiselle Catherine got a child by me, but it can't be God's will that I should marry her and make the child ridiculous!

COSTE  Calm yourself. I'm deeply shocked by what you have just told me. Do you mind answering some questions?

LEGUERCHE  I've been raising my voice, Monsieur Coste. It won't happen again.

COSTE  You were right to do so, Monsieur Leguerche. My response was wrong for I wasn't aware of all the facts.

LEGUERCHE  That's what I thought — that you did not know the whole story. — Otherwise you would have wanted to meet me before now.

COSTE *nods.*  —— How did it happen — your coming here that night?

LEGUERCHE  I had arranged to meet Juliette that night. It wasn't the first time, either. Such things don't matter when you are engaged and are going to get married — at least not in our circles. You can't wait until you have your own butcher's shop. True love is no respecter of time. Anyway, no one was ever put out by my visiting Juliette here. Once, the gardener kicked up a fuss the next morning over a damaged vine trellis — but a couple of nice cutlets soon pacified him. That was the way I always got in — up the trellis and in through a window Juliette left unlocked. That's the way it was that night, too. I climbed in, dropped from the windowsill onto the floor, and was feeling my way towards Juliette's room at the end of the passage, on tiptoe, but it still must have made a noise, for a door in the middle of the passage half opened — and a white arm pulled me into the room. It was Mademoiselle Catherine.

COSTE  Catherine had designs on you?

LEGUERCHE  I resisted — as long you can resist when you're being held tight and covered in kisses.

COSTE  You had to spend the night with her?

LEGUERCHE  At any rate until it was too late to go to Juliette. That's what started this whole damn affair.

COSTE  Juliette?

LEGUERCHE    When I was delivering the meat next morning she naturally demanded to know where I had been. I made up some excuses, but when she threatened to break off our engagement, I finally confessed. It was with a heavy heart, Monsieur Coste — I beg you to believe me. — It's not done to speak ill of any lady, especially not one who has taken a fancy to you.

COSTE    Was Catherine in love with you?

LEGUERCHE    I don't know what to make of it, Monsieur Coste. It seemed so — but then again, it was as if she thought I was someone else, someone quite different. Finally, for the sake of my conscience, I had to imagine it was Juliette I was with.

COSTE    But that wasn't enough for Juliette?

LEGUERCHE    She was so jealous, she was hopping mad. She wanted to run to Monsieur Coste and denounce Mademoiselle Catherine. The cheek of it! It was all I could do to stop her. So she swore revenge, and since Catherine was pregnant, she was able to exploit that. Juliette could tell immediately, and she didn't let up, once she had that to go on. An indiscretion you can cover up — but not a child. I can't blame Juliette entirely. We both kept quiet and saved Monsieur Coste a lot of embarrassment. It's surely not unreasonable to expect Monsieur Coste to show his gratitude?

COSTE    How much do you demand?

LEGUERCHE    Well, Juliette and I figured out that — considering that —

COSTE    — considering that under no circumstances do I want my niece to be connected with a butcher's boy!

LEGUERCHE    Mademoiselle Catherine is doubtless just as anxious to avoid that.

COSTE    I have evidence that that is the case.

LEGUERCHE    That's how it is, Monsieur Coste. On that basis we can come to an arrangement that satisfies all parties. For Juliette and me, it's a question of being able to get married. To set up a little butcher's shop — or perhaps Monsieur Coste could see his way clear to providing more generous support? Don't misunderstand me, Monsieur Coste, we're not insisting. We're only trying to get ahead — and as quickly as possible.

COSTE    What do call more generous support?

LEGUERCHE *takes two slips of paper from his pocket.*   This would be enough to set up a simple, basic shop — and here I've worked out what a better equipped one would cost — initial capital outlay included, of course. *Hands him both slips.*

COSTE *gives them a cursory glance.*   You can count on the better equipment. *Rises.* Please follow me. *Opens the front door, right.* I must ask you to excuse me for a few minutes, Monsieur Leguerche. *Ushers Leguerche out — closes the door behind him. Remains standing by the door — clasps his brow. Goes quickly to door, upstage right — opens it.* Madame Jattefaux!

*Enter Jattefaux.*

COSTE    Your defence of Catherine's credibility has just been totally demolished. The truth is very different and you will have to accept it. It's a lesson I will have to learn, too, and remember — that an innocent angel-face can tell worse lies than any villain with a face as ugly as sin.

JATTEFAUX    What has aroused your suspicion?

COSTE    Not suspicion, Madame Jattefaux, not a bit of it — I no longer suspect. I no longer need to grope in the dark with assertions and counter-assertions merely creating insoluble confusion. Until some third person pops up and makes the situation crystal clear.

JATTEFAUX    Who accuses Catherine of lying?

COSTE *points to door, downstage right.*   He's behind that door, waiting to be compensated for having bestowed his favours: the butcher's boy, Leguerche.

JATTEFAUX    How did he come to —

COSTE    To Catherine?

JATTEFAUX — to make such an absurd claim — that

COSTE    — that fits the facts so precisely that I declared myself ready to pay for his silence!

*Jattefaux flops into armchair.*

COSTE   Or is it all a product of his imagination, these happenings that may indeed be possible, but which we find incredible: that a young girl, reared in a household like this, should entice a butcher's boy into her room at night while he is creeping along the passage to his lady-love, the kitchen maid.

JATTEFAUX *stunned.*   Here? In this house?

COSTE   While you were sleeping — while I was sleeping — while we thought Catherine was sleeping, like on any other night.

JATTEFAUX   But how could it be that I heard nothing —

COSTE   No cries of help from Catherine? Because she didn't raise any — since she wasn't ravished by some debauched intruder who found her door ajar. Wouldn't she have raised the whole house if she'd been subjected to force?

JATTEFAUX   I'd have been the first to hear her.

COSTE   And everyone else under this roof, Madame Jattefaux. But there wasn't a sound. Nothing — until the child appeared — to bear witness, belatedly, to what happened that night.

JATTEFAUX   Do you believe the butcher's boy?

COSTE   There can be no doubting his word. Leguerche is honest — in his own way. It's certain he is the father of Catherine's child.

JATTEFAUX   Then why did she say it was Lieutenant Marrien?

COSTE   Because she was afraid to admit it was the butcher's boy — that it was a butcher's boy she had thrown herself away on. That had to be hushed up. So this diabolic plot was hatched, in cold blood. She invents a lieutenant as her seducer — from Paris — one of the best families. She spots him in town — knows he is not stationed here — happens to learn his name — and then pins the blame on him after he's disappeared back to Paris. All very clever. Only one flaw in her calculation — I wasn't content with just the lieutenant's name — he would have to appear in person. He arrives, protests — and Leguerche takes his place. The lie is uncovered — leaving its originator exposed as — a strumpet!

JATTEFAUX —— What's to become of Catherine?

COSTE   That's the last thing on my mind. Right now my task is to inform the lieutenant of what this Leguerche can be bribed to keep silent about. Disgust will seal Lieutenant Marrien's lips. That way the thing can be hushed up, for I can't afford to have it publicly known. Please ask Lieutenant Marrien to come in.

*Jattefaux rises — exit left.*
*Coste waits — looking left.*
*Enter Marrien, left.*

COSTE *invites him to sit, sits himself.*   My journey has become unnecessary — I won't be accompanying you to Paris.

MARRIEN   How should I interpret your sudden change of mind?

COSTE *smiles weakly.*   The case against you is dismissed, Lieutenant. The court has apprehended the real perpetrator.

MARRIEN *also smiles.*   I hope the culprit is someone you are glad to have caught, and that congratulations are in order.

COSTE   How do you mean?

MARRIEN   That now you've finally found whoever it was love led astray, may he be welcome to you as a husband for your niece.

COSTE   Even if he wanted to marry her, he would still not be welcome.

MARRIEN   At least it would legitimatize the child.

COSTE   Only for any such legitimacy to expose it to public derision.

MARRIEN   Who is the father?

COSTE   The butcher's boy, Leguerche.

MARRIEN   A butcher ——?

COSTE   The butcher's boy Leguerche who delivers the meat. A coarse lout who takes women where he finds them — a sort of rustic Don Juan. Idolized by the servant girls. What do say to that?

*Marrien stares at him.*

COSTE   There's worse to come. Not only is he a butcher's boy, he has all the airs and graces of a gentleman. He didn't disclose what had happened at the time. And now he was put up to it by his fiancée, who used to be a chambermaid here, and whom he left in the lurch that night to devote his attentions to my niece. He was expected elsewhere. He had his Juliette — he had no need of Catherine. But Catherine forced him into her bedroom. Juliette was deprived of her rights. Catherine stole them — and was punished by having a child by Juliette's lover. He is the real father — Leguerche by name, butcher's boy by trade!

MARRIEN *with an effort.*   Why do you tell me all this?

COSTE   For reasons that should be obvious. A Leguerche is all too aware why. No one must breathe a word — it's simply too sordid. People would revel in it — at the expense of others who would burn with shame. And that includes me. As for your knowledge of this affair, I must ask for your discretion, just as the butcher's boy is prepared to be discreet, in his fashion.

MARRIEN   How has — Leguerche — reacted?

COSTE   By taking the money and not boasting of his conquest.

*Marrien remains silent.*

COSTE   Are you surprised that I've paid him off? He's more than just an accessory — he is the father. To take legal action against him would be pointless. Besides, the poor devil intends to put the money to good use — he's going to set himself up in his own shop and marry his Juliette. What have you got against Leguerche?

MARRIEN   Nothing, but ——

COSTE   He'll relish his newfound independence and keep his mouth shut. It's all agreed. *Points, downstage right.* I'll go through the formalities with him later. That will settle his account — once and for all! *Turns back to Marrien.* I expect, by the time you arrive back in Paris, you will have already forgotten all the bother that was inflicted on you here. At any rate, I must ask you to try to forget. Will you promise me that, Lieutenant Marrien?

MARRIEN   You should not ask me that —

COSTE   You think it an insult that you were wrongly accused — is that why you refuse?

MARRIEN   You misunderstand me. Not a word shall ever pass my lips. The only thing I regard as insulting is that you doubt my discretion.

COSTE *rises — goes to Marrien — proffers his hand.*   I have no reason to do so — not now, not ever.

*Marrien rises — takes Coste's hand.*

COSTE   It never happened, Lieutenant Marrien. As sure as I hold your hand in mine, I have put it totally out of my mind. There is such a thing as burying the living when their conduct becomes intolerable. So the person whose accusation brought you here will also be silenced. Goodbye, Lieutenant Marrien.

*Marrien bows — but does not leave.*
*Coste looks at him enquiringly.*
*Marrien meets his gaze — smiles.*

COSTE *uncertainly.*   What — ?

MARRIEN   I would like to put a question to Mademoiselle Catherine — how she learned my name.

COSTE *amazed.*   You want to speak to her?

MARRIEN   It's not idle curiosity —— but it's true I am curious to find out how one can become acquainted without ever meeting.

COSTE   She saw you in town that day.

MARRIEN   But one doesn't see a person's name!

COSTE   Think of it as pure chance.

MARRIEN   A chance in a million, surely. I'm intrigued as to how it happened.

COSTE *shrugs.*   You are entitled to an explanation. I respect your wish. *Rings.*

*Enter Servant.*

COSTE   Mademoiselle Catherine's presence is requested.

*Exit Servant, rear.*

COSTE *to Marrien.*    My business dealings with Monsieur Leguerche call. Shall we see each other again?

MARRIEN    I shall take my leave now. *Bows formally.*

COSTE    Bon voyage, Lieutenant Marrien. *Exit, downstage right.*

*Marrien stands beside armchair, sunk in thought.*
*Enter Catherine — goes without hesitation to centre of room — looks at Marrien.*

MARRIEN    You are very surprised to find me still here?

CATHERINE    Why should I be surprised?

MARRIEN    It had been arranged for me to leave with your uncle. We should have left already.

CATHERINE    But you have not left.

MARRIEN    We are not going to Paris together now, Monsieur Coste and I.

CATHERINE    Will you stay here?

MARRIEN    I shall go alone on the next express. It leaves this evening.

CATHERINE    Do you never have more than a day's leave?

MARRIEN    I have only today, that is correct — but even if I had longer, I know of no reason why I should stay on here.

CATHERINE    Why did you not leave at once?

MARRIEN    I do have one reason which justifies postponing my departure for a few hours.

CATHERINE    Just like the last time you were here.

MARRIEN *laughs.*    That time I was at the mercy of the timetable, for there was no earlier train to Paris — but the reason I'm staying today is deliberate. I want to talk to you.

CATHERINE    About all the experiences we shared?

MARRIEN   That would be a short chapter, soon told in few words. I feature in it only by virtue of my name. But my name is something very close to me, its fortunes and my fortunes are identical. So I take no little interest in what happens to it, since that involves me, too. It seems to have played an extraordinary prank on me this time, without my being aware of it. Where did my name present itself to you in full — Jean-Marc Marrien?

CATHERINE   In church.

MARRIEN   One doesn't talk in church. Least of all about oneself. An individual loses his identity in the great mass of the faithful. He is absorbed in the communal devotions. Did my name desecrate the sanctity of the church with some blasphemous utterance?

CATHERINE   It revealed itself to me as the organ pealed out and we prayed.

MARRIEN   I prayed?

CATHERINE   Along with all who knelt as the priest elevated the Host.

MARRIEN   At the most sacred moment?

CATHERINE   At the most sacred moment I lowered my eyes — and read your name.

MARRIEN   Where?

CATHERINE   You had laid your cap on the ledge in the pew — and it was written in the cap: Jean-Marc Marrien.

MARRIEN   We were kneeling next to one another?

CATHERINE   We were still kneeling when the blessing was pronounced.

MARRIEN *deeply affected, falls silent, then laughs.*   So if I had put down my cap with the crown instead of the lining showing, I would have avoided any complications. Truly an action which bears no relation to the consequences!

CATHERINE   The cap lay as it was destined to lie.

MARRIEN   Was I acting under compulsion, then?

CATHERINE   It had to be, after we had looked at the rings in the jeweller's window.

MARRIEN   I did look at the jewellery display — there were rings too.

CATHERINE   We both looked at the rings at the same moment.

MARRIEN   You were keeping a check on what I was looking at?

CATHERINE   I felt it.

MARRIEN *again falls silent — then amused.*   And as chance — extravagantly — had it, we were thrown together a third time that day — at the opera.

CATHERINE   In a box.

MARRIEN   Where was I sitting?

CATHERINE   In the front row, one of the middle seats.

MARRIEN   And you?

CATHERINE   In the seat next to yours.

MARRIEN   Then I left before the end of the performance and stumbled in the dark.

CATHERINE   In the dark you touched my arm, which was bare.

MARRIEN   I touched you?

CATHERINE *points to her arm.*   Here.

MARRIEN   But that was quite unintentional.

CATHERINE   After we had looked at the rings together — and knelt before the priest in church — and sat together that evening for the festivity at the opera?

MARRIEN   But what does all that signify?

CATHERINE   That we were married — first the rings — then the blessing in church — then that evening the music to celebrate by!

*Marrien looks at her.*

CATHERINE    And that night our marriage was consummated, like all others.

MARRIEN *collects himself.*    The marriage you believe took place was not consummated as weddings are supposed to be, where man and wife spend the wedding night together. It was not the man you married in your imagination who came to you that night. Do you not recall a —— butcher's boy called Leguerche?

*Catherine at once alters her expression — looks at Marrien wide-eyed.*

MARRIEN    He was your lover that night — I was put forward in his place. He is presently negotiating with your uncle in the next room. He will hush things up — for money. You have nothing to fear from him. But I could take steps to silence you if you continue to proclaim me the father of your child — which you seem determined to do.

CATHERINE *horrified.*    Has someone come to slander me?

MARRIEN    If truth be slander — then he is slander personified — in person and therefore undeniable. In the form of a butcher's boy. I give way to my rival — Monsieur Leguerche.

CATHERINE *terrified.*    It's not ——!

MARRIEN    Shall I summon him to see if you recognize him? To refresh your memories of that night — in which you shamelessly betrayed the husband you had married that same day with all due pomp and ceremony?!

CATHERINE    I did not betray you!

MARRIEN    No?

CATHERINE    You were with me — and I conceived our child!

MARRIEN *falls silent — then smiles weakly.*    When you speak it only creates confusion. I almost believed for a moment that was a fact, but there is no basis to it whatsoever. Of course, you have not betrayed me — there is nothing to betray. Nor have I any business informing you of this butcher's boy Leguerche's appearance or behaviour. We are both on the wrong track — Mademoiselle Coste.

CATHERINE *timidly.*   Now you call me Mademoiselle.

MARRIEN   How should I address you?

CATHERINE   I have a child.

MARRIEN *slowly.*  Catherine ——

CATHERINE   It's not the child of a — butcher's boy. Who is this Leguerche? How did he come to be in my room? It was not him I heard when the leaves rustled on the trellis. I heard — another. The window was not rattled by a hand I did not recognize. The boards in the passage creaked only under the steps I was expecting. Would I have opened the door to an utter stranger — someone I abhorred, like all strangers who ever pursued me? The man I desired to lie with me — was it not the man I loved with all my soul? Whose look pierced my heart like a blazing dagger when he merely glanced my way — at noon, in front of the jeweller's shop. Who quickened my pulse as I knelt beside him under the great dome of the church? And whose touch on my bare skin, with all the instruments of the orchestra resounding and transporting me above all earthly things, thrilled me into submitting to him totally? What in the sight of heaven has ever occurred that is more real than my marriage to Jean-Marc Marrien? Was it not so inscribed by God's hand in the great Book of Destiny itself? Who dares break this marriage — and murder a child, for it dies if my love for its father is destroyed? —

MARRIEN *calmly.*   Your child will live, Catherine.

CATHERINE *quickly.*   When will you see it?

MARRIEN   Is it a fine child?

CATHERINE   It resembles you so!

MARRIEN   Resembles me?

CATHERINE   It must resemble you — mustn't it?

MARRIEN *nods.*   A day that seems like any other suddenly turns our life upside down. A train leaves too late, and between arrival and departure one glance in a jeweller's window, a visit to church, an evening at the opera, and our destiny is shaped. Your destiny, Catherine — mine too, perhaps.

CATHERINE   Did you only realize that today?

MARRIEN   I did not know you loved me.

CATHERINE *goes to him and lays her hand on his arm.*   Jean-Marc, I loved you with all my heart.

MARRIEN *without moving — looks straight ahead past Catherine.*   And I am beginning to love you, Catherine, with all my soul.

CATHERINE *steps back.*   What are you saying?

MARRIEN   I love you.

CATHERINE *goes to door, upstage right.*   Say it again.

MARRIEN   I love you truly, deeply — resolutely.

*Catherine leaves. Marrien remains motionless.*
*Enter Coste and Leguerche, downstage right.*

COSTE *notices Marrien.*   You haven't gone yet, Lieutenant Marrien?

MARRIEN *turns to him.*   I do not intend to.

COSTE   Does your regiment not need you?

MARRIEN   That remains to be seen.

COSTE *to Leguerche.*   Well, Monsieur Leguerche, we can finish our business now. You need not trouble to come back again to collect the money. I'll write you a cheque you can take with you. That's the simplest way to conclude matters. *Sits at desk and writes.*

*Leguerche looks at Marrien.*
*Marrien meets his glance.*

COSTE *rises and shakes the cheque to dry it.*   You can have it as soon as the ink dries. Don't lose it.

LEGUERCHE   That's not something you lose.

*Marrien steps between Coste and Leguerche.*

COSTE *about to give the cheque to Leguerche.*    Here it is.

*Marrien quickly seizes it and tears it up.*

COSTE *taken aback.*    What's the meaning of that?

MARRIEN *to Leguerche.*    Nothing — *To Coste* — yet everything.

COSTE    What am I supposed to think, Lieutenant Marrien?

MARRIEN    That I am the father of Catherine's child.

# ACT THREE

~

*Coste and Marrien, seated*
*Coste looks down — shakes his head.*

MARRIEN   Are you opposed to my proposal? Catherine is not of age. You are her guardian. That has considerable weight if you raise any objection.

COSTE   Catherine has always been a law unto herself. She won't pay any attention to the opinion of others now.

MARRIEN   I don't believe you should accuse Catherine of mere wilfulness, Monsieur Coste.

COSTE   Don't think I accuse her of being stubbornly wayward. That would be to admit to a total lack of understanding, and I would have no choice but to stand aside and leave you and Catherine to your own devices.

MARRIEN *eagerly.*   Is there anything you are still unclear about?

COSTE   No — nor could anyone informed of the facts fail to see that she was acting under compulsion, and what that compulsion was.

MARRIEN   A compulsion which now extends to me. Must I not obey?

COSTE   Your conduct entitles me to judge you by the highest standards of chivalry, so I can only agree — yes.

MARRIEN *happily.*   You fully understand?

COSTE   You feel you were the stimulus which caused Catherine to throw off her emotional restraint. Her susceptibility on that particular day was such that it only needed a spark to set off the reaction, and that spark was when your glance lighted on her.

MARRIEN   My glance!

COSTE   She loved you at first sight — overwhelmed by emotions which had found their true object. All that followed was coloured by that. The imagined exchange of rings at the jeweller's —

MARRIEN   Our betrothal!

COSTE   Your presence in the church together, construed as a marriage ceremony —

MARRIEN   The priest pronounced the blessing!

COSTE   The opera, that you both attended in the same box, must have seemed like a wedding celebration —

MARRIEN   Celebrated by a thousand guests in the opera house!

COSTE   It all happened, yet at the same time it isn't true. You might call what links you and Catherine a mystical union. A union made in heaven, no doubt — but not one that can be easily recognized in reality.

MARRIEN   In the eyes of the world, there is no impediment to the marriage of Lieutenant Marrien and Mademoiselle Coste!

COSTE   You see no difficulty?

MARRIEN   What difficulty?

COSTE   Catherine — has a child.

MARRIEN   What if that upsets my commander? What if he discharges me from the regiment? I'll enter service abroad — in the colonies. Or set up as a farmer in the tropics — without a uniform — but with Catherine.

COSTE *shakes his head.*   It won't be your commander who objects.

MARRIEN   My family? Will it offend them? Does it make me unworthy of human society if I marry Catherine — who has a child?

COSTE   You will not sink lower in anyone's estimation on account of what you propose — on the contrary, it will reveal the nobility of your character to all who learn of your motives in marrying Catherine. But can you be constantly explaining in order to make others understand and forgive? Are you justified —

and think of Catherine! — in dragging through the mud the marvellous tale which is your love?

MARRIEN    I would fight to defend it though I were struck dumb.

COSTE    Even if you do remain silent, and Catherine too, there is another who will speak out.

MARRIEN    Who?

COSTE    Leguerche.

MARRIEN    What — will he say?

COSTE    Something that could not fail to ruin your social position and destroy your relationship with your family: that your wife has a child fathered by a butcher's boy.

*Marrien stares ahead blankly.*

COSTE    Lieutenant Marrien, there are limits to how reality can be altered. The deepest dream is like a death wish. You have your life before you. Society will forgive you — it will even pay tribute to your love story — but if you declare yourself the father of Catherine's child, it must be unchallenged.

MARRIEN    I am its father.

COSTE    You are not, Lieutenant Marrien — not as long as you tear up cheques which would seal the other's mouth.

MARRIEN *looking up.*    Once more you want to wound Catherine's honour?

COSTE    Does Catherine not remember — not want to remember — her night with Leguerche?

MARRIEN    Was it not me she was expecting?

COSTE    It was the butcher's boy who came.

MARRIEN    He never came to Catherine.

COSTE    You both deny it?

MARRIEN Who calls Catherine and me liars?

COSTE Are those the weapons you will use against Leguerche? He will not quit the field without putting up the most furious resistance.

MARRIEN *calmly.* Who else should quit the field?

*Enter Jattefaux, upstage right.*

JATTEFAUX Is it true that Catherine is going away?

COSTE Catherine?

JATTEFAUX She says she has to leave at once. Is that your wish, Monsieur Coste?

COSTE Going where?

JATTEFAUX She doesn't say.

COSTE Simply going away?

JATTEFAUX Were those not your instructions?

COSTE I haven't talked to her about going anywhere. Is she going with you, Madame Jattefaux?

JATTEFAUX I assume so, though she hasn't said as much directly. She just keeps on repeating: we both must leave right away — and rushing to pack her trunk. She seems really afraid to stay a moment longer, the way she is acting.

COSTE *looks at Marrien. Then at Mme. Jattefaux.* Please calm her. Tell her to stop packing — *With raised voice.* — for nowhere in the world is she safer than in this house.

*Jattefaux leaves.*

COSTE How do you interpret this sudden decision of Catherine's? A journey into the unknown — with you.

MARRIEN With me?

COSTE   She intends to flee with you, Lieutenant Marrien — a thorny path that can only end in desolation.

MARRIEN   Flee from whom?

COSTE   From a bloodhound who will not let up till he has his prey in his clutches and has been paid off.

MARRIEN   Catherine must not leave —

COSTE   I can protect her!

MARRIEN   Only you?

COSTE   Because I am ready — to settle things with Leguerche.

*Enter Catherine upstage right.*

CATHERINE   Madame Jattefaux tells me I must stop packing. Must I?

COSTE *hesitates.*   It was not my instruction — I merely passed on Lieutenant Marrien's request — not to let you leave my care. *Quickly to Marrien.* Did you not say explicitly that she should not leave?

*Catherine turns her gaze on Marrien.*

COSTE   Lieutenant Marrien's reasons are thoroughly sensible. He has asked for your hand in marriage. I had no hesitation in entrusting you to a person of such noble integrity. First, though, there are certain formalities to be dealt with. The regiment must be informed, his family, too. If we pay scrupulous attention to all the essentials, we will gain time, and the date of the wedding can be brought forward. *To Marrien.* Does your leave extend beyond today?

MARRIEN   No, just today.

COSTE *thoughtfully.*   You mustn't overrun. Return to Paris at once. By this evening you will be with your family and can tell them of your decision — tomorrow morning you inform your commander. Catherine stays here with me until you send me positive news from Paris. Then I bring Catherine to you, as safe and sound as when you left. *To Catherine.* Will you help me persuade Lieutenant Marrien, Catherine?

CATHERINE *slowly.*    Are you leaving me today — because your leave is up?

*Marrien remains silent.*

COSTE    He has to in the line of duty, Catherine.

CATHERINE    Can you fully devote yourself to your duty — if you leave me here alone?

*Marrien remains silent.*

COSTE    Orders are orders, Catherine, Lieutenant Marrien has to go.

CATHERINE    Are you not worried by the danger — you leave me in?

*Marrien stands motionless.*

COSTE    What danger can there be, while I have both the will and the means to — settle certain affairs in Lieutenant Marrien's absence?

CATHERINE    If I am alone, will they not — steal our child?

MARRIEN *firmly.*    I will not return to Paris — before I know you are safe — both you, Catherine, and the child.

*Enter Servant, left.*

COSTE    Who is it —?

SERVANT    Monsieur Leguerche wishes to speak to Lieutenant Marrien.

*Marrien is about to go to Catherine.*

CATHERINE *raises her hand to stop him. Smiles.*    You will — protect the child from him. *Takes backward steps towards door, upstage right. Leaves.*

*Exit Servant.*

COSTE *pauses.*    Do you wish to receive him?

MARRIEN *to Servant.*    Monsieur Leguerche.

COSTE *at Marrien's side.*   Lieutenant Marrien, let me deal with Leguerche.

MARRIEN   The man explicitly wanted to see me.

COSTE   What will you say to him?

MARRIEN   How do you talk to — a shadow?

COSTE   Can you ignore his existence?

MARRIEN   Would it be a mortal blow if I refused to recognize him?

COSTE   His highest hopes would be dashed.

MARRIEN   Thousands could try the same ploy to extract money from me. I'm no public benefactor.

COSTE   He's the only one who can substantiate his claim.

MARRIEN   His claim on me?!

*Coste shrugs — exit, downstage right.*
*Marrien leans against armchair.*
*Servant opens door, left.*

SERVANT   Monsieur Leguerche.

*Enter Leguerche.*
*Exit Servant.*
*Leguerche clears his throat to announce his presence.*
*Marrien flops into armchair.*
*Leguerche sits on armrest of other armchair.*
*Marrien stares fixedly down.*

LEGUERCHE *chuckles.*   Two slaps like I've just had — quite incredible! Left, smack! — right, smack! — twice, with the full weight of her hand, before I could duck. Then not even allowed to wait until the welts had faded — no, made to grab my hat and pushed out into the street with my cheeks still aflame.

*Marrien gives a slight cough.*

LEGUERCHE    That was all the thanks I got from Juliette. When I told her how my visit to Monsieur Coste had come unstuck at the last minute. After Monsieur Coste and yours truly had already come to a very satisfactory agreement. But almighty idiot that I was, I wasn't quick enough. The Lieutenant beat me to it.

MARRIEN *offhandedly*.    To what?

LEGUERCHE    Grabbing the cheque. While it was waving in the air, I hesitated for a fraction of a second — and my chance was gone. The Lieutenant was in proud possession of the cheque.

MARRIEN    Which I tore up.

LEGUERCHE    I have a theory about that I'll come back to later, if I may. First I want to express my regret, looking back, that a settlement was prevented in the way just described.

MARRIEN *ironically*.    Simply because you didn't get hold of the cheque quickly enough — otherwise everything would be fine?

LEGUERCHE    That's how I see it — my fault, solely because I'm not as adept physically. A butcher's boy is not very — supple. You, Lieutenant, are more agile. With your build, you've got the advantage over me — on all counts.

MARRIEN    What do you mean?

LEGUERCHE    With your sweetheart.

MARRIEN    I have become engaged to Mademoiselle Coste.

LEGUERCHE    Congratulations are in order, no one can deny. She's quite a catch — Monsieur Coste's niece. Many's the one who's been licking his lips at the thought of her fortune. There have been dozens dancing attendance on her, trying to hit the jackpot. All given the brush-off, one after another — until a certain lieutenant pops up — from Paris — and wins the race at a canter. What would any onlooker think?

MARRIEN    You have some particular thoughts on the matter?

LEGUERCHE    It's the same old story, nothing special. A respectable girl gets herself in trouble — so some fine father has to be bought for the child. You can even get a lieutenant if the price is right.

MARRIEN   And that is the case here?

LEGUERCHE   You've been bought — by Monsieur Coste for his niece — absolutely. You've done it for the money. Show me a young lieutenant who doesn't have debts. Paris — gambling — women! Perhaps you were in a real fix — at risk of being drummed out — and Monsieur Coste's offer was a godsend. I don't blame you — makes sense to leap at it. A man's got to live. So rake in the shekels and line your pocket. But others have to live, too.

MARRIEN   Who?

LEGUERCHE   You can't have it all for yourself. You've got to give me a cut.

MARRIEN   I see I must clear up some misunderstandings.

LEGUERCHE   Fire away. You can speak openly. Haven't I already proved I know how to keep my mouth shut?

MARRIEN   Marrying for money holds no attraction for me. I am already very rich, and have no desire to add to my wealth.

LEGUERCHE *stares at him open-mouthed.*   Then why — are you — marrying — Catherine?

MARRIEN   I am marrying Catherine — because I love her.

LEGUERCHE   You — don't — need — money?

MARRIEN   From Monsieur Coste? Nothing.

LEGUERCHE   You — won't —give — me — any money?

MARRIEN   Not a sou.

LEGUERCHE *wipes his brow. Mutters to himself.*   They're trying to pull a fast one behind my back. Watch out, Leguerche, they want to make a fool of you again. You're too slow on the uptake. They're always quicker and snatch away what you almost had in your hand — *To Marrien.* Why won't you pay me anything?

MARRIEN   Do I owe you anything?

LEGUERCHE *anxiously.* I had to swear to Juliette I wouldn't come back to her empty-handed. Then we could get married — set up shop — a butcher's shop — all tiled — a freezer — and meat — meat — meat — *Malevolently, to Marrien.* And even before it's built you want to — to hack it to pieces?

MARRIEN I never promised you any money.

LEGUERCHE I had it, Lieutenant. I as good as had it — from Monsieur Coste. You robbed me. You tore up the cheque. Now you must make good the damage, Lieutenant.

MARRIEN Your claims on Monsieur Coste are equally unfounded.

LEGUERCHE *taken aback.* Are you the father of the child? — *Laughs.* Your sweetheart's child?

MARRIEN *calmly.* I already told you.

LEGUERCHE *scornfully.* And not me? Since when not? Since a lieutenant came strutting along in his fancy uniform? And the sun and the moon and the stars just — disappeared with a bang? No, they didn't. Everything is just as it was ordered in the beginning — a father is a father — and his child is still his child. What's the honourable gentleman trying to tell me — that the Virgin Mary's wasn't the only immaculate conception?

*Marrien remains silent.*

LEGUERCHE *goes up to him.* Aren't I a good enough rival? A lawyer might fit the bill — or someone else high up the pecking order? Who wants no money. Who's satisfied with just the honour of — being the first. To hell with that! A butcher's boy is what you've got. Common as muck. Wants hard cash. Spent a night with a lady — so what? You can forget about that, but not what came of it — the child. That's my trump card. I can cash in on that. Are you going to pay up, Lieutenant?

MARRIEN *has risen — backs away behind armchair.* Don't come near me!

LEGUERCHE Are your fingers itching to get round my throat? Strangle me — that will silence me. Then the world outside won't hear me bellow out that I am the father — *Again laughing* — of your child!

MARRIEN Go away!

LEGUERCHE   So you abandon the idea of murdering me? Then you must pay the price: money — money — and once again, money. Don't answer yet — take time to think it over. Important decisions shouldn't be rushed. And the sum involved has gone up. You admit you are very rich — I admit I am extremely poor. You admit you can't stand the sight of me. I admit you can buy me off. The price is a butcher's shop, in a house that belongs to me. The whole house. Mine from cellar to attic. With a garden. And no mortgage. Are you listening?

*Marrien remains silent.*

LEGUERCHE   That will cost you a pretty penny. Can't be helped. You shouldn't tear up cheques. You're being paid back for your own stupidity. It needn't have cost so much — I'd made a very reasonable demand ——

MARRIEN   Get out!

LEGUERCHE   It's your own fault the price has risen. But if I understand you aright, Lieutenant: what price would you not pay for your child?

MARRIEN   Get out!

LEGUERCHE   I'll be back. Twenty times round the house — then I'll be back.

MARRIEN   I'll set the dogs on you!

LEGUERCHE   Dogs don't bite butchers.

MARRIEN   You won't be allowed in.

LEGUERCHE   I'll find a way in. *Exit left.*

*Marrien stares after him.*
*Coste comes out quickly, downstage right.*

COSTE   You sent him away — you were in a rage?

*Marrien turns to him.*

COSTE   You ended up raising your voice — I heard it through the door. You're as white as a sheet, Lieutenant Marrien. How did it go with Leguerche?

MARRIEN   He — gave me time to think it over.

COSTE   Think what over?

MARRIEN   Whether I should use dogs on him or the whip.

COSTE   You really threatened him?

MARRIEN   Should I have knocked him down without a word?

COSTE *breaks off.*   You thwarted my plans, Lieutenant Marrien, when you refused to return to Paris. Why did you stay?

*Marrien stares at him.*

COSTE   You don't answer?

MARRIEN   I didn't go — to prevent an attempt on Catherine's life behind my back.

COSTE   By whose hand?

MARRIEN *seizes his hand.*   By this one, Monsieur Coste, that up to now has only bestowed blessings on Catherine's head.

COSTE   And is it now become a fist to threaten her?

MARRIEN   Why do you want me to go to Paris?

COSTE   I'll be perfectly frank: I want to find Leguerche and satisfy his demands.

*Marrien remains silent.*

COSTE   Money is the key. For him. For us, Lieutenant Marrien. In this case, the power of money becomes miraculous. A man will disappear — the earth will simply swallow him up — as soon as he has money in his hands. Leguerche will never have existed — and you are free to live.

MARRIEN *slowly.*   To pay Leguerche is to recognize Leguerche.

COSTE *falteringly.*   And not to pay him is — to wipe out his existence?

MARRIEN   Are you ready to dishonour Catherine by paying Leguerche?

COSTE *astonished.*   What are you saying, Lieutenant Marrien? Do you really think the power of thought can make a man disappear, like a puff of smoke, as soon as you put him out of your mind? He may be dead in your mind — you may be convinced of it — but he's still flesh and blood in the real world. Leguerche will still exist — full of hatred and close to the two of you. You'll always be yoked together — unless you cut loose. And you can — by giving the butcher's boy his money!

MARRIEN *as if awakening.*   Will he repeat his demand?

COSTE   He gave you time to think it over. How long?

MARRIEN   Not long. Minutes.

COSTE   And then it's dogs and the whip?

MARRIEN   Are dogs and the whip enough?

COSTE   Enough to plunge you and Catherine into a state of unending turmoil. How can you keep something secret if you start thrashing people?

MARRIEN   Is keeping a thing secret enough to — undo — what happened?

COSTE *goes over to him.*   You may not see a way out of this quandary, but there is a way, and that's to forget yourself. Live for the moment. Start afresh. Forget what's happened. Are you not resolved to take the most drastic measures? What of the regiment? The house in Paris? You are ready for whatever lies in store — I can see deep into your heart. Love for Catherine has shaken the very core of your being. Your conduct warrants neither praise nor reproach from me, for it soars sublimely beyond my judgement. Defend the sphere you and Catherine inhabit. Few find the path to such rarefied heights. Keep all intruders out! As for Leguerche, he shall be flung down into the depths — with the money I will give him! *Exit, downstage right.*

MARRIEN *stands irresolutely, then quickly off, left — returns with cap, cloak and sabre; leaves them on armchair — runs to door, upstage right, flings it open.* Madame Jattefaux!

*Enter Mme. Jattefaux.*

MARRIEN   Where is Catherine?

JATTEFAUX    She's lying down. She felt faint.

MARRIEN    Can she get up at all?

JATTEFAUX. She is very weak.

MARRIEN    Can she hear what you say?

JATTEFAUX    I've had no response from her so far.

MARRIEN    She must hear. Tell her that Lieutenant Jean-Marc Marrien must see her at once.

JATTEFAUX    I shall tell her. *Exit.*

*Marrien waits by the door.*
*Enter Catherine.*

MARRIEN *holds out his arms.*    Catherine!

CATHERINE *in his embrace.*    Jean-Marc!

MARRIEN    How did it begin?

CATHERINE    Don't you know?

MARRIEN    I have forgotten everything so I might hear it first from your own lips. Where did we first meet?

CATHERINE    At noon, in front of the jeweller's.

MARRIEN    We were mesmerized by the rings. What then?

CATHERINE    I knelt at your side in church.

MARRIEN    Our marriage ceremony. And then?

CATHERINE    You took me to the opera.

MARRIEN    Our wedding celebration. And then?

CATHERINE    At night you came to me.

MARRIEN    I truly did come to you. I hurried through the garden — the gravel crunched under my feet — I climbed up the vine on the trellis — opened the window — then I was standing in the passage. Did I find the door?

CATHERINE    I had already opened it.

MARRIEN    I slipped into the room. You were shimmering in white. I held you close to me. With these arms!

CATHERINE    These arms made love to me.

MARRIEN    What did I say?

CATHERINE    Don't you remember?

MARRIEN    Did I ask you at last for your name?

CATHERINE    I had kept it from you all day — in the night I revealed it.

MARRIEN    Say it now.

CATHERINE *whispers.*    Catherine.

MARRIEN    That's what you whispered in my ear, lying beside me.

CATHERINE    Then you revealed yourself, too.

MARRIEN    My name?

CATHERINE    Say it now.

MARRIEN    Jean-Marc.

CATHERINE    We said our names a hundred times, so we would know each other.

MARRIEN    You —

CATHERINE    Catherine —

MARRIEN    Catherine!

CATHERINE    You —

MARRIEN    Jean-Marc —

CATHERINE    Jean-Marc!

MARRIEN    And so we know each other — ourselves alone — from that first day when love overpowered you — and would bestow the gift of life on me — life such as I had not lived until that moment! *Changes his tone.* We must leave. Are you ready?

CATHERINE    I need only close my trunk.

MARRIEN    No trunk. That would cause delay. We would lose time. I cannot wait for trunks to be brought down. We are fleeing, Catherine, you and I.

CATHERINE    We have to flee, I know that.

MARRIEN    Where to? Let Heaven decide over which island it spreads its blue canopy. Aren't there islands in the sea where no people live? Do you know of any, Catherine?

CATHERINE    Let us sail across seas.

MARRIEN    Fearlessly, past crags that resemble grotesque human faces. I shall spit into the ugliest of them, like that! ——— *He breaks off.*

*Leguerche has appeared behind the French window.*
*Marrien stares at him.*
*Catherine follows his glance.*
*Leguerche opens the French window — enters — closes it behind him.*
*Marrien steps protectively in front of Catherine.*

LEGUERCHE    Twenty times around the house — I counted every one — and at an even pace. *Advances two steps.* Like that — one — two. Not a drop of sweat and my heart is not pounding. No cheating. I kept to what I said. Now I'm back.

*Silence.*

LEGUERCHE    Well?

MARRIEN    How — how did you get in?

LEGUERCHE    Over the wall — through the garden. You think I don't know all the secret paths? I've used them often enough.

MARRIEN   Who —— are you looking for?

LEGUERCHE   Maybe Juliette — maybe —— Catherine. Whoever offers herself to me. How's it to be this time? *He steps to one side to see Catherine better.*

*Catherine stares at him, transfixed.*
*Marrien looks at Catherine.*

LEGUERCHE *stares at Catherine — nods.*   Here we are again, then. In the brightness of day — not like the last time. Then it was pitch-dark — you couldn't see your hand in front of your face. Now it's light.

MARRIEN *to Catherine.*   Don't look at him ——

LEGUERCHE   Don't interrupt me —— are you going to pay up? *To Catherine again.* There are memories that need refreshing. It would be shameful of me not to remember —— to spit on favours granted and enjoyed. I'm not a savage.

MARRIEN *to Catherine, who remains motionless.*   Be strong! Leave now ——

LEGUERCHE *to Marrien.*   You're not going to pay, are you? —— And I understand why not. How much is she worth? A king's ransom? *Stepping towards Catherine.* Beyond rubies! *To Marrien.* Listen to me — I know by experience — *taking hold of Catherine* — I've been embraced by these arms, lain on these silky soft breasts, sunk into this body so that you never want to emerge again, held tight in a vice-like grip by these lusty young limbs. Didn't I have to tear myself away from you, Catherine, when dawn came?

MARRIEN   Go! Let me deal with him ——

LEGUERCHE   So you can pay me? —— I want no money! I'm not falling for that — *Strikes his forehead* — not here — *With an expansive gesture.* — and certainly not after what I've experienced with her. No deal, not even cash down. No more haggling, Lieutenant. It's pointless complaining. You've had your chance, now it's too late. You see, I've got to know Catherine! —— My head is full of her, no room for — Juliette. Juliette? — back into the gutter where she belongs! Where was I? With you two! With you, Catherine —. I mustn't forget a thing, so I'll follow you. That will be my life from now on — haunting you. Following your tracks. Where you are, I will be. If you're sitting at a table, I'll join you. When you're lying in bed, I'll be staring through the window. If you go to America, I'll be a stoker on the ship. Hide in some tropical forest, and I'll be up a palm tree, watching! —— And when they ask what chains bind me to you —

I'll tell them the whole story, to their astonishment: that's my child they are raising — I made that child — in the course of one unforgettable night with her — me, the butcher's boy, Leguerche! —— Let the persecution begin. I'll be waiting at the gate, and when you leave the house I'll be dogging your footsteps, sticking to you like a bur. *He throws open the French window — crosses the terrace and disappears below.*

*Marrien stares after him.*

CATHERINE *groans.*    Don't let him ——

MARRIEN *cries out.*    What, Catherine?

CATHERINE    —— Don't let him kill our child!

*Marrien looks about in extreme agitation. With a bound he is at the armchair — tears sword from sheath — rushes after Leguerche.*
*From below, a blood-curdling cry is heard.*
*Enter Coste, downstage right.*

COSTE *to Catherine.*    What was that?

*Catherine is struck dumb.*

COSTE *notices the open French window.*    Where is Lieutenant Marrien?

*Marrien returns to terrace. Corte awaits him. Marrien enters.*

COSTE    What — have you done?

MARRIEN    I have —

COSTE    What — good did that do?

MARRIEN *slowly.*    If there are some acts so terrible that they cut us off from the world — this had to be one of them.

*Coste hurries past Marrien across terrace — exit.*

MARRIEN *at Catherine's side.*    Now we can live. *They kiss.*

# Clairvoyance

## (*Hellseherei*, 1929)

A Comedy of Manners in Three Acts

# CHARACTERS

Victor
Vera
Lady
Sneederhan
Maid

*All three acts take place in Victor and Vera's drawing room. Three doors: one to left, one to right, one to rear into hallway — its upper half is glass-panelled.*

# ACT ONE

LADY  *in hat and gloves — waits in drawing room. Having started the gramophone, she sits on the arm of an armchair, bobbing her foot to the music. The record finishes. Lady peels off a glove, lights a cigarette. — Vera and maid appear in the hallway. Vera hurriedly takes off her hat and gloves, gives them to maid. The maid says something to Vera — Vera quickly opens the glass door.*

VERA *entering.*   It's you?

LADY   Are you surprised?

VERA   Why shouldn't I be surprised?

LADY   Well — my car is down below. You can see the red from miles off.

VERA   I didn't see a thing. Have you been waiting long?

LADY   Half a dozen gramophone records and half a cigarette.

VERA   You must forgive me —

LADY   I didn't say I was coming. I was out and about in the car. It's a nice day. I came to call —

VERA   I can't go with you now.

LADY   — to fetch Victor.

VERA   Has Victor got time?

LADY   For business matters?

VERA *as if suddenly remembering.*   Your building plans —

LADY   Just as soon as I've made up my mind on the site. We'll inspect it again today — if Victor gives the go-ahead, the excavations can begin tomorrow.

VERA    Victor is so happy to be building your villa.

LADY    I couldn't have found a better architect.

VERA    Shall I call his office?

LADY    He should be here any moment — for lunch.

VERA    Is that the time already?

LADY    Midday.

VERA    I couldn't eat a thing.

LADY    That's quite a protest.

VERA    Against the barbaric custom of eating by the clock. I'm not hungry — I'll eat when I am. Anything else is a sin against nature. If we forget that, we're parasites — not human beings.

LADY    You're all on edge, Vera.

VERA    Just because I'm telling the truth?

LADY *goes to her — strokes her hair.*    It's not like you. Blondes are never on edge — annoyed sometimes perhaps, and unable to hide it. Do tell me what it is.

VERA    I'm not annoyed —

LADY    Yes, you are. Very much so. And miles away. You don't see my red car in front of the house. You barely remember my building project. Something has happened to you this morning, and not just something annoying. Believe me, I know about these things. It's best if you tell me all — now, before it festers any more — like blood poisoning. Get it off your chest.

VERA *hugging her.*    Provided you stay here — all through lunchtime.

LADY    Why do you insist on that?

VERA    So you won't stay?

LADY    I'll stay. I was going to eat with you anyway. But why is it so important?

VERA    Because — Victor mustn't notice anything.

LADY    Notice what?

VERA    My tears — they would give me away at once!

LADY *pauses.*    What is it — you've done, Vera?

VERA    Why do you think I've done something? I love Victor. How could it even occur to me to inflict a wound on myself? I'd bleed to death. Do you think I want to die? I want to live. That's why he mustn't know — and I don't want to know!

LADY *tentatively.*    Has — Victor done something?

VERA *rising. Curtly.*    No.

LADY *lighting a cigarette.*    And yet I'm indispensable — to keep the conversation going over lunch — otherwise, with just you and Victor, you'd plunge into a bottomless pit.

VERA    I wouldn't be able to control myself — he would ask me, and I would own up.

LADY    You're totally in control of yourself — look how you've roused my curiosity yet haven't revealed a thing. We'll have a high old time, the three of us. *Towards glass door, listening.* Is that Victor?

VERA *startled.*    Not yet!

LADY    Your maid. *To Vera.* You really are trembling, Vera!

VERA    And I will — when I see Victor ——

LADY    I'll wait for him downstairs and whisk him straight off to the site. Calm yourself in the meantime. We'll meet up at the theatre this evening.

VERA    No. He'll think that odd. He'll want to see me now. Your excuses will make him suspicious. There must be nothing odd. Not now. Not ever. Promise me that, if you care for me at all.

LADY    I'm your friend, Vera.

VERA *impulsively.* The ring is gone!

LADY *almost laughing.* A ring? Is that all you've lost?

VERA But you know the one. The ring with the blue sapphire in the antique setting.

LADY Your most beautiful ring.

VERA A present from Victor the day we got married. He placed it on my finger with words God can surely never forget. It was the most solemn act of the day. For him too. After all, he uttered the words. We were standing in the room, alone. He said in the quietest of voices: from this moment on there is only you and me in the world — a bond between two people is more than any congregation of the living and the dead. I shall hold it sacred. Amen. And I repeated the 'Amen' more devoutly than any priest.

LADY And *that's* the ring you've lost?

VERA Disappeared, without trace. As if the earth had swallowed it. I was wearing it — and suddenly I was no longer wearing it. The finger was bare — no ring beyond the knuckle — nothing.

LADY And this happened this morning?

VERA *taken aback.* This morning?

LADY Surely that's why you are in such a state?

VERA It's been gone for weeks. I even know the exact day I lost it. It was when the president of the Architects' Club held his big party. Victor had something else on that evening and I had to go alone. The ninth of March. The date is stamped on my memory.

LADY *after a moment's thought.* And — at the ball —

VERA — I was wearing the ring, just as Victor wanted. He always decides which jewellery goes with which dress. He has an eye for it. He often tries out new combinations for hours on end — that's when I feel as if I'm a work of art he is creating.

LADY I hope for your sake he never completes it.

VERA   Because he would love me less if he did?

LADY   Less —? *Breaking off.* When you left the party, was the ring —

VERA   When I left the party — in a hurry and long before it had finished — I pulled on my glove over the ring in the cloakroom — I know I did for I gazed at it for a moment — with a feeling that suddenly rose up — a mixture of alarm — and anger — and shock — the shock you feel when you've been really disillusioned ——

LADY   And what caused this feeling you've just described, during the president's ball?

VERA   One of the guests used Victor's absence to make stupid insinuations about modern marriage: everyone does their own thing — madame alone at the ball — monsieur at some hotel, not alone — life's too short to think there's only one 'special one' — just follow your intuition and seize the moment. I can't forget a single phrase, every one cut me to the quick.

LADY   Empty words, Vera, just what men say on such occasions.

VERA   I didn't want to take it seriously either. But I couldn't help it. Finally, my head was spinning. I knew perfectly well how mean, how insulting it was to suspect Victor in the slightest — yet I left early and went home —

LADY   — to find Victor there?

VERA   He hadn't got back yet.

LADY   So you concluded he must be guilty?

VERA   I didn't think anything at all. Once I was home I could breathe again. I went into the bedroom — and before getting undressed I wanted to take off the ring. It wasn't there. Victor's wedding present had disappeared.

LADY   So — you must have lost it on the way home from the ball.

VERA   I searched every room — searched the stairs — then from the door to where I had got out of the car: no trace of the ring. I searched half the night — until I heard Victor arriving. I decided to leave the empty jewel-box where it was and say nothing. I pretended to be asleep — and kept watch: Victor didn't open it and locked it away, empty, in the wall safe.

LADY   Since when you haven't mentioned it to Victor?

VERA   I didn't want to upset him. I didn't want to upset myself. It would have brought back memories of that evening. I couldn't say anything. Anyhow, the ring would surely turn up. Surely I had only mislaid it. Like the glove which was also missing the next morning, and still is. I was so worked up that evening, I must have jinxed everything: the glove — and the ring. They must both be in the flat — so I thought — and I searched high and low —— today I think differently ——— I've stopped thinking!

LADY   You're now convinced the ring is gone for good?

VERA   After I was told today where the ring is — I've lost it for good!

LADY *baffled.*   So the ring has been found —— it's being kept somewhere —— but you don't want to get it back?

VERA   Again, I don't know. Anyway, I couldn't get it back any more, for I've destroyed the clue that leads to it. It was within reach, now no one can track it down.

LADY   Is that what you'll tell Victor?

VERA   I'm only telling you, you're my friend.

LADY   Who — has the ring?

VERA   Some little jeweller in some side street.

LADY   How did it get there?

VERA   The person who found it took it there.

LADY   To sell it?

VERA   To have it valued.

LADY   And sell it later?

VERA   He's already forgotten about it.

LADY   It's been at the jeweller's that long?

VERA   It was found just after I got back from the ball — on the kerb, where I had got out of the car. I took off my glove to pay the chauffeur — and since I was in a hurry, the ring came off as well. I dropped the glove without noticing — with the ring inside it. Then I rushed into the house.

LADY   While someone picked up what you had dropped.

VERA   A young man — arm in arm with his girlfriend — strolling along the street. Suddenly his companion cries out: something white — and points to my glove. Her young man bends down — flourishes the glove, says jokingly: not on offer as a pair, so thanks, but no thanks — and drops it. It makes a metallic sound when it hits the pavement. That makes the girl curious, she says: there must be something inside it. He retrieves it — has a feel — turns it inside out and finds the ring. The girl and her young man can't agree on the ring — they know nothing about jewels and settings — and he agrees to show the ring to a jeweller next morning to tell them what it is they've found. He does so: the young man enters the shop — there's only the jeweller's daughter there — her father is ill. She says she will show him the ring. The young man consents — but is distracted later and forgets to return — the girl doesn't show the ring to the jeweller — he's not well — everything is forgotten: and there the ring remains, wrapped up in tissue paper in the corner of a cupboard in the jeweller's shop — unnoticed — unscathed.

LADY   You've managed to find all that out — all the details?

VERA   I even know what the jeweller is suffering from — sciatica. The young man wears a bowler. The girl is deceiving him.

LADY   Have you called in the police?

VERA   I'd sooner have confessed to Victor.

LADY   So who put you on the trail?

VERA   It just occurred to me — something really crazy — and I still thought it crazy while I was doing it. I went to see a clairvoyant.

LADY *amused.*   You went to a —

VERA   A so-called clairvoyant — that's where I was this morning. You read in the papers about experiments that have worked. Maybe I would be lucky and find out where the ring is hidden in the flat. Of course, I didn't believe it for a minute — but it cost ten marks to try — and I paid the ten marks.

LADY   And the man immediately fell into a trance.

VERA   I had to write down in one clear sentence whatever was bothering me.

LADY   So you wrote —?

VERA   That I lost my ring on the evening of the ninth of March.

LADY   Nothing else?

VERA   And then, with all the concentration I could muster, I had to think of the ring.

LADY   You wouldn't have found that difficult.

VERA   No. I gave the clairvoyant all the support I could. Afterwards he praised me as an especially gifted medium

LADY   And what did the result of his clairvoyance turn out to be?

VERA   What I told you.

LADY   All that information you got — from him?

VERA   In detail, right down to the kind of hat — and the sciatica.

LADY   That's really eerie, and conjured up in broad daylight, too. Weren't you spooked out?

VERA   I was — when he answered my second question. I got carried away enough to put it to him after he begged me to let him experiment with me some more. Free of charge this time — just to see what happened — and since I was apparently a psychic medium of rare ability. I must have been out of my mind to write it down.

LADY   What did you write?

VERA   That I missed my husband on the evening of the ninth of March.

LADY   And his response?

VERA   He covered his eyes — and I concentrated so it almost hurt. What he said came very rapidly: I see a man — and he describes Victor in every detail, to a T! — he is in a large building — in a room — at first alone — still alone — a curtain is drawn back — a woman steps forward — in a kimono — damask, with a dragon design — the woman turns to close the curtain behind her — I can't see her face — the man rises from the divan he was lying on — he goes to the woman — embraces her from behind — kisses her neck ————— *Shudders*. At that I broke the chain that linked his thoughts with mine — jumped up from the chair and fled out the door as if I were at the mercy of some devil!

LADY *after a pause*.   You're not going to take this charlatan seriously?

VERA *vehemently*.   Not without evidence!

LADY   How can he produce that?

VERA   When the ring is found.

LADY   Where?

VERA   At the jeweller's.

LADY   But you would take that to mean — the clairvoyant's second supposition was correct.

VERA   I would know everything.

LADY *again after a pause*.   You want to know — nothing?

VERA   About Victor?

LADY   I don't mean it personally. As a matter of principle. Just suppose: a man is deceiving his wife. The woman doesn't find out.

VERA   What if it were the death of her if she did find out?

LADY   One can get divorced.

VERA   A woman with a burning love for her husband in her heart?!

LADY   Her passion would cool down.

VERA    If she were one of those impersonal people you mentioned. But those aren't real human beings. I am. I love Victor as only I can. He is the temple I pray in. The noisy street outside — it mustn't be allowed to intrude with its filth. The temple is sacred, since time immemorial. Any shrill noise would shatter the dome that protects us — Victor and me. I'll fight with all my might against attack and defeat. There is no world outside — not for Victor and me!

LADY    I admire your determination to reject reality — as if it didn't exist.

VERA    What is real? This wallpaper is real, behind is rough stone. Are we really living between bare walls? We embellish our home — and our love — so we can live in the midst of this reality — which is ten times worse than death if we let it intrude.

LADY    At the expense of the ring in this case.

VERA    It's gone. It can't reappear. I've made sure of that.

LADY    But might you not want to make certain — one day, out of curiosity — whether the clairvoyant was right in what he saw?

VERA    First I would have to find all the scraps of paper I threw out of the car window on the way back. That's equally impossible.

LADY    What did you tear up?

VERA    What I had to write down while he was talking. He insisted on it. You get a written record. Mine is scattered to the winds.

LADY    You don't remember anything at all?

VERA    I couldn't find the shop of some obscure jeweller or other without written instructions.

LADY    So the ring is gone, then. How will you explain its loss to Victor?

VERA    I won't. I left the jewel-box out for him — he locked it up. Let him tell me where my ring is.

LADY    Perhaps it is best to deny all knowledge.

VERA    Will you betray me?

LADY    If you don't betray yourself he'll never know what really happened.

VERA *to herself.*    For that — would be the most dreadful thing.

LADY    What?

VERA    The truth.

LADY *kisses her, shaking her head. Towards glass door.*    Victor!

VERA    He won't be able to tell from looking at me now. I've already confessed everything — to you.

VICTOR *behind glass door — gives hat and coat to maid. — Enters — with a bulky parcel. To maid.*    No — I'll keep the parcel. *He puts it down on an armchair — kisses Vera, pats the parcel.* For you. *Greeting the Lady.* It quite took my breath away when I turned into the street: everything looked different. What had happened? A dash of red — lighting up the whole street — what a fabulous contrast to the surroundings. A luminous rich red against the slate-grey house-fronts and — hey presto — the street was beautiful. A revelation — thank you!

LADY    Because my car is outside?

VICTOR    Of course it's your car. Seen from a purely objective perspective, which runs parallel. But the aesthetic effect of it! It defined the whole street. Perfectly positioned! Don't you know that's the secret of great works of art? They have a point which contradicts everything else. A black collides with the yellow of a painting. That mobilizes the painting's energies — and they pour out. It needs the black to make the yellow yellow. Irresistible. It gives it its distinctive accent. *To Vera.* Am I very late? — Did you arrive together? — Have you been shopping?

VERA *hesitates.*    Yes.

VICTOR    So was I. That's what held me up. At first I couldn't find anything suitable. *Undoing the string around the parcel.* Where were you?

VERA    Buying silk.

VICTOR *straightens up.*    So was I. I didn't see you in the store.

LADY    There are several floors.

VICTOR *to Vera.*   You didn't buy the —?

VERA   No — I bought nothing.

LADY   Vera was helping me. I was looking for some damask.

VERA   Which is in a different department, that's true. I was after the plain white silk. Second floor, on the right. Where the sales assistant was signally lacking in intelligence. Nothing would deflect him from his conviction that wedding dresses should be made of one single material. Not a combination of plain and lustrous. I finally shouted: it's not for a wedding dress — and the fellow goggled at me like a seal. Don't ask me why. *He unrolls both lengths of material.* Here's what your gown will be made from.

VERA   For — the fancy-dress ball at the Architects' Club?

VICTOR   Exactly, my child. You like it?

VERA   So white —

VICTOR   Nothing but white. Snow-white, like snowflakes. Except: the top half matt and the bottom half shimmering. There you have my creation of a costume to adorn you and please me. Can't you imagine the effect?

VERA   Very — uniform ——

VICTOR   Protest away — my satisfaction will be all the greater when I've convinced you. Let our friend be a judge of its success — how fortunate we're not alone. So there can be no question of me overriding your own good taste. Try draping this round your shoulders. Let me help. *He drapes the material round her shoulders.* That's one half — now the other length for the skirt — if you'd just spread it out with your hands — like a crinoline bustle.

VERA   What's it meant to look like?

VICTOR   Velázquez. A copy of his famous princess. But all in white.

VERA *stands as instructed.*   Do you like it?

VICTOR *steps back. To Lady.*   Well? The verdict?

LADY *shakes her head.*

VICTOR   A bit boring. Lifeless.

LADY   Monotone.

VICTOR   That's the word I wanted. Devastatingly monotone. A wash-out — no resistance. Doesn't work. Why not?

LADY   Because one tone merges with the other.

VICTOR   Correct. Now remember what I said about the car in the street — how it gave it its distinctive accent. There — the grey of the street, here — the white. Characterless without a contrast to set it off. Here it has to come from the hands — jewellery — a ring. Blue — that would enliven the white — bring it to life. You must wear your old ring with the blue sapphire with the white gown.

VERA *gazes at him dumbfounded.*

VICTOR   That's the secret of this costume — let me now reveal it. My starting point was the blue ring. For once its unique character shall be seen for what it is. All the white shall flow radiantly towards it and in turn be stimulated and nourished by it. The effect of my creation will be overwhelming, I promise you. I'll fetch the ring.

VERA *in great consternation.*   After we've eaten, Victor —

VICTOR   I can't wait. I feel I've made a fool of myself in front of our visitor — the ring shall restore her respect for me. *To Vera.* Don't move.

VERA   I feel faint, Victor — I'm so hungry ——

VICTOR   Five minutes, no more.

VERA *to Lady.*   Would you not —

VICTOR   Try it on for you? Certainly not. *To Lady.* Her dark complexion doesn't suit what was conceived with Vera's blond in mind.

LADY   Vera is exhausted.

VICTOR   What from?

LADY   It's been a very stressful morning for her.

VICTOR   Looking at silk.

LADY   Aren't I hard to please when I've set my mind on something?

VICTOR   Brocade.

LADY   And five minutes could be crucial in influencing my decision.

VICTOR   About what?

LADY   One's moods changes — and I might no longer care for that particular plot of land.

VICTOR *in consternation.*   But surely you'll take it?

LADY   If you can spare the time — I wanted you to help me make up my mind. The car's waiting downstairs.

VICTOR *thinks for a moment, runs to door left — flings it open.*   Is lunch ready? No. *Points to Vera.* She hasn't fainted. It will all be done before we eat — I'll fetch the ring. *Fishes a bunch of keys out of his pocket — exit right.*

VERA *rooted to the spot.*

LADY *shrugs.*   I couldn't prevent it.

VERA *snaps out of daze — stamps her foot.*   And he won't get a word out of me.

VICTOR *returns — with the jewel box open and empty.*   Had I already taken the ring out for you?

VERA   Ring — what ring?

VICTOR   The one that was in this box?

VERA   Isn't it there?

VICTOR   Look — empty.

VERA   Yes — empty.

VICTOR   Are you not wearing it?

VERA    There are my hands.

VICTOR    In your dressing table?

VERA    But you won't let me.

VICTOR    Which means — the ring must be — *He breaks off.*

VERA    May I take this off now?

VICTOR *scratches his head — ponders.*

VERA *puts down the lengths of silk in armchair.*

LADY    Have you lost — something valuable?

VICTOR *preoccupied.* Apart from its value —— the value is certainly a consideration —— it's valuable enough to attract a thief ——

VERA    But who would steal anything in our house?

VICTOR *still brooding.*    Who could have ——?

VERA    You surely doesn't suspect the staff?

VICTOR *looking up.*    Why not the staff? If someone got hold of my keys?

VERA    Don't you always take them with you?

VICTOR    That only leaves burglary. Someone broke in and used a tool to open the safe.

VERA    There's always someone here.

VICTOR    They were in cahoots with the cook or the maid.

VERA    I'll vouch for them both with my life.

VICTOR *mockingly.*    Who can you trust?

VERA    Someone who doesn't steal.

VICTOR    In this case?

VERA    The maid and the cook.

VICTOR *vehemently.*    But not the thief who plundered the safe.

VERA    Why, is more missing?

VICTOR    Why should more be missing.

VERA    You said plunder.

VICTOR    Isn't it enough for one ring to be stolen — my present to you the day we got married?

VERA    You didn't take good care of it, Victor.

VICTOR    You're right, it's my fault. Hold me responsible. Remind me of my duty. I must retrieve the ring for you. *He goes to telephone.*

VERA    Who are you ringing?

VICTOR    The police — detectives. This is a serious crime — the police must investigate.

VERA    You're going to involve the police?

VICTOR    To take fingerprints. Invisible to the naked eye, but the thief will have left tracks behind. They'll uncover the truth.

VERA    There was no thief!

VICTOR    Then where is the ring?

VERA    I — I lost it.

VICTOR    —— Why did you lie at first?

VERA    Because — I was ashamed.

VICTOR    —— When did you lose it?

VERA    At — the President's Ball.

VICTOR    During the ball?

VERA    Or after the ball.

VICTOR    You don't remember exactly?

VERA    When you lose something, you don't notice it at the time.

VICTOR    But afterwards, at home, you were certain — and you left the empty box for me to shut away?

VERA    Because I was so ashamed.

VICTOR    —— What did you do afterwards to try to get the ring back?

VERA    Nothing.

VICTOR    Nothing? Nothing, Vera? You treated the loss of the ring as if it were a mere bagatelle? You just let it go? Lost all trace of it?

VERA    Yes.

VICTOR    Do you expect me to show the same indifference?

VERA    If you love me, Victor — yes.

VICTOR    I'm beginning to — wonder — about your love — the way you can let such a unique memento go.

VERA    It's for the sake of my love that I relinquish the ring.

VICTOR *shrugs.*    What is lost can be found. It shall be found. They're very much mistaken if they think I'm a millionaire and all and sundry can get to keep any ring they find. A search operation is called for, we'll pull out all the stops. Even if it's in pieces and I have to put it together again, I won't quit until I've found every last bit. *To Vera.* And then I'll forge it anew and make you a present of it a second time. *Calling through the glass door.* My hat and coat.

LADY *going to Victor.* You won't be coming with me in the car, then?

VICTOR You start lunch — it's imperative I deal with this first. I'll be right back. *He goes into hallway. The maid helps him into his overcoat. Exit Victor.*

VERA Victor!

# ACT TWO

*From door left: Vera — exceedingly agitated, looks around helplessly. She sits down at desk — scribbles a few lines of a letter — Lady enters left — lights cigarette.*

LADY  You ate very little.

VERA  Not a thing.

LADY  You positively fled from the table.

VERA  Yes.

LADY  The maid will think we've been quarrelling.

VERA  What could come between us?

LADY *remains silent.*  — What made you run off in a panic?

VERA  Victor might come back.

LADY  Do you want to confront him here?

VERA  Neither here nor — *She chokes.*

LADY *from behind Vera.*  Are you writing?

VERA *nods.*

LADY  What are you writing?

VERA *shifts to one side.*

LADY  May I read?

VERA *nods again.*

LADY    *reads — cradles Vera's head.*    A farewell letter — punctuated with tears.
Poor — little Vera.

VERA *seals the letter — holds it out to Lady.*    Will you deliver it?

LADY    You entrust this delicate mission to me?

VERA    So he can't pretend he didn't find it. This way I have a witness to back
me up.

LADY    Why would he want to pretend?

VERA    So as not to lose me. He would miss his puppet, someone to try out his
new ideas on. He needs a toy he can manipulate, someone who doesn't
contradict him. That's my role.

LADY    You underestimate what you mean to him.

VERA    Not a bit, since noon today. How did he react to my pleas? With derision.

LADY    He was very distressed.

VERA    Was I any less distressed? Did I not make it as clear as day that I was
imploring him? Even someone deaf as a stone could have read my quivering lips.
He can hear perfectly well, yet he was deaf to my begging.

LADY    You must put yourself in his position.

VERA    What position?

LADY    He unsuspectingly goes and opens the safe — takes out the jewel-box in
question — opens the lid and finds it empty.

VERA    Well then?

LADY    Isn't he right to be startled?

VERA    How could I hold that against him?

LADY    First he thinks it's burglars — then you admit to losing it.

VERA    In all honesty.

LADY   The fact that you made no attempt to find it must naturally have been incomprehensible to him.

VERA   I would have been surprised if he had he thought any differently.

LADY   Then what are you accusing him of?

VERA   Of being deaf towards me — blind towards me — uninterested in me. He lets me implore him and doesn't do what I'm begging him to do. The whole story of the ring — it's unimportant now — whether he finds it or not. What is crucial is that my devastation leaves him cold. He doesn't love me.

LADY   He loves you in a way that —

VERA   He's never loved me.

LADY   Child —

VERA   Not the way I believed he did when I allowed myself to be loved by him. If I leave him today, the gap will be filled by — someone else — somebody who lets him do as he likes. But I would advise her to offer some resistance, not to let herself be moulded like wax in his hands as he pursues some preconceived ideal. Then she'll be happy with him. — You're laughing?

LADY   What you say is very true, and something I —

VERA   Something you?

LADY *breaking off — sitting down beside her.*   Vera — how will you live without him?

VERA *lost in thought.*   Can I — live without him?

LADY   You'll get over it.

VERA   To think of him — with a woman, coming out from behind a curtain — in a kimono — with a dragon design ——

LADY   How could anyone know that?

VERA *looks up.*   You think he won't find the ring?

LADY *smiles, shakes her head.*

VERA　He will?

LADY　No.

VERA　But he'll search — he swore he'd search until he gets it back, if necessary piece by piece.

LADY　If your prohibition still holds —

VERA　I prohibit it!

LADY　Then the ring remains missing.

VERA *taken aback.*　Have you the power ——

LADY　Even if it costs me my villa — which he shall not build if he goes against your wish.

VERA　You'll — do that for me?

LADY　Is that what you want?

VERA　A hundred times over! — Are you quite sure your threat will work on him?

LADY　I'm not — wax in someone else's hands.

VERA *throwing her arms around her neck.*　How can I ever repay you?

LADY　How?

VERA　With friendship — unto death and beyond.

LADY　Sometimes even life lasts too long.

VERA *letting go.*　Where should I be when you speak to Victor?

LADY　Not here, naturally.

VERA *looking around.*　Where ——?

LADY *presses a bell-button. — Enter maid.* Wrap up the parcel and take it to my car.

MAID *exit with silk and wrapping.*

VERA To return the silk?

LADY No, to the dressmaker's — to have the costume made up as Victor wanted.

VERA To think of such a thing now!

LADY What do you want to be thinking about when you see Victor again?

VERA *pensively.* It will all be forgotten by then —

LADY — except for your fancy-dress ball and getting ready for it.

VERA *runs into hallway — claps her hands.* My things.

*Maid helps her on with her coat.*

VERA *returns.* What about the letter?

LADY You don't want him to read it any more?

VERA I'm not leaving after all.

LADY Then it's pointless. *She puts it in her pocket.*

VERA *leaves — turns back.* Don't be too harsh with him.

LADY *laughing.* I won't shout.

VERA I mean — don't reproach him.

LADY You mean, there are extenuating circumstances?

VERA Just restrict yourself to one sentence: the ring or the villa.

LADY You think that's plausible enough for him to swallow?

VERA   You're not going to tell him —

LADY   What?

VERA   Why I don't want to see the ring again?

LADY   I'm smarter than you give me credit for.

VERA   Thank goodness for that. *Exit quickly with a sigh of relief.*

LADY *waits — turns on gramophone.*

VICTOR *appears behind glass door — takes off his coat — enters.*

LADY *gives him a cursory glance.*

VICTOR   Your car — that passed me by?

LADY *nods.*

VICTOR   Without you?

LADY *nods.*

VICTOR *goes to left — opens door — looks in — closes door.*   Where is Vera?

LADY   In the car that passed you by.

VICTOR   Going where?

LADY   To the dressmaker's — for a fitting.

VICTOR *angrily.* Now's not the time!

LADY *points to gramophone — puts her finger to her lips. The record finishes.* Another record?

VICTOR   If you don't mind —

LADY   And if I do?

VICTOR   What then?

LADY *closes the gramophone.* There, you see, I too am obedient. That's what you lords of creation expect, isn't it? *She holds out her hand, which he kisses.* Yes, Vera is having her costume made up.

VICTOR *sarcastically.* Then it will be a race to see whether she gets her costume before I get the ring.

LADY One could take bets.

VICTOR I would certainly win.

LADY You would assuredly lose.

VICTOR It's as good as found. Ninety-nine per cent certain, so — guaranteed. I've got the best detective agency on the job, searching high and low. First: they'll comb the pawnshops, since whoever found it may have pawned it — that's usually the case since it's the simplest way to dispose of things. Secondly: an advertisement in the papers — with a not inconsiderable reward as an enticement. Thirdly: posters on the advertising columns with a precise description of the object — easily remembered by any passer-by. The whole town will be bombarded with appeals for information about the ring. The fun starts in half an hour.

LADY I fear all three initiatives are doomed to fail.

VICTOR Then a fourth, which I forgot to mention, will do the trick. The villain who found the ring may have sold it. Where do you sell a jewel? At a jeweller's. So all the jewellers will be searched from top to bottom — from the wholesale merchants to the backstreet pedlars.

LADY In that case your efforts will certainly be crowned with success.

VICTOR The man who runs the agency is in absolutely no doubt. The ring is not valuable enough to split the stone from its setting. It will still be intact — somewhere or other. As we shall see.

LADY I advise you to restrict your researches to the jewellers.

VICTOR Why do you suspect that only jewellers ——

LADY I don't suspect — I know.

VICTOR    That the jewellers ——?

LADY    That one specific jeweller has the ring.

VICTOR    Which one?

LADY *shrugs.*

VICTOR    You know which jeweller ——?

LADY *shrugs again.*

VICTOR    Why won't you tell me?

LADY    Because it is immaterial — since you won't be retrieving the ring.

VICTOR *stares at her.*    And why — won't I be — retrieving the ring?

LADY    Because Vera does not wish it.

VICTOR    Vera knows ——?

LADY    Vera knows what I know, for I know it from her.

VICTOR    ———— Is she making fun of me — and my anger?

LADY    She's in deadly earnest. As you can read for yourself. *She gives him the letter.*

VICTOR *tears it open — reads — looks up.*    I don't understand a word. Do you?

LADY    I know the letter.

VICTOR *reads again.*    I'm leaving if you don't —

LADY    If you don't stop searching for the ring.

VICTOR *startled.*    Is that why she's gone off in the car ——?

LADY    No. Really no. She went for a fitting — and she'll be back because you won't be continuing your search. I was able to promise her that. The letter is now superfluous. *She tears it up.*

VICTOR *after a pause.*    What in Heaven's name has happened to the ring to make it untouchable even though it's within reach?

LADY    It's not very complicated — but it is funny, Victor. Indirectly, via the ring, it came to light that you visited a lady in a kimono with a dragon design — a visit you made, to be exact, on the ninth of March, in the evening, while your wife was dancing at the President's Ball. That's what the ring revealed. Correct or not?

VICTOR *nods, wide-eyed.*

LADY    Well, if so, the ring will be at the jeweller's. That's why finding it is dangerous, since then the — other thing — must also be correct — as far as Vera is concerned — and she can't bear that thought.

VICTOR *despairingly.*    Explain why, in five words —————

LADY    I'll need ten. And there's something rather uncanny involved that you will have to take on trust. What is a clairvoyant? Sometimes a very awkward customer who can cause embarrassment with his second sight mumbo jumbo — it should be banned. It encroaches on one's privacy and peace of mind. Not everything has to be exposed — first a ring, and then —

VICTOR    Did Vera find out?

LADY    After the revelation of how the ring had been found and had ended up at the jeweller's —

VICTOR    By clairvoyance??

LADY    She was at her wit's end and went this morning.

VICTOR    I thought you were buying silk?

LADY    That was a lie. Vera was scared stiff of the truth. I wanted to take you off to the site to get you out of the way.

VICTOR    ———— Is Vera convinced this man is really able to see things — wherever or whenever they may have happened in the past?

LADY    She didn't put it to the test — and doesn't want to either, so she won't have to believe in the soothsayer's other disclosure.

VICTOR    Which is ——?

LADY    That you were trying to embrace the kimono with the dragon design.

VICTOR *groans.*    The logic is irresistible —: you can't have one without the other. Win one — lose the other. Vera leaves home — and the ring reappears. —— Can't Vera be persuaded?

LADY    Can you destroy the proof — a solid ring?

VICTOR *groans.*    In half an hour ——

LADY    You will call off the hounds — and accompany me to the site.

VICTOR    How will Vera take it if I have suddenly changed my mind ——? Won't she become suspicious?

LADY    Since I threatened not to let you build my villa if you didn't respect Vera's wish, your decision was an easy one. Was it not?

VICTOR    It's my dream — to have you settle here.

LADY    You can count on it coming true, now you know on what condition.

VICTOR    Vera's peace of mind.

LADY    Without that the dream melts into thin air.

VICTOR *kisses her hand. Starting.*    Is that Vera?

LADY    Go and eat, and then come in — very cheerful, and somewhat chastened.

VICTOR    I am wax in your hands.

LADY    Then I can still mould you until you please me.

*Exit Victor.*

VERA *in the hallway — takes off her coat. Enters.*    Is Victor —

LADY    At breakfast.

VERA *happily.*   How can he eat?

LADY   After a good deed, a good meal. Heroes get hungry.

VERA   Has he —

LADY   — overcome his reluctance. Drawn a line under various — conflicting calculations.

VERA   That's the way businessmen talk.

LADY   He assessed the situation soberly, like a business deal. Simply weighed up the pros and cons — ring or villa? The villa was a clear winner.

VERA   Since when is Victor so calculating?

LADY   Since I urged him to make the reckoning — in order to fulfil my promise to you.

VERA *tentatively.*   And you succeeded —

LADY   You'll be convinced when you see him.

VERA   — without hinting at the untold danger if the ring is found — at the jeweller's?

LADY   Do you think I'm going to mention your clairvoyant and make you look ridiculous in the eyes of your husband?

VERA *timidly.*   It's no more ridiculous than —

LADY   Than Victor's resolve to abandon his search for the ring once and for all.

VERA *ecstatic.*   Really and truly?

LADY   As God is my witness.

VERA *kisses her passionately.*   I thank you — you've restored Victor to me!

VICTOR *enters from left, eating an apple. Seemingly composed.*   Well — what's the verdict?

VERA *stares at him.*

VICTOR   Your costume fitting for the ball — are they making a good job of it? Do they need my assistance?

VERA *happily.*   I gave them exact instructions — like a Velázquez princess.

VICTOR   Then they can't go wrong. Are you reconciled?

VERA   With whom?

VICTOR   With whom? With the sheer white that you will be enveloped in.

VERA   Are you reconciled?

VICTOR   With whom?

VERA   With whom? With the sheer white that lacks a certain accent to set it off.

VICTOR   Accent?

VERA   The blue ring on my outstretched finger.

VICTOR *slaps his forehead.*   Ah, the tale of the ring — that had slipped my mind. I'm glad you reminded me. You know the position, don't you? *Indicating the Lady.* Madame set out the options. If an architect can't build, it would be the death of him. Architecture demands sacrifice. The ring must be sacrificed. *He telephones.* Four nine zero four nine. *To Vera.* Hear for yourself — I've no secrets. *Into telephone.* Victor here —— that's right, the architect. You recognized my voice? But then, you are a detective. The latest? I do have one important development to report. I no longer require your services. What? No, no further enquiries. Yes, I'm terminating the contract. Why? It's — not worth it. The cost is too high. It knows no bounds. You guarantee success. For that very reason. You don't understand? You intend to investigate until it's found — that would turn me into a pauper. That's why I fear your guarantee. You've already incurred costs? Shelved other commissions? The consultation? Those costs I'll meet — send me the bill. *He hangs up. To Vera.* You heard all that? Alarm over — no more talk of the ring.

VERA *goes to him.*   Did you do it partly for my sake?

VICTOR   What can I say?

VERA    And not just for business reasons — for your villa?

VICTOR    For the one — and the other — but ultimately to restore domestic harmony.

VERA    Really?

VICTOR    It's true, believe me.

VERA *kisses him.*

LADY *Putting on her gloves.*    Now may I have Victor?

VERA    I feel so relieved, I don't mind being left alone.

LADY    So we can take our time?

VERA    Just as Victor wishes.

LADY *to Victor.*    And what do you wish?

VICTOR    A thorough inspection — it might take some time.

LADY    Agreed. Let us go.

VERA *follows both into hallway.*    Drive carefully. And for goodness' sake, Victor, don't let her go at breakneck speed. I'll be worried to death while you're gone.

LADY    Haven't you worried enough for one day?

VERA    That's all dead and buried — what can happen to me now?

LADY    Nevertheless, you shouldn't tempt fate —

VERA    Nevertheless, I'm madly happy. Drive however you want! *She slams the glass door shut. — Victor and the Lady disappear in the hallway. — Sounds from below of the car starting.*

VERA *paces up and down — runs her fingers through her hair — flings herself on the sofa — dangles her legs.*

MAID *enters through glass door.*    A gentleman to see you, Ma'am.

VERA    Me?

MAID    Yes, Ma'am.

VERA    Did he not give his name?

MAID    No, Ma'am.

VERA    What does he look like?

MAID    Not like — a gentleman.

VERA    What then?

MAID    More like a man.

VERA    Who wants to see me?

MAID    I'm not sure if Madam should see him.

VERA    Send him away.

*Exit Maid*

VERA *stretches out again and hums.*

MAID *returns.*   The man — insists on seeing Madam.

VERA    But if he is as awful as you say he is?

MAID    Perhaps Madam could inspect him through the glass door.

VERA *stands — goes to glass door. Starts back. Gasps.*   Sneederhan —!

MAID    Shall I —

VERA *stammers.*   Show him in.

*Exit Maid. Sneederhan appears in the hallway: he is wearing a long, shabby, grey coat, black boots, lace gloves — full beard, glasses. — Maid shows him in.*

VERA *transfixed.*

SNEEDERHAN *stands in doorway, his glasses glittering, watching Vera. He strides across to her and holds out a gloved hand.* Thank you again. That was the most wonderful séance ever. You placed yourself completely in my hands. It was as if your thoughts were music — with every note I played, one image after another rose up from the depths. I count it a great success. Thanks to you. Heartfelt thanks. *He takes off his gloves and puts them down on a table. Returning to Vera — in the most matter-of-fact tone.* Did you feel at all fatigued afterwards? Headache? Irregular pulse? Did you notice anything like that?

VERA *recovering.* Have you come to enquire about my health?

SNEEDERHAN One perseveres. Amidst all the whirling confusion one must never lose sight of the goal. An ocean of foam pounds against this rock, but in vain. — How do you feel?

VERA *ironically.* Wonderful!

SNEEDERHAN Just as I thought. You pass every test and trial with consummate ease. It was predestined — a shining exception, demonstrably proven. Are you not delighted when I sing your praises?

VERA Enraptured!

SNEEDERHAN I seldom make compliments. But this was truly mind speaking unto mind without impediment. The world has no secrets from us. — May one avail oneself of the copious seating arrangements?

VERA Do you intend to continue your experiments with me here?

SNEEDERHAN *sits down in an armchair — beckons to Vera to do likewise.* Impossible in a boudoir overflowing with furniture. I need a bare room — like mine. Do you remember?

VERA Of course.

SNEEDERHAN After all, it's only an hour or two since you visited me.

VERA I don't understand why you've come. Won't you tell me?

SNEEDERHAN ———— Have you the ring?

VERA *remains silent.*

SNEEDERHAN   Well — what's your answer? Have you?

VERA *collecting herself — forcefully.*   Yes!

SNEEDERHAN *nods.*   That goes without saying — there is no mistaking what I saw.

VERA   No!

SNEEDERHAN   What?

VERA   Everything you saw was right.

SNEEDERHAN *fervently.*   And it was all true — the person who found the glove on the pavement — discovers the ring inside — goes off to the jeweller next morning and leaves it there, never to return? — That's what really happened?

VERA   Precisely.

SNEEDERHAN *stops short.*   How can you know? One could hardly check out that whole previous sequence of events?

VERA   I know — because everything else fits.

SNEEDERHAN   As you think back, it all becomes real for you?

VERA   Absolutely.

SNEEDERHAN *rubs his hands.*   The evidence is piling up. — Then you followed the route I specified: down the long dark street — across the square towards the left — turn right at the public convenience —

VERA *almost crying out.*   No — to the left!

SNEEDERHAN *astonished.*   Not right at the public convenience?

VERA   And not across any square — nor down any long street — nor even in any town!

SNEEDERHAN   Now I'm completely confused. Murky darkness closes in on all sides — erasing memory. I no longer see anything.

VERA    Have I blotted out the route?

SNEEDERHAN    Everything is whirling — swallowed up in a fog. — Why did you do that?

VERA    Because — I don't want to know!

SNEEDERHAN *pulling himself together.*    Ah, signs of agitation after all. The normal reaction. Let's ignore that. The only thing of importance is that the ring has been found.

VERA    That's important for you?

SNEEDERHAN    Invaluable. I can present the court with a piece of evidence that will refute the accusation made against me.

VERA    You've been accused?

SNEEDERHAN    By some numskull of a public prosecutor. According to him what I do is fraudulent. I take money for old rope. I abuse the credulity of my fellow men. I should laugh, only the ignorance of my opponent makes me sad. But he has the power, he can have me thrown in jail — so I have to defend myself. With witnesses, who can speak on my behalf. *Bows before Vera.* In the courtroom I shall call you as a witness.

VERA *recoils.*    You — can't do that!

SNEEDERHAN    Aren't you overcome with joy at helping truth triumph?

VERA    I — won't come.

SNEEDERHAN *smiling.*    Afraid of the lawyers and judges in their wigs and black robes? There's nothing terrible underneath. They're just people like the rest of us.

VERA    I — shall refuse to testify!

SNEEDERHAN    The judicial authorities will scarcely permit that. Witnesses have to speak out.

VERA    When — is the court case?

SNEEDERHAN　In the middle of April.

VERA　We won't be here then. Victor and I will be abroad.

SNEEDERHAN　Whoever doesn't appear the police come after.

VERA *her voice shaking.*　The — police ——?

SNEEDERHAN　So appear on time and discharge the obligation that chance has put your way. Or that was preordained — and I can only add, providentially. For five minutes after you left I received the summons. Your perfume was still in the air, we had just finished our séance — which is not answerable to any of the allegations of the public prosecutor. With the success of this one incredibly beautiful experiment I shall refute all accusations. Let the crowd in the great courtroom hold its breath as you raise your hand and — on seeing the ring retrieved by my psychic powers — every eye shall reflect the radiance of celestial knowledge!

VERA　———— I'm afraid — I must disappoint you. I — don't have the ring.

SNEEDERHAN　I beg your pardon — what don't you have?

VERA　The ring — that I should display.

SNEEDERHAN　You mean — that's not it you're wearing?

VERA　Never again — it's missing and stays missing, just as when I lost it.

SNEEDERHAN　What — do you mean?

VERA　That the route you sent me on was the wrong one — it didn't lead to the goal.

SNEEDERHAN　Did you follow my instructions to the letter?

VERA　Left at the public convenience — or right — or straight ahead. There was no jeweller's shop anywhere.

SNEEDERHAN　—— Where is the piece of paper?

VERA *almost mockingly.*　Torn up.

SNEEDERHAN   Why?

VERA   In a rage — at believing the nonsense you served up.

SNEEDERHAN *looks straight ahead — nods — turns his gaze back to Vera.*   That contrasts with your first statement — that you had the ring again.

VERA   What is this — a court case already? Are you the judge? Who gave you permission to interrogate me?

SNEEDERHAN   I don't lay claim to any such right — in principle I condemn such presumption —

VERA   And in principle I condemn total strangers' interference in my private affairs.

SNEEDERHAN   There is a public interest at stake.

VERA   Who dares say that?

SNEEDERHAN   The public prosecutor. He's interested in any kind of deception — *With emphasis* — any kind of proven deception. Perhaps his interest in this case will extend to a witness who has committed perjury. A long prison sentence. *Rising.* But I don't want to anticipate —

VERA *bursts out.*   But can the ring be found?

SNEEDERHAN *smiling.*   Here, in this house?

VERA   At a jeweller's?

SNEEDERHAN   Using all the powers at the court's disposal? Inside twenty-four hours every jeweller's shop will have been searched. If in vain — it's my head on the block. *Drawing himself up.* But it won't be! *Exit through glass door.*

VERA *stares blankly in confusion. — From below the same loud sound of a car-horn. — Vera trembles. — From behind the glass door Victor's head peers tentatively. After watching Vera briefly he resolutely throws open the glass door.*

VICTOR *bustling exaggeratedly.*   Just back for ten minutes. The site looks fabulous. We're going ahead. I'm fetching the plans — she's gone ahead — I've to go to the hotel. *He takes hat and coat into hallway — returns — rummages around and extracts rolls of paper from a drawer.* Here they are. *Looks around.* Incidentally, I've a contractor coming just now, wants to supply me with ten thousand bricks. Quite a pile, eh? *Going to Vera.* Is everything all right? You look —*Breaks off.* I don't want to keep him waiting. Will you be in the conservatory? I'll look for you there when I've finished. *He leads her off right.*

VERA *exit.*

VICTOR *closes the door behind her with a sigh of relief. Goes quickly into hallway — beckons to left and enters with Sneederhan.* How do you know who I am? You called me by name on the stairs.

SNEEDERHAN   I turned back when the lady addressed you as Victor.

VICTOR   From which you deduce —?

SNEEDERHAN   With a kind of inspiration — that you are the person I need to speak to.

VICTOR *casually.*   Something about a ring — I didn't fully understand.

SNEEDERHAN *inquisitively.*   Yet you didn't hesitate to invite me in?

VICTOR   First may I enquire: to whom do I have the pleasure of speaking?

SNEEDERHAN   Sneederhan.

VICTOR *questioningly.*   Pardon?

SNEEDERHAN   I helped your wife get back the piece of jewellery she had lost.

VICTOR *surprised.*   Are you — the jeweller?

SNEEDERHAN *smiles.*

VICTOR   Have you brought the ring? It must disappear at once. Give it to me. How can I reimburse you? *He puts his hand to his wallet.*

SNEEDERHAN   That's a very telling sentence, I must remember it. Disappear — — I am Sneederhan the clairvoyant, your wife consulted me this morning.

VICTOR   That was rash of her.

SNEEDERHAN   It seems so. Now the avalanche has been set in motion — it's most often a tiny stone that sets it off.

VICTOR   You really are full of frightening metaphors. What avalanche has been set off?

SNEEDERHAN   The arm of the law is about to descend on me — but your wife's hand, adorned with the ring, shall intervene and force it to desist.

VICTOR   You seem to assume I know what this is all about, but I don't.

SNEEDERHAN   All you need to know to understand my warning is that the lady of the house is about to commit an irreparable offence.

VICTOR   What?! What are you saying?

SNEEDERHAN   In legal terminology: she's about to commit perjury, quite manifestly so.

VICTOR   And who — is she about to deceive?

SNEEDERHAN   The judge — who will question her about the whereabouts of the ring.

VICTOR   Somebody — stole it?

SNEEDERHAN   Withheld it.

VICTOR   Who?

SNEEDERHAN   Its owner.

VICTOR   Her own ring?

SNEEDERHAN *in a leisurely manner.*   Let me take off my gloves — Are the seating arrangements here for a purpose?

VICTOR *indicates an armchair — sits down himself.*

SNEEDERHAN   What do you know about the ring?

VICTOR *beginning to show some signs of consternation.* That my wife happened to lose it — searched for it in vain — and this morning was talked into —

SNEEDERHAN — and this morning had revealed to her the whereabouts of the piece of jewellery. The revelation came from me.

VICTOR I was not actually meant to know anything about it —

SNEEDERHAN Very soon everyone will know when reports of the court case fill the newspaper columns.

VICTOR And what is the case about?

SNEEDERHAN About Sneederhan — the crook — swindler — charlatan — who extracts fortunes from people's pockets — with his con trick: clairvoyance. Burn him at the stake. — Burn all Galileos. As they always have!

VICTOR Have they brought a charge?

SNEEDERHAN For taking money — ten marks a session. Is that profiteering? Is my home a palace? Am I dressed like a fop? Do I live like a lord? I could earn thousands — I am a man of science. I do research — hard work. What I do is what I am.

VICTOR But one may raise doubts —

SNEEDERHAN From doubt comes progress. Put me to the test. I welcome the accusation. I will defend myself — and public opinion will be staggered by the defence I shall launch.

VICTOR Are you so sure of your case?

SNEEDERHAN Since this morning. Working with your wife was marvellous. She is a medium of undreamt-of intensity. I felt the release of powers I never suspected I possessed. I discovered myself — no doubt about it. — A pity she broke off the second experiment.

VICTOR The first must surely have been enough.

SNEEDERHAN Perhaps she was exhausted after so much concentration. Who can tell?

VICTOR    No one is interested in that.

SNEEDERHAN    Yet the first experiment was a total success. I revealed the path to take to find the ring — she could do it in her sleep — and she did do it! — Why is she hiding the ring from me?

VICTOR    You've spoken to Vera?

SNEEDERHAN    Before you arrived — in this room — except she was sitting here and me there.

VICTOR    Of course she didn't go for the ring. She wasn't lying at all.

SNEEDERHAN    Will she go for it later?

VICTOR    No, she won't.

VICTOR *insistently.*    Why not?

VICTOR    She never will — Mr Sneederhan.

SNEEDERHAN *after a pause, gruffly.*    Are you my enemy?

VICTOR    I hardly know you.

SNEEDERHAN    Not my personal enemy — an enemy of the occult?

VICTOR    I know too little about it to be in a position to reject it.

SNEEDERHAN    Yet you are possessed by the urge to destroy — it suddenly darts out and attacks me.

VICTOR    Why would I want to do that?

SNEEDERHAN *fanatically.*    You think the dark powers do not exist? They are life itself — what we call life is their shadowy reflection. You'll soon find out — they shall shatter the monotonous routine of your lives when I reveal their true power. It may be just a ring — but with its gemstone it becomes a star that dispels the dismal gloom. Get the ring — whole worlds are at stake!

VICTOR    What an outburst! In the next room —

SNEEDERHAN *mockingly.*   —— sits your wife —

VICTOR    — cursing the ring that you unearthed!

SNEEDERHAN *remains silent.*

VICTOR *goes to him.*    You may be a visionary with psychic powers — but you're also flesh and blood, with all the human attributes — common sense and understanding as well as feelings and instincts. Don't you sense that what is going on here needs to be — approached from a different angle? After all, it's strange, is it not?: a woman loses a piece of jewellery — and a very important one for her, at that — finds it, but doesn't want to take it back. There must surely be a special reason for that. Admit that — and let the rest be silence. It would be best — for all concerned. For you too, Mr Sneederhan. You risk a great deal. Let's assume your prediction is incorrect. You've been accused of fraud. You say you can provide evidence to the contrary. But after an exhaustive search the ring is not found. The jeweller denies all knowledge. You are disgraced — more than that: convicted. The sentence will be a heavy one. — I'm willing to help you. Make yourself scarce before the trial. Flee abroad. I'll pay for it. Look round there for some solid trade and give up clairvoyance. It's the devil's own trade you are plying. Mankind has enough on its plate without any further insights into human weakness. Avoid the avalanche. When can you leave? *Taking out his wallet.* How much?

SNEEDERHAN *calmly.*    What is a scoundrel?

VICTOR    What?

SNEEDERHAN    Someone who is not continuously prepared to sacrifice himself — and those close to him — to his god.

VICTOR    Who else do you want to sacrifice?

SNEEDERHAN    The two who have a secret that keeps the ring from me. The court shall extract it from you. I swear it!

VICTOR    Are you — a murderer?!

SNEEDERHAN    If scientific enquiry is murder — then I am a murderer. *He takes his lace gloves — exit through glass door.*

VICTOR *stares after him. Long perplexed, he finally telephones.*    Palace Hotel —— the number — *Slaps his forehead.* For Heaven's sake, the number ——

# ACT THREE

∼

*Victor waits, scarcely able to control his impatience: to distract himself, he alternates between unrolling the building plans left on the table and peering into the hallway. Finally, at his wits' end, he snatches up the telephone and is about to phone when a car horn sounds below.*

VICTOR *rushes to glass door — thinks better of it — pauses. — In the hallway Lady and maid. Maid opens glass door. Enter Lady. Exit maid.* Thank God you've come.

LADY   It sounded like a cry for help on the phone.

VICTOR   No more, no less. SOS in dire distress. Waves already breaking over the deck. Catastrophe inevitable! — Why are you laughing?

LADY   I'm glad you're so desperate.

VICTOR   You find it funny?

LADY   It suits you. I feel compassion and want to stroke you like a little child.

VICTOR *instinctively takes a step back.*

LADY   Not permitted? Well, I won't force my affections on you. — *Coolly.* Why didn't you come to me if you need my advice — or my active help — so urgently?

VICTOR   I didn't want to be seen —

LADY   Visiting me in the hotel?

VICTOR   It could give rise to misunderstandings —

LADY   Which you now wish to avoid —

VICTOR   In this situation, emphatically so!

LADY *after a pause — calmly.*   I am not aware of any change in the situation.

VICTOR   Since we parted — you went ahead in the car, I came to fetch the plans — then havoc — an earthquake shook everything to pieces, even what was scarcely in place: — I'm doomed to lose Vera!

LADY   Is — Vera not here?

VICTOR   No.

LADY   Up and gone — for good?

VICTOR   To the dressmaker's. I sent her away — under the pretext of wanting to approve her costume before the final cut — but it's only a reprieve. I already feel the rope tightening around my neck.

LADY   Who wants to hang you?

VICTOR   A person by the name of Sneederhan. A madman — fanatic — a whirling dervish foaming at the mouth — a murderer!

LADY   What role do you allocate him in our — comedy?

VICTOR   The trouble-maker par excellence. No way of getting rid of him. He'll stop at nothing — he'll have us all on toast.

LADY   No possibility of a happy ending, then?

VICTOR   Like the Gordian knot that is cut through in the legend? Those times are past. No such flamboyance allowed these days. It's proof — evidence — that counts. The ring proves this Sneederhan's visions are authentic.

LADY   So the clairvoyant now appears on the scene.

VICTOR   Already has — twice, here, in person. The first time to ask Vera if his prediction was correct — then to warn me against Vera's perjury.

LADY   She has to swear under oath?

VICTOR   In court. In the case against this Sneederhan and his black arts. The public prosecutor is after him as a con-man, but he's fighting it tooth and nail.

And his trump card — his pièce de résistance — is his miraculous discovery of Vera's lost ring. Vera will be called as a witness.

LADY    That's certainly an unanticipated development.

VICTOR    But the consequences are only too foreseeable. If Vera does not produce the ring herself first —

LADY    She can't. She's destroyed all trace of it.

VICTOR    — then the court will get hold of it. The ring appears — and my lovely world disappears. *He sinks into an armchair.*

LADY *goes to him — strokes his hair.*    Victor — could you never leave Vera?

VICTOR    Never! What Vera means to me — what Vera has begun to mean since it entered the realms of possibility that — or rather the impossibility, for then the ground would rock beneath my feet, the very foundation I need to build on — a betrayal of devotion and trust — I wouldn't be capable of drawing another straight line!

LADY    Do you regret it?

VICTOR *shakes his head — kisses her hand.*

LADY    You've nothing to regret anyhow. A damask kimono with a dragon design — that you enfold in your arms — but that refuses to surrender? Is that why you are so depressed?

VICTOR *looks up despondently.*    Is not all hope gone?

LADY    I will not expose myself to scandal — I'd leave town first.

VICTOR    You mustn't!

LADY    I couldn't let you build the villa for me.

VICTOR    I must build it!

LADY *her face close to his.*    Why must you?

VICTOR    Because you promised me.

LADY   What did I promise?

VICTOR   Everything.

LADY   When — our villa is built.

VICTOR   Our — villa ————

LADY   I want it built —— *Drawing herself up.* —— And since that's what I want, that's what will happen.

VICTOR *Throwing up his hands in despair.*    The plans have become muddled in all this turmoil — I can only work if —

LADY   If the foundation is not shaken.

VICTOR   Vera's faith in me!

LADY   What's to shake that? The fable of the ring? Who can believe that? Do you? Surely you're not serious? The public prosecutor will be proved right. Depend upon it. Face the prospect of the trial with your peace of mind restored. Vera will go and give her testimony — the truth. She distrusted the psychic from the start and she tore up the directions to where the ring was allegedly to be found as soon as she left him. Hence, she doesn't have the ring, and that's that.

VICTOR   And if the court instigates a search ——?

LADY   Let it — and expose the quackery once and for all. Nothing will be found — certainly not the way this charlatan operates.

VICTOR   I tried to bribe him — to go abroad.

LADY   Out of sympathy with the wretch. That won't arouse any suspicion.

VICTOR   You think not?

LADY   The ring is no concern of yours. And Vera remains determined not to find it. Don't get yourself worked up — who believes in the big bad wolf in this day and age?! Do you think the wolf is at the door?

MAID *enters.*   Mr Sneederhan would like to speak to sir and madam.

VICTOR   With who?

MAID   With madam —

VICTOR   — and me? *He looks at the lady helplessly.*

LADY   Show Mr Sneederhan in.

MAID *exit.*

VICTOR   Do I really have to receive him again?

LADY   You do if you want to get rid of him for good.

SNEEDERHAN *appears behind glass door — gesticulates questioningly when he sees the lady — the maid shrugs — Sneederhan decides to enter.*   Change of ladies?

LADY   Same gentleman. Aren't you satisfied with that, Mr Sneederhan?

SNEEDERHAN   You know my name —

LADY   — and all about your occult practices. The public prosecutor's charges interest me most.

SNEEDERHAN *snorts.*   The public prosecutor — I wouldn't want to be in his shoes.

LADY   Why, what will happen to him?

SNEEDERHAN   Disgrace.

LADY   So confident, Mr Sneederhan?

SNEEDERHAN   So sceptical, beautiful lady?

LADY *looks to Victor.*

VICTOR   You needn't bring up anything I may have said to you. I got carried away by your mumbo jumbo and replied in kind. There were no witnesses. Who are you? What do you want?

SNEEDERHAN   I won't repeat myself either, except for meeting you again. That's part of the matter in hand, which is well under way, with a happy ending in sight.

VICTOR   That sounds very promising. And what's the solution?

SNEEDERHAN   The ring has been found!

VICTOR   And you call that a — happy ending?!

SNEEDERHAN   To put it mildly. I call it the triumph of the occult powers. Giving rise to peals of laughter all round. While the wise man merely smiles. *Looks around. A chair perhaps* —? *He pulls an armchair up close to Victor and Lady.* Something so real it's almost a miracle. Can you understand that? Seeing the world from the inside? Reflecting the cosmos? The terminology of a new science. The radiant beginnings of a new dawn. Salutation! — Then what happens? Stunned, I trudge home — my experiment a failure. My best experiment to date — a flop. Or perhaps not a flop? Since there was no longer any importance attached to getting the ring back — the ring I had discovered. And that was the case, was it not? Anyway, that's immaterial. The piece of paper with the instructions showing the way had been torn to shreds and scattered to the winds. Gone — but not irretrievable!

VICTOR   You mean you were able to collect the shreds —?

SNEEDERHAN   Back between my own bare walls, the darkness lifted — I could think again — and I remembered that I always take a carbon copy of what my medium writes. With this evidence I shall compile my great book and vindicate the new science. I am duty bound to take great care, and this I did.

VICTOR   You took the carbon copy —?

SNEEDERHAN   As my guide, and it worked like magic. I had seen only too clearly — even if your wife disputes it, you do turn right at the public convenience. There's no street to the left. Right — right again — and the jeweller's on the right — with him sick — while his daughter, who had mislaid the ring wrapped in the glove, found it again — and showed me it: a blue sapphire in an old-fashioned setting. The glove size thirty-eight — two buttons —white kid.

VICTOR   ———— Do you have the ring with you now?

SNEEDERHAN   Why would they hand it over to me? Does it belong to me? I detected it. It's safe. Very safe.

VICTOR   How — safe?

SNEEDERHAN   It may only be collected in my presence. Indeed, it can only be collected in my presence, for only I know the way. Is your wife at home?

VICTOR   Why? What do you want from my wife?

SNEEDERHAN   To come with me to the jeweller's and get her ring back. To be confirmed in writing on the spot when it's handed over, as witnessed by the jeweller and his daughter. That's for deployment in court. Can we leave at once?

VICTOR   My wife — isn't here.

SNEEDERHAN   Will there be a long wait?

VICTOR *to Lady.*   Hadn't Vera got travel plans?

SNEEDERHAN   Travel plans that her husband doesn't know anything about?

VICTOR   I was mistaken — she's not going until tomorrow.

SNEEDERHAN   So the matter can be settled before then.

VICTOR   She's very busy today getting ready. You know how it is with women.

SNEEDERHAN   And after her trip — how long?

VICTOR   She'll be gone for ten weeks — twelve.

SNEEDERHAN   My case comes up in two weeks.

VICTOR   Then you'll have to get by without my wife.

SNEEDERHAN   If that's what she wants.

VICTOR   You want to question her?

SNEEDERHAN   I shall wait. Here — or at the front door.

VICTOR    And — if she refuses?

SNEEDERHAN    Then it's up to the public prosecutor to elicit the truth.

VICTOR *remains silent.*

SNEEDERHAN *stretches out comfortably in armchair.*

LADY *lights a cigarette. A lengthy pause ensues.*    Mr Sneederhan — please accept my apologies. The way you were described to me left a false impression. Hence my hostility towards you. That prejudice has now been totally dispelled.

SNEEDERHAN    Very flattering — for you.

LADY    For me — of course, only for me. I've learnt my lesson. I have sat in silence, like a pupil at the feet of the master. Did you not see how moved I was?

SNEEDERHAN    I barely touched on the heart of the matter.

LADY    But enough to astound me. You have set yourself and your science a lofty objective. Nothing will stand in your way — nothing must stand in your way.

SNEEDERHAN    So the light has dawned?

LADY    Crushing all dissent. Further resistance would be wicked. I support your claim on the ring. Let it be procured. Today. Now.

VICTOR *stares at Lady.*

SNEEDERHAN *smiles triumphantly at Victor.*

LADY *to Victor.*    As you see, I am resolved to desert to the other side. My decision is final. One's own private resentments are no grounds for opposing a man of science.

VICTOR *stammers.*    You mean you want to ——

LADY    Support Sneederhan, help him win his case. And without prevarication. Vera must testify — unequivocally — with the ring on her finger.

VICTOR    Is that not the end of everything that ——?

LADY   Now is not the time to discuss that.

VICTOR *despondently.* You're right —— there would be no point any more.

LADY *to Sneederhan.* You won't mind who goes with you? It doesn't have to be my friend, does it?

SNEEDERHAN   It can only be handed over to its owner.

LADY   Or her authorized representative.

SNEEDERHAN   Namely?

LADY   Her husband.

VICTOR *starts.*   You expect me to ——??

LADY   Agree to this small task. *To Sneederhan.* Is it far to go?

SNEEDERHAN   A few minutes by car.

LADY   My car is below. *To Victor.* Get yourself ready. You'll need identification papers. And there's to be a written report, as evidence. The court won't tolerate incompetence. Is that your passport?

VICTOR *without thinking has taken out his wallet — opens it for inspection.*   And my Architects' Club membership card.

LADY *to Sneederhan.*   Does that suffice?

SNEEDERHAN   It's enough to identify him.

LADY   So the jeweller won't raise any objections to handing over the ring. *To Victor.* Mr Sneederhan is ready to leave.

SNEEDERHAN *facing her.*   Let me say this before I go. People seldom change. Women least of all. One has to rise above prejudice, weigh the evidence, and if it's convincing judge accordingly. It goes against the grain to abandon the barricades and shake hands with the enemy. Yet the greatest cowardice can produce the greatest heroes. A bastion has just fallen. Undaunted by the shame of capitulation, of submitting to me. I stand erect, my head held high. But I shall never forget my defeated rival. The beautiful lady I leave behind — my new convert, my disciple! *He goes into hallway and stands with his back turned.*

LADY *to Victor.*   What are you waiting for?

VICTOR   An explanation ——

LADY   So curious?

VICTOR   I see the villa sinking into an unfathomable abyss.

LADY   Are you giving up?

VICTOR   Are you not tearing up all the plans?

LADY   I don't change my plans that quickly — and I never abandon the barricades.

VICTOR *hopefully.*   We —

LADY   We shall see. *Brusquely.* You must go.

VICTOR *goes into hallway — takes hat and coat — exit with Sneederhan.*

LADY *pores over plans.*

VERA *enters hallway — takes off her hat and coat — has the maid carry a large cardboard box into the room. Exit maid. Enter Vera.*

LADY   What is that?

VERA *preoccupied.*   In the box? My costume — to try on.

LADY   Will he like it?

VERA   Who?

LADY   Victor.

VERA   What?

LADY   Your costume.

VERA   He designed it.

LADY   But the finished article.

VERA   But will it be finished?

LADY   He has no doubts.

VERA *mockingly.*   He may not have —— *Breaks off.* Why are you here?

LADY   Why shouldn't I be here?

VERA   No red car?

LADY   It's currently in a somewhat unfamiliar neighbourhood.

VERA *absent-mindedly.*   An unfamiliar neighbourhood ——

LADY   First there is a long street —— then across a square — then it turns right at the public convenience. Right — not left.

VERA *pricks up her ears.*   At the ——?

LADY   The prescribed route, Vera. Now it's stopping at the jeweller's shop.

VERA   At the ——?

LADY *looks at her watch.*   Just about now. They've arrived.

VERA   Who ——?

LADY   Victor and Sneederhan.

VERA *with a pained smile.*   You wouldn't joke if you knew what has happened in the meantime. — Anyway, I tore up the piece of paper.

LADY   Your copy — Sneederhan had a carbon copy and is using it to find the way.

VERA *beside herself.*   They're after the ring? —— Though Victor promised he would never look for it?!

LADY   He was forced to break his word.

VERA   What could force him?

LADY   Sneederhan's threat to take you to court and disclose your perjury.

VERA   He betrayed me to Victor?

LADY   Totally. And Victor was obliged to protect you from dangers you were consciously exposing yourself to.

VERA *holding her head in her hands.*   Can the ring really be found this way?

LADY   It has been found. Your Sneederhan found it. And now it is being handed over to Victor and the transaction witnessed in writing.

VERA *bursts out.*   While I try on my costume for the ball —— that I will never go to!

LADY   Both of you shall go.

VERA   Can the dead dance?

LADY   Who is dead?

VERA   My heart, it's stopped beating — it will never beat again ——!

LADY   Why not?

VERA   For then everything else has to be true — just as it is with the ring that has been found!

LADY *after a pause — calmly.*   It isn't true.

VERA   Let it not be true — I'm afraid of the truth.

LADY   It's not the truth.

VERA   How can you prove me wrong?

LADY   Because I know the truth.

VERA   The kimono with a dragon design.

LADY   Is mine!

VERA *remains silent. In disbelief.*   Yours —?

LADY   If you want proof that a kimono of that description is mine, come with me to the hotel.

VERA   It was you Victor was with ——?

LADY   On the ninth of March, when he let you go to the President's Ball alone. I wanted to consult him about the plans for the villa. Victor put business before pleasure.

VERA   He didn't tell me —

LADY   Why should a man bore his wife with whatever job he's taken on? Victor is considerate. The thought of him working while you were dancing might have upset you.

VERA   I — see that. Victor is quite secretive. And I don't begin to understand building plans.

LADY   That accounts for his behaviour, then.

VERA   And you're not mistaken about — the date?

LADY   The ninth of March. I have it in writing. Read for yourself — Meeting with Victor. *She takes a notebook from her bag and opens it.* Well?

VERA *reads.*   The ninth of March.

LADY   In the evening. At my hotel.

VERA   And you didn't put that in later, to reassure me?

LADY   There would be no room, between the other entries. I don't fake.

VERA   Forgive me. *Still reading.* Who is Alfred — on the tenth!

LADY   That's — *snaps the notebook shut and puts it away* — indiscreet.

VERA   I'm so confused.

LADY   But your suspicions are subsiding?

VERA *still brooding.*   Still —— he kissed you on the neck?

LADY   What did he do?

VERA   That's what the clairvoyant saw — and he would have seen more if I hadn't run off.

LADY   Who would have dared do more?

VERA   Victor.

LADY   Your Victor? You think I would allow my best friend's husband to deceive the wife who loves him — the wife he loves? You two belong together like leaves on a tree. Anyone attempting to come between you will have me to reckon with. Let them shake till their arms grow stiff — there'll be no falling leaves. I'm fond of Victor — I freely admit it — because he's bright and cheerful and — your husband. Don't you see: if I felt anything more than friendly companionship — wouldn't I try my utmost to keep it from you — and not reveal that Victor was with me on the ninth of March? What do you say?

VERA *embraces her.*   That it's my good fortune he was with you!

*Victor, in the hallway, peers into the room.*

LADY *gestures to him meaningfully over Vera's head.*

VICTOR *takes off hat and coat — enters, hand buried in jacket pocket.*

LADY   I have confessed our great adventure. Now it's my partner's turn to speak. Vera demands a full confession. Where were you on the ninth of March? In the evening?

VICTOR *stammers.*   Vera ——!

LADY *goes from Vera to Victor, close up, eye to eye.*   That's the silliest answer imaginable! *In a changed tone.* You weren't at the President's Ball? You cancelled because you had a rendezvous elsewhere.

VICTOR *devastated, to Vera.* Is it really all over ——?

LADY *sharply.* Everything will be over — *With self-control.* — if you can't recall that you visited me at my hotel on the evening in question. If you prefer not to recall that, then I've been lying. I've no desire to be called a liar. If that's the case — farewell.

VICTOR *bewildered.* I'm supposed to have ——

LADY You're supposed to repeat what I thought it advisable to acknowledge. Our harmless tête-à-tête on the ninth of March. Or was it not harmless, as I've described it to Vera?

VICTOR *comprehends.* Was that — the ninth of March? In the evening? The evening of the President's Ball? I couldn't go. *To Vera.* What reason did I give you for not being able to go?

LADY You didn't give a reason — you never do — when you have business meetings.

VICTOR Then of course I said nothing.

LADY You brought me the building plans and we studied them in detail. I yawned frequently.

VICTOR And how you yawned!

LADY And I soon dismissed you — I was exhausted.

VICTOR And I stayed in the bar and — *He stops.*

VERA And?

VICTOR You were asleep when I got home!

LADY *sotto voce.* Bravo.

*Pause.*

VICTOR *breaking the silence.* Why all the questions?

LADY    Because Vera associates the ring with — things you no longer need to know about. The shadow has passed. *Stroking Vera.* Has it not?

VERA *gives a peculiar nod.*

LADY *to Victor.*    So open your hand.

VICTOR    The world is full of wonders. Glove and ring wrested from the wreckage. Praise be to Sneederhan! *He flourishes both items.* It's your ring, Vera. *He holds it out in his hands.*

VERA *gazes at him.*    It is the ring. *She doesn't touch it.*

VICTOR    Your going to Sneederhan was a stroke of genius. The man has magic powers. I was sceptical almost to the end — then finally convinced when everything turned out the way he had foretold. Incredible. Now the poor fellow has been put on trial, and you can help him. He wants you as a witness. And you really can confirm that he was not mistaken.

VERA    Is he never mistaken?

VICTOR    Fifty per cent of the time certainly. Which he freely admits. He's usually let down by his medium.

VERA    I was a good medium.

VICTOR    As the ring proves. Won't you put it on?

VERA    Not yet.

VICTOR    It doesn't go with that dress anyway. *He puts it down on the table, takes up the plans. To Lady.* What about our plans?

LADY    I wanted to make the decision today.

VICTOR    Where should we sit down?

LADY    Best at the hotel.

VICTOR    As you wish — you are the client.

LADY *to Vera.* That's how down-to-earth he is when it's a business matter. *To Victor.* Let's go.

VERA *eyeing the cardboard box.* This — is the costume for a first fitting. Your approval is not needed. The atelier wants to do more work on it. *To Lady.* I need your help — Victor will leave us alone. Wait in the conservatory until I call. It won't take long. We'll soon have settled everything. *She pushes Victor out of the door right — closes it behind him — and promptly starts to undress. While opening the box she says* What do you think?

LADY What do you mean?

VERA What do you think of my figure?

LADY It's flawless.

VERA No defects?

LADY You're perfect, just as you are.

VERA Really?

LADY Young, firm flesh — enviable.

VERA You're not just saying that?

LADY I don't believe in flattery — I acknowledge what I see.

VERA I'm relieved.

LADY Why do you ask?

VERA Because I must know if I'm attractive enough to — give a man all he desires.

LADY Victor?

VERA Only Victor.

LADY *remains silent.*

VERA *begins to slip on the costume.*  If you could help me —— It's not sewn up yet, you'll have to use the pins. Don't hurt yourself.

LADY *already busy.*  And I'll be careful not to wound you with pinpricks.

VERA  My wounds would be of less consequence.

LADY  Are you more afraid for me?

VERA  It would leave a stain.

LADY  A drop of blood?

VERA  The ignoble thoughts that are lodged in my mind.

LADY  What are you thinking of?

VERA  Of Victor and the dragon lady.

LADY  Is that what you were — picturing to yourself?

VERA  You're already angry. I know nothing happened. Everything was — quite harmless. Just as you said. And Victor confirmed everything. Nothing could have happened to hurt me.

LADY  That I can guarantee.

VERA  You can vouch for the past — but no one can determine the future in advance.

LADY  And what might happen then?

VERA  Then it might happen that — then it even must happen that —

LADY  That Victor ——?

VERA  That you meet Victor —— in secret —— and I'm to blame for your relationship.

LADY  Now I really have pricked myself!

VERA   Does it hurt? The other thing will hurt even more, the way I will insult you with my suspicions whenever I see you and Victor together.

LADY   You know how I feel about Victor.

VERA   Today companionship — tomorrow passion.

LADY   Vera!

VERA   For sure. I shall bring you together. Whether you want it or not. You'll see in my eyes what I think, whenever I see you. There's a terrible power in such things — stronger than your resistance. Your meeting is fated.

LADY   But why do you think that?

VERA   It's happened that the ring has been found — so the other thing will happen too!

LADY   That's all a figment of your imagination.

VERA   But with dire consequences. Or would I not have to kill myself if I found I had driven you into each other's arms — with my fantasies? If I had made my best friend into a cheat — and my husband a deceiver? The shame of it would choke me — I'd drop down dead. You'd be quite right to kick me aside — like some criminal who had brought about the whole disaster. You want to love each other, don't you?

LADY *uncertain.*   I reject your suspicions —

VERA   To no avail. You're saddled with them. No escaping them. When are you meeting Victor?

LADY   There is no rendezvous.

VERA   Not yet. But soon, for I will keep on asking you: when? Then you'll remember, then you'll be properly enmeshed and writhing helplessly in the clutches of deception. Do you want to betray me with Victor?

LADY   I don't want to —

VERA    Don't do it. Anyhow, it might clash with Alfred on the tenth of March. Even if you keep a schedule, you might inadvertently mix them up. Then you would lose both. This way you keep Alfred. Agreed?

LADY    That's uncalled for —

VERA    As is any further discussion.

LADY    What — do you want me to do?

VERA    Find another architect for your villa.

LADY    In other words?

VERA    In other words?

LADY    We part company.

VERA *rings the bell.*

MAID *enters.*

VERA    The lady will be leaving. Please show her out.

LADY *gazes at Vera — glances at the door right — shrugs — exit.*

MAID *follows — exit.*

VERA *goes to table — tears up the plans, then opens the door right — rings again.*

MAID *enters.*

VERA    Please fetch my husband. He's in the conservatory.

MAID *exit right.*

VERA *takes up position; fingers spread, she opens out the skirt of the dress.*

VICTOR *enters from right.*

VERA    What do you think?

VICTOR *looking around.* Are you — alone?

VERA Do I please you?

VICTOR Where is —— *He opens the door left — looks in.*

VERA Is this how you wanted it?

VICTOR What?

VERA The costume?

VICTOR Has she gone — without me?

VERA All that's missing is the distinctive accent — the blue of the ring. Fetch it from the table.

VICTOR *goes — discovers the plans in pieces.* What's this?

VERA Your plans — torn up.

VICTOR Who can have done that?

VERA Who here can have done it?

VICTOR ———— Vera??

VERA Otherwise you couldn't have finished my costume. Will you finish it now?

VICTOR *takes the ring — approaches Vera uncertainly.* Yes, I will finish it — with the ring.

VERA Here is my finger.

VICTOR Will you receive it — as you once did?

VERA Should I receive it as I once did?

VICTOR As never such a ring has been found before, Vera! *He draws Vera close. — In the hallway the maid goes from right to left — returns with a letter.*

VICTOR    For me?

MAID    For madam. *Exit.*

VERA *takes the letter — opens it — reads.*

VICTOR    A letter in a large buff envelope?

VERA    From the court. Summoning me as a witness.

VICTOR    Now will you take the oath?

VERA    Fervently, Victor. I'll take any oath for Sneederhan!

*Agnete*

(1935)

# CHARACTERS

Heinrich K.
Agnete
Stefan M.
Frau M., Stefan's mother
Fräulein Feustel, secretary

# ACT ONE

*All three acts take place in the library of Stefan's house. Tall bookcases separated by old dark paintings. To the left, a fireplace with carved armchairs on either side. Elsewhere a leather sofa and leather easy-chairs, a small metal table. To the right, wide French windows leading to the garden terrace. To the rear, a sliding door; another narrower door beside the fireplace on the left. The blue and green striped awning over the terrace subdues the morning light in the room.*

*The sliding door opens slowly and Stefan emerges from his study, closing the door behind him. He approaches the small table on which there is a framed photograph. He focuses on it intently, finally bending down to be able to see it better. Even that is not enough, so he lifts it and holds it close to his eyes. Still not enough, so he takes it over to the French windows where there is more light, and remains sunk in contemplation for some time. At last he returns the photograph to its place, goes to the sliding door, half opens it and calls out.*

STEFAN    Let's leave it at that, Fräulein Feustel.

*Fräulein Feustel's voice, querying.*

STEFAN    No, we'll call it a day.

*Enter Fräulein Feustel.*

STEFAN    And not just today, Fräulein Feustel. Maybe the rest of the week, or longer. Just how long I really can't say — it could be a break of a fortnight, a month even. Would it be possible for you to go on a trip somewhere?

FRÄULEIN FEUSTEL *taken aback.*    Where to?

STEFAN    To your relations? There would be nothing for you to do here, so any time spent there would not be wasted.

FRÄULEIN FEUSTEL    I could always visit my brother without advance notice.

STEFAN   You've mentioned him before — and the gardens around his house. They will all be in bloom now. Perhaps you could think of it as your vacation taken a little early, unless you've already made other plans.

FRÄULEIN FEUSTEL   I've always aimed to fit in with whatever suits you.

STEFAN   Then let your holiday begin now. Right away, Fräulein Feustel. Do you need long to pack?

FRÄULEIN FEUSTEL   It will only take a few minutes.

STEFAN   You won't need to come back here after you've taken me to the station. After all, I won't be alone any more. You could take the next train. Would that be possible?

FRÄULEIN FEUSTEL   There's only one train in the morning.

STEFAN   Can you still catch that?

FRÄULEIN FEUSTEL   It leaves ten minutes before the train you are expecting arrives.

STEFAN   That needn't stop you. I'll position myself on the platform where he can't fail to see me in case I don't recognize him.

FRÄULEIN FEUSTEL *hesitates.*   I don't know if I should —

STEFAN   He can't miss me at the barrier. How could you help me anyway? You've never seen him and couldn't point him out to me. And he knows he is being met. He'll pick me out even in a crowd. You need have no qualms about leaving me. I won't move from the spot.

FRÄULEIN FEUSTEL   I must hurry —

STEFAN   Do, Fräulein Feustel. We mustn't be late. And don't forget to let me know where you are. I might want to summon you back here urgently. Would you be able to come at once?

FRÄULEIN FEUSTEL   It's not that far. I could be back the same day.

STEFAN   Then I would resume work at once — *he fall silent, ponders. Exit Fräulein Feustel, left.*

*Stefan goes into his study, begins to clear his desk, putting books and papers in the drawers and locking them.*
*Enter Frau M., left. She stops in the middle of the room, observing Stefan.*
*Stefan has finished clearing his desk and emerges from the study, sliding the door shut behind him.*

STEFAN *turns and peers into the room.*   Is someone there?

FRAU M.   It's me, Stefan. Can't you see me, Stefan?

STEFAN   Now I know where you are. *He approaches her.*

FRAU M.   You're sending Fräulein Feustel away. On holiday, she tells me.

STEFAN   Yes, she agreed to my suggestion. Is she having second thoughts?

FRAU M.   No, she's packing. But why are you sending her away? She doesn't know why. *Anxiously.* Do you need to spare your eyes more than before?

STEFAN   They are no worse. The fog is no more impenetrable.

FRAU M.   I get so worried, like just now when you —

STEFAN   There's no need to be scared. I'll never go blind. *He makes her sit down on the sofa and sits down in an easy-chair.* Where I get this strength from — this strength that conquers all weakness — the strength to see, but in a different sense from what is normally conferred on us, a sense that is more — revelatory — *He takes the photograph from the table and hands it to Frau M.* It comes from him —

FRAU M. *takes the photograph and studies it.*

STEFAN   — and now he is not here, I'm bereft. I can't think. I couldn't dictate a word to Fräulein Feustel.

FRAU M. *looks up.*   Do you love him so much?

STEFAN   Does that really describe the bond between us? The power this child — my child — has over me is something I find more and more amazing. How can I describe it, something happening in my innermost being. I feel closer to life. The gap you find opening up — in my case especially — is suddenly bridged over. My view of the world had darkened and I was close to using all the gifts I had been given to — take flight. That was the danger. Flight — aloft — into those cold, rarified regions where everything is moribund and the lifeless miasma a merciless killer. The flight of the intellect ends in death. The endless quest — is that its goal? I was close to those icy regions when a child's voice called to me. And I obeyed. I obeyed the voice of a child, I could do no other. I turned back and I found life again, the life I thought had disowned me. For I have a child. Is there any more valid proof of life?

FRAU M.    You have a beautiful child, Stefan.

STEFAN    Who exerts a power over me to which I submit, totally. The work I undertook has its own laws. How can I continue with it when the source of those laws — of life itself, which is the absolute key to our work — has left the house empty? Do you understand?

FRAU M.    It's not hard to understand, Stefan.

STEFAN    I tried to sustain myself by looking at this photograph, but it was hopeless. So hopeless that I sent Fräulein Feustel on leave and put off all thought of work until laughter has returned and I can see the hair on his head there glistening again. That will be a light in the darkness, dispelling the gloom. *He broods silently.*

FRAU M. *replaces the photograph. Sighs.*    It's not good for the child either.

STEFAN *attentively.*    What, mother?

FRAU M.    Him staying in another house but in the same town. And the move, all of a sudden. Even a child registers that at once: how frightening when something happens that shatters everything one knew. The fright lasts longer than the shock. The child should have been spared that.

STEFAN    If there had been time to take stock —

FRAU M.    One should have taken stock, however little time there was. Now everything that has happened seems to me to have been misguided. As for what will happen — it can never be the way she wants it to be.

STEFAN    Which is — what?

FRAU M.    That we should never divulge when Lena died.

STEFAN    But she insists on it. We promised.

FRAU M.    We agreed too quickly, as with everything else she demanded.

STEFAN    It settled her. She was distraught.

FRAU M.    Stefan, this is about Heinrich — it's not about Agnete. It's Heinrich who's returning from captivity. From a Russian prison camp. For him, this world of ours is shattered. Is this the homeland he knew? Hardly. And the one who could give him fresh hope now, and who inspired him through those long hard years, is no longer alive.

STEFAN    What he wrote was so confident and full of brave plans, for Lena's sake.

FRAU M.    He shouldn't have been kept in the dark about Lena's death. We should have rejected Agnete's proposal. You can't say someone is alive if they're long dead and buried. She may not have been able to tell him the truth then, when his fever was at its height, lest it kill him, but you should have written and told him later. Man to man, to help him over his despair.

STEFAN    I was ready to.

FRAU M.    I know. But Agnete wouldn't permit it.

STEFAN    But we can understand why, surely?

FRAU M.    Understand, yes, but we shouldn't have gone along with it. She has the best intentions, but she won't succeed.

STEFAN    Can one say that? Did she not save Heinrich's life by going to him — and then by not telling what she was meant to tell? That Lena was dead.

FRAU M.    Up to that point her actions deserve the highest praise. She sets off into the wilds — a country in the grip of winter — a field hospital in Poland. The feverish patient is crying out for his fiancée — her visit can only assist his recovery, the doctor had also written — and to soften the horrific blow, it is her sister who must break the news that the one he is so desperately hoping for can never come. Doomed to die in the south, in the mountains where she still hoped for a cure. A lonely grave, high up in the mountains. It was not the right time to bring such tidings. It would have been tantamount to murder. Agnete was right to keep silent. Who doesn't understand that? — But when the fever had passed, when he can fight again, who can understand that he still must not be told? He would have withstood the shock and held her memory sacred. From suffering comes strength. Life is not destroyed by the pain of a single blow. Heinrich is young.

STEFAN    In his letters he laughs at all his inflictions — being wounded, then imprisoned.

FRAU M.    Because he can paint a picture of going home. Lena will be waiting for him. Standing on the platform — more beautiful than ever, radiating happiness and beckoning to Heinrich, like a song rising up to the very firmament above all the roar of people and machines.

STEFAN    He'll guess, when he sees me. I won't have to tell him.

FRAU M.    And it will be a hammer blow, worse than any he encountered in the field.

*Silence.*

FRAU M. *shaking her head.*    I can't do it.

STEFAN    What, mother?

FRAU M.    Tell this lie. I can't twist the truth to raise the dead.

STEFAN    It's hard to follow Agnete's idea.

FRAU M.    Death must be kept separate from life. Even if there were reasons — valid reasons, ten times more convincing than the reasons Agnete gave: the day of somebody's death is immovable, it's part of eternity, unchangeable. Lena breathed her last four weeks before Agnete went to Heinrich, not four weeks after. How can one deliberately confuse the two?

STEFAN    Agnete doesn't want to deprive him of the belief that Lena still made the effort to see him, even though she was already ill and suffering.

FRAU M.    She only told us yesterday that Heinrich didn't recognize her and took her for Lena.

STEFAN    Yes — and she relived it all, everything that happened, when Heinrich's telegram arrived.

FRAU M.   She went white as a sheet. I'll never forget the way she stared at the telegram, transfixed.

STEFAN   The whole house of cards that she had so happily constructed suddenly collapsed.

FRAU M.   No, Stefan, not mere cards, more like blocks of stone that could crush him rather than protect him — all with the best of intentions, but fatal nonetheless — unless we prevent the final deception that Agnete thinks will help him.

STEFAN   You mean we shouldn't tell Heinrich the wrong date?

FRAU M.   What good does it do to keep the right one from him?

STEFAN   Agnete told us: Lena's self-sacrifice — dragging herself over a vast, icy wasteland to bring him comfort and speed his recovery. That must surely reconcile him to his fate. After all, it would have been heroic — if it had happened. That's the source of consolation. Aren't you convinced?

FRAU M.   No. Not any more. Yesterday Agnete took us unawares. Today none of her arguments stand up. Not in the cold light of day. It's time for the plain, sober truth. Banish all the giddy dreams and illusions — they only create havoc, and it will be our fault.

STEFAN   What havoc do you foresee?

FRAU M.   It will grow with every new denial of what truly happened. He will find out, one day he will find out, and then the whole edifice — his consolation — will collapse. The wound reopens. He'll bleed again. How much blood does a heart need to keep beating?

STEFAN   Agnete thinks he need never know.

FRAU M.   That's impossible, Stefan. Impossible for him not to rake over every last detail. How she suffered. How she died. The day, the hour of her death. Was she bathed in sunshine at the end? Was his name on her lips when she breathed her last sigh? That's all he will want to know. Isn't it understandable? He finds his homeland reduced to rubble. There is more life in the departed. So he'll resort to his memories of Lena. And not only in his mind. It will drive him on — to the churchyard in the mountains, to visit her grave. And there it is, engraved on a stone — and it is not what we said it was. The stone speaks and makes liars of us all.

STEFAN    There can be no doubt Heinrich will want to see Lena's grave.

FRAU M.    And that will be the end of the silent devotion — what had been soothed and settled will be churned up again. His pain at the loss, he'll feel it all over again — and we will reproach ourselves for not having told him, along with everything else, on the day of his return. He would have borne it. Was it any crueller than Lena's death? That Agnete passed herself off as Lena?

STEFAN    Isn't that eclipsed by the fact that Lena's very existence has been extinguished?

FRAU M.    He'll feel the sting — but he'll feel a thousand stings if it's only revealed it to him later. It's more merciful to conceal nothing. Consign it all to the past, let nothing more emerge that can wound. No doubts, no uncertainties. If he is to find his way into the present again, let nothing poison it. For there is a future, for each of us. If we will only lay the shadows to rest. Don't trouble Heinrich again, don't dissemble with Lena's name.

STEFAN    But there is the oath Agnete extracted from us — it was almost an oath, was it not? — not to give anything away.

FRAU M.    It's no betrayal, for we only want what she wants — to help Heinrich. To get through this difficult first day, and beyond — something Agnete hasn't thought about. She's still looking into the past and trembles at the thought of him coming to claim the living person she constantly made him believe was alive, even to the point of assuming her very identity. She'll be overwhelmed by guilt, now that the bolt of lightning she held back for so long finally strikes him with double force.

STEFAN    There can be no question of any guilt.

FRAU M.    No guilt attaches to her, but she doesn't know that. Hence the confusion and all these plans that will never work. None of them will. They will only make things even darker, more impenetrable. The child is gone. This is no place for children's laughter, she says. A man returns from the desolate graveyard that is Russia and finds himself — in a house of the dead. Lena has just died for his sake — children should not be romping around in a house of mourning. So she removes the child.

STEFAN    He is very lively — and happy as the day is long.

FRAU M.    Which would be more of a consolation to Heinrich than anything we can say. The child has no conception of grief — it would help dispel Heinrich's grief. What can you or I or Agnete say that would register with him? Our doleful commiseration would only exacerbate his pain. Laughter? That's a child's privilege. This wonderful child, that nature has created in defiance of our mortality, this child can lead Heinrich out of his desolation and into the living light of day. It can do what is denied to us. The child must be here — here, when Heinrich's life starts afresh, provided we don't spoil things.

STEFAN    Spoil things?

FRAU M.    You send Fräulein Feustel away. You interrupt your work. With the house empty since your child left, you are unable to concentrate. So your vital work comes to a standstill.

STEFAN    I'll be able to devote myself exclusively to Heinrich.

FRAU M.    No good will come of that. He needs to see that life goes on, activity never ceases. You can't talk someone into a sense of confidence, or the courage to face life. They need an example to follow. Let Heinrich be part of all that shapes our life here — your work; the child and its high spirits; Agnete's aura. It will gradually restore his energy, galvanize him to triumph over his afffliction. — Don't deprive him of the child.

STEFAN    It was what Agnete wanted.

FRAU M.    She must change her mind and fetch the child back. For your sake — and Heinrich's.

STEFAN    You'll talk to her?

FRAU M.    The moment she gets back. She's only delivering the child.

STEFAN    And you'll tell her there can be no deviation from the truth from now on, for Heinrich's sake?

FRAU M.    It will be a relief to her too, and let her see things in a different light — and let the dead rest in peace.

STEFAN    Then nothing can stop her taking your advice. It's to everyone's advantage.

FRAU M.   There's nothing she can say that could persuade me otherwise.

STEFAN   So I needn't have sent Fräulein Feustel away.

FRAU M.   No, Stefan, you will go on with your work. —— What are you thinking?

STEFAN   I had a sudden image of Agnete. It may be her agitation is as unrelenting as ever. I'll have Fräulein Feustel ring you from the station to see if she should still leave.

FRAU M.   Let her stay — you shall work. The child will come. Rest assured.

STEFAN *rises.*   It's as if the ground were rising and falling beneath my feet. Everything suddenly swaying. Why this uncertainty?

FRAU M. *rises.*   I feel the same. It's because we're in agonies of expectation since yesterday, inwardly quaking.

STEFAN   As you said: someone returns from a land strewn with corpses only to enter a mortuary. I shall tell him Lena is dead, but no more. It's not for me to reveal the rest — the story Agnete concocted about her death.

FRAU M.   I will. I'll tell him everything, straight away. — Is that Fräulein Feustel knocking?

STEFAN   I must go.

FRAU M.   It's hard.

STEFAN   The hardest thing I've ever done, mother. Going to meet a friend, and then to deliver an almost mortal blow. *He stretches out his hand to her.*

FRAU M. *draws him close. Then opens the door, left.*   Don't keep Fräulein Feustel waiting. *Leaving.* Fräulein Feustel —— *Exit.*

STEFAN *follows, closes the door behind him.*
*Enter Agnete through French windows. Hat, short veil, gloves, carrying a bunch of flowers. Listens for sounds that might disturb her — then, hearing none, puts the flowers in a vase and carries it over to the small table. Replaces the photograph with the flowers. Locks the photograph in a chest and pockets the key. Stands and breathes a sigh of relief. Wearily removes her hat and gloves.*
*Enter Frau M, left.*

FRAU M.   Agnete, I didn't hear you come in.

AGNETE   I came through the garden. A short cut. I didn't want to be late. Has Stefan left? He will have, of course, long ago. Otherwise he would miss the train when it comes.

FRAU M.   Stefan will be there on time. *Taken by surprise.* Flowers?

AGNETE   The flowerbeds are full of them.

FRAU M.   And you've picked the brightest ones.

AGNETE   For their glowing colours. Don't they look almost funny amid all the books and the dark pictures?

FRAU M.   Do you want to introduce a sense of fun?

AGNETE   A friendly first impression, that's all. To make your eyes light up — or is any warm welcoming sign forbidden?

FRAU M.   Not by me. Nor by Stefan.

AGNETE *taken aback.*   That's true — I did advise against. But flowers — flowers don't talk. And they smell lovely and freshen the air. What a delight when you breathe in. That all helps make an impression.

FRAU M. *has gone over to the table.*

AGNETE *watches her.*   The scarlet ones are the strongest. Be careful, they can make you dizzy. Their pollen can be poisonous.

FRAU M. *straightening.*   The photograph is gone.

AGNETE   To make room for the vase.

FRAU M.   Where did you put it?

AGNETE   I didn't put it back up.

FRAU M.   Can't you find a place?

AGNETE   I've locked it away. In the chest. Here's the key. I'll hold on to it.

FRAU M.   Do you want to hide it?

AGNETE   It shouldn't be on view as long as Heinrich is in the house. He mustn't see anything that might cause pain — like a child's laughing face. Will he ever learn to laugh again? It can only increase his grief to see what is lost to him.

FRAU M. *remains silent. Shaking her head, she sits down in an armchair beside the fireplace.*

AGNETE *almost fiercely.*   Aren't we obliged to show all the consideration we can?

FRAU M.   One thing cancels out the other.

AGNETE   What have I overlooked?

FRAU M.   That there's more life bursting from these colours than from the silent photograph of a child.

AGNETE *remains silent.*

FRAU M.   Stefan has sent Fräulein Feustel away.

AGNETE   Where to?

FRAU M.   Where she can spend her leave.

AGNETE   When was that arranged?

FRAU M.   It so happened she had to take her leave now.

AGNETE   Had to?

FRAU M.   Since Stefan wasn't able to carry on with his work.

AGNETE   What was stopping him?

FRAU M.   The changes that have taken place.

AGNETE *hoarse-voiced.*   What changes?

FRAU M.   You've removed his child. He misses it. Part of himself has been torn away. How can the rest live?

AGNETE *as if relieved.*    He's worried about the child. He needn't be. It was perfectly happy when I left. At home with all the new things right away. He won't be homesick at all. He has his toys and I built them all up around him. You can see he understands — in his play. He was playing with his train-set. He knows it has to move smoothly along the rails, over the points, with no jolts or bumps: for Uncle Heinrich is in the train and is very sick. So sick that he is not even allowed to see little children — like him, who's not grumpy and complaining that he's not at home any more. First the sick people have to get strong again, then it's the healthy people's turn. Our child is healthy. Stefan should know that!

FRAU M. *calmly.*    Bring him the child back.

AGNETE *stammering.*    Bring the child back here ——?

FRAU M.    Call it what you will — I see it as a mission, a mission that a child can perform. A blessing for Stefan, his father — and for Heinrich, his father's best friend. One shouldn't rob them of the support they both need to reconnect with life, each in his own different way, but both of them searching for happiness. Don't stand in their way.

AGNETE *heatedly.*    If it were a blessing for Stefan I would go and fetch the child back straight away. Stefan has every right to be close to it — that right is unshakable, like the earth's foundations. Remove one stone if you dare, and you put everything at risk and will be struck down. It is Stefan's right that is being protected.

FRAU M. *in wonderment.*    What is Stefan's right?

AGNETE *after some thought.*    That this child should be spared anything that might dim its lustre. Such as the presence of Heinrich. Dejection on the face of an adult is a terrible sight to the young. A man of suffering can only be an object of fear to a child. Does it ever recover from such an impression? The devastation is lasting. I removed it from such a sight — it was the only way I knew not to ruin everything.

FRAU M.    Was it not for Heinrich's sake?

AGNETE    That's what I said yesterday. Yesterday it seemed to me that Heinrich would be hurt if we were evasive. I didn't want to reveal the real reasons in front of Stefan. After all, I was confused too. So much to think about. A telegram, out of the blue. Who would be prepared for the return of the dead?

FRAU M.   Nobody thought Heinrich was dead.

AGNETE   He sent news, but sometimes none for long stretches. They died in their thousands in those murderous Russian camps. Was he safe? With the wounds he had, and no one to tend them? I was prepared for him not to have survived.

FRAU M.   If he survived and never lost heart — that was your doing, Agnete.

AGNETE *resolutely.*   That was my doing — my achievement! — I did more than anyone should ask of a fellow human being, however deep one's despair. I lied that a dead woman was still alive. I took every care with the deception, and to prevent any other news reaching him that would have destroyed him. I intercepted letters that revealed everything — the year, the day, the hour. It was left to me to pass them on, since only I knew where he was being held prisoner — from his letters to Lena, the only person he was still writing to. I read all those other letters — and never replied. No report of her death reached him — so Lena lived on. And he could too, in the stifling heat and the icy cold of the east, and not die and be buried in some foreign field. — Is that not enough, the things I have done? Enough to ask this one small reward: to let me decide as I think fit? — Must I produce even more reasons to plead my case — reasons that would remove the seeming confusion I'm caught up in, at a stroke?

FRAU M.   The lies —

AGNETE   Yes, I lied — I lied — I lied.

FRAU M.   — they don't count. They saved a life.

AGNETE   I don't want any inflated thanks.

FRAU M.   It might soon be small thanks you get for it.

AGNETE   Who would accuse me? Stefan? You?

FRAU M.   Someone who already owes you one debt of gratitude, but the other thing Heinrich would not understand.

AGNETE   What other thing?

FRAU M.   The other secret — about Lena.

AGNETE     What more can he find out?

FRAU M.     When she died. The date of her death. The year, the day, the hour.

AGNETE     *stares at her. Then with unconcealed shock.*     Then he would also know it was not Lena who visited him — but me?

FRAU M.     Will that be the most unbearable thing of all?

AGNETE     No, not for him — for me! I couldn't bear it!

FRAU M.     Are you still so distressed that he didn't recognize you?

AGNETE     That was the first deception, and everything else followed from it!

FRAU M. *shaking her head.*     That should be your least concern — it was his obsession and he was delirious at the time. Your deceptions later were worse, but the intention was good and that excuses them. But this would be worst of all — something Heinrich merely dreamt.

AGNETE     Is it not a dream he must be allowed to keep alive? The loved one, her illness already looming over her, struggling across the snow-covered steppe to find him and tell him: so what if it costs me my life, what do I care — if you see me one more time, my beloved, and I see you? — Can one destroy such an image? Must it not endure? To the broken spirit an immutable source of life — and it was that, as we know, for he did not succumb. He cannot do without this image — it's all that is left to him, it mustn't be destroyed.

FRAU M.     And yet the blow will fall, and all the harder when it does than if it fell now.

AGNETE     Whatever he tries to find out, we can prevent it. Besides, years have passed since it all happened. We're the only ones left, and we're not likely to let anything slip — *Almost laughing* — and destroy a beautiful dream.

FRAU M.     Stone defies the passage of time. Don't forget the stone that bears different figures. Cut deep in the stone, impervious to the weather.

AGNETE *freezes. Then falteringly.*     Lena's grave. Up in the mountains.

FRAU M.     For him, a place of pilgrimage, one he will soon undertake. Sooner than we think. Is our connection any closer? Even you — you are only her sister.

When he finds out, he will only pause here briefly. Though he doesn't know the whole story. That the stone will teach him — and more: that human hearts are so stony that they perpetuate the torment and open up old wounds that were already healing over. And Heinrich will go over the whole story again, tormented by questions that throw up deeper doubts, even the deepest, deep as the grave: did she love him? What can one believe if even death can be twisted?

AGNETE *stunned.*   He'll go on a pilgrimage —?

FRAU M.   Forestall him. Don't leave him in his delusion. Only unhappiness will come of it. He's bound to be on edge, hypersensitive — this was more than just a war, it was sheer horror. Whatever reserves he has left will collapse when Stefan gives him the news. That is the moment to begin afresh. Suffer no more. The grief must not return. He will come to love life again — yield to its allure, and all is possible. Infinitely so. Let Heinrich live again. —

AGNETE *still dazed.*   Live here —

FRAU M.   We don't want to lie. Neither Stefan nor I. Every lie eventually costs one dear — it's unworthy to make such calculated deceptions. Stefan agrees. We talked it through. I will tell Heinrich. I can explain if he complains about what he was told earlier —

AGNETE   Wait — first I must move the stone from the grave, then he can make his pilgrimage.

FRAU M.   You mean you're still resolved to —

AGNETE   More than that: I mean that I shall resist to the end — that even stones lie!

FRAU M.   You can't dispute the date of Lena's death, ever.

AGNETE   She was alive that day. More alive than ever. In Heinrich's arms!

FRAU M. *half raises her arms in consternation, then feebly lets them sink.*

AGNETE *behind an armchair, clasping its wings as if for support — speaking in a low voice.*   The news came that the swamps had brought on his fever. It was not long after the start of the campaign. But already in enemy territory. The swamps lay in wait for their victims, as if nature were in the grip of a destructive fury unleashed by the convulsions of mass slaughter. The fever took hold, laid him low, threatened to consume him. He struggled against its ravages, refused to let it snuff out his youth. He cried out for help, without help he was doomed. Only one could help in this battle — Lena. She must come, stay at his side, ease the pain, erase it. So the young doctor wrote who was treating him and had befriended him. A matter of the utmost urgency with Heinrich's life at stake. The one called upon must come without delay, or it would be too late. —— The one called upon could go nowhere. She herself lay helpless, far off, an eternity away. —— Was that the message he should receive? Shatter the glass before he could drink from it? That he had already raised to his lips to cool his raging thirst and revive him? It would have to be broken to him gently, the end of that flickering hope. —— And so I became the messenger, my task to soften the blow, the terrible bombshell that threatened to destroy him. —— I didn't hesitate. It was an emergency, the doctor said. The steady pounding in my head drove me on — on — on — lest he despair. I thought: it's already taken too long, I must go faster or he'll think no one is coming. That Lena was somehow less than eager. Or worst of all: that he might die without proof that only death could hold her back — proof that I could provide, after fighting my way through storms and freezing cold — thinking of only one thing — to reach him as he struggled for a sign of that loyalty. —— That was the important thing, only that — I almost forgot everything else. That alone drove me on: to find him still alive and be able to excuse her — my dead sister. —— It seemed like a race against death. I seized every opportunity that came my way — stopped carts and climbed up, exposed to the elements — or cut across fields. And death fought back, hurled snow in my face, blinded me. I groped my way forward with my eyes shut. Snow-drifts piled up, I clambered over them. I persevered, to the end — and one day: journey's end. *Takes a deep breath, sits down in armchair. Resting her chin on her clenched fists, as if talking to herself.* It was a manor house — turned into a field hospital. It suddenly loomed up in front of me, like some dark castle in the air. Not a sound. It was almost empty, for the troops had pushed further forward. Those newly wounded at the front weren't sent back here, there were only a few patients, and they would return to the front when they were well enough. So the nurse said who showed me in. But before that she had told him I was there. She knew as soon as I enquired about Heinrich — I couldn't say another word, she left me standing there, went off, and when she returned she said: Your fiancé is expecting you — he'll quickly recover now that you are here. —— I was in such a state of suspense that before I could contradict her I was following her along endless corridors with my heart beating louder than the sound of our footsteps on the flagstones — till we reached a door at the end of the last corridor, there was hardly any light, the nurse took my hand and whispered: here is the handle, it's hard to find, it's so dark. Then she left me alone. She was wearing a wimple with wings which seemed to fly back along the corridor like some ungainly bird, until the sounds died away. So I saw her disappear into the void and felt the cold of the metal handle in my hand, icy cold that made me shiver and remember the terror I had felt rushing to get there: while he was still alive — and I threw open the door and cried out in relief: *Heinrich!* —— when I saw him propped up in the bed. *Pause.* He fell back at once on the pillows, seemingly lifeless. But he was mumbling something. To understand him I had to bend down close to his face — and then I did understand what he was saying : so you've come — to our wedding? And he didn't open his eyes when I asked him if he — recognized me. Asked him to look at me. All he said was: I see you. It's our wedding. The cathedral flooded with light — candles consecrated on the altar, a choir singing. The solemn ceremony. Then all the guests, crowding around us. We are a handsome couple. You are wearing a myrtle garland like a crown. Your long veil billows like a sail as we hurry out of the hall. Then we leave on our travels. We travelled — travelled — travelled, and now we are — Where are we? Are we still in this world? Where are your garland and veil? Have you taken them —? *She stops. Then finishes calmly.* The nurse giving him the wrong information, then me calling out his name so excitedly — can only have confirmed what he had been expecting with almost unshakeable belief: that Lena must have come; for he needed her, if he was to live. I didn't want to kill him. ————————

*Silence.*

FRAU M., *who had listened with eyes lowered, slowly raises them to Agnete.*

AGNETE *her stance unchanged — continues.*    The nurse saw me run out of the building as dawn broke. I ran — I kept running — blindly — finally people helped me find my way home — till I got here. *Looking at Frau M.* No, not here. I only came here later, when I was — looking for a father for the child.

FRAU M. *groans.*    Stefan ——

AGNETE    I knew he was fond of me —— and I abused that. I probably said it was loneliness that had led me to him, but he wasn't disinclined. Then I pressed for marriage — and Stefan was very happy when the child was born — something you found somewhat puzzling — born so early yet strong and healthy.

FRAU M.    So that's the solution to the puzzle of the birth.

AGNETE    Just as all puzzles are eventually solved when you persist in your probing.

FRAU M.    Why didn't you reveal yourself to Heinrich later, for the child's sake? He would have — *She breaks off.*

AGNETE *disconcerted.* The shame of it! — To think I could compel Heinrich — Heinrich, who didn't love me —. Make a mere trick out of what was surely the grace of God — or was it not that?

FRAU M. Think of Stefan.

AGNETE *growing more impassioned.* Think — think — think — there's just too much to think of. I've had to be continually on guard not to betray myself in some way or other — and no time to think things through. When I try to, my head spins: what way is there out of this agonizing dilemma? It's breaking my heart.

FRAU M. *after long reflection.* Heinrich hasn't forgotten that day?

AGNETE His wedding day?! The momentous day stamped on his memory as the day life reclaimed him? No, he hasn't forgotten. He soon recovered and was off into battle again. Where he was wounded and carted off into captivity. Which he endured, however gruesome. After all, he was now married and had new duties. His wife, his country, his homecoming — powerful links to life, are they not? Feel them strongly enough and your courage will never fail you. And in every letter he wrote the flame burned bright and constant. He commemorated every anniversary of that sacred, unforgotten day, and never failed to dispatch the letters. Once he escaped, for that was the only way to get hold of a messenger. He was recaptured and tortured even more. But the anniversary had been celebrated.

FRAU M. You never showed us his letters.

AGNETE And let you read what I could not tell? And what I did not admit to until yesterday — that I had stood in for Lena. I already suspected that admission would not be enough to make you understand everything I had to do. Why take the child away? Why shouldn't its laughter dispel the gloom? I knew you wouldn't approve. *Again heatedly.* Shall I fetch it back? To put the finishing touch to my torture? Whose is the child I bore? Not the one who calls himself its father — and who is that beside him? The confusion! — That the child must deny his own blood and say father to the one and not the other. Must I witness that, played out before my very eyes till I'm so tormented I snatch the child back and scream: you have only one mother — nothing else counts in this life! *Pause. Continues.* That's why I wanted to hide the photograph, so that no one sees it and suddenly remarks on the likeness, for it is unmistakable. A mere coincidence? But my blood runs cold — I'm exposed, unmasked straight away. I have no resistance left. I don't want to hide my secret any more — rather relieve myself of it like something disgusting. There, take it — just leave me alone! *Falls on her knees before Frau M.* I'm not worthy: I've committed murder a thousand times in my mind — wished that any of the murderous hail of bullets might strike him down. Death in battle is a fine thing — how many have sacrificed themselves willingly, joyfully! That should have been his fate too, then he would not return. I prayed, and killed him in my prayers. But my prayers were not answered. I did not find grace! *She is racked with sobbing.*

FRAU M. *gazes slowly around the room. Then resolute, having made up her mind. Looks down at Agnete and gently strokes her hair. Quietly.* What became of Heinrich's letters?

AGNETE   Torn up and burnt!

FRAU M. *emphatically.* I burned them!

AGNETE *Raises her tear-stained face.* You?

FRAU M.   Leave that to me.

AGNETE   But how can you —?

FRAU M. *firmly.* What must be done — I can do!

AGNETE   Can you reduce a stone to dust?

FRAU M.   The stone remains. The only solid thing in this whole desperate business. Everything else is a misconception — a misunderstanding — a mistake — shrouded in mystery. I shall block every way of knowing, foil every threat. It will become quite obscure — and finally disappear — as it must — for my son's sake.

AGNETE *stares at her.* You love your son that much, your Stefan?

FRAU M.   Is your love any less — for your son?

AGNETE *rises.* Why do you ask me?

FRAU M.   Did you not ask me? I gave you my answer at once.

AGNETE   Must I answer?

FRAU M.  When you are put to the test, as I have been, then you will know the answer, only then. *She rises.* Take heart when you meet Heinrich. It was wartime when it happened, when we have no power over what we must do. We can only submit, body and soul. We have no choice. But when the storm is past, everything has been scattered to the winds. Everything, Agnete! *She embraces her and kisses her.*

AGNETE *takes up her hat and gloves. With a sudden surge of emotion.*  Can I not go to my child and stay with it?

FRAU M.  How would you explain that to Stefan?

AGNETE *slumps.*  I shouldn't have explained anything. *Goes to door, left.* I don't want to explain. *Exit.*

FRAU M.  *remains motionless. Then goes along the bookshelves, fondly stroking the spines of the books. Ends up at fireplace — leans against the mantelpiece and contemplates the intricate pattern in the carpet at her feet. — Noises behind the door, left, attract her attention. She snaps out of her reverie, steps away from the fireplace and waits in tense expectancy.*

*Enter Stefan, left; he shuts the door behind him.*

FRAU M.  Is Heinrich —?

STEFAN  He's by himself in the garden. He didn't want to come into the house yet. *Looking worn out, he sinks on to the sofa.*

FRAU M.  Was it so distressing?

STEFAN  It was terrible. When the train arrived I was standing in a crowd in front of the barrier. That way he couldn't miss me, even if I didn't pick him out at once. I had chosen my place well, for he spotted me at once. Except he didn't call out to me. He called Lena's name. Shouted it — delightedly, at the top of his voice. I couldn't understand. He waved, waved his hat, as if there really was someone there who was expecting him — Lena. It was a mystery to me, until I saw who it was he thought was Lena. The crush of people flooding towards the exit had thrust this woman right up beside me. She was wearing a bright flowery dress and a broad, light-coloured hat. He couldn't ever have mistaken her for Lena, but from a distance it must have seemed just possible: that she was dressed so gaily to welcome him — and with me beside her — that made the mistake even more likely. —— Then he was standing in front of us, and while she was promptly claimed by a party of happy acquaintances getting off the train, his eyes turned to me, already full of apprehension, and he started to say *Is Lena* —? but broke off. That was all he said. —— I don't even know if he heard when I said we were going to my house — that Agnete was now my wife and that we had a child. ————

FRAU M. *quickly.*    Did Fräulein Feustel not ring?

STEFAN *rising.*    She didn't leave.

FRAU M.    Why, what stopped her?

STEFAN    I saw no point any more. I had realized that Agnete could be made to see her measures were too extreme. You explained why to me, and every objection disappeared. — How can she not accept your better judgement? The child comes back — so why should I dismiss Fräulein Feustel? I gave her the day off. She returns this evening. Tomorrow life resumes. Also for Heinrich's benefit.

FRAU M. *with an effort of will power.*    We must let her do as she thinks fit.

STEFAN    Agnete?

FRAU M.    Do everything as she instructed. I've changed my mind. She's given me — *She breaks off.*

STEFAN    Given you new reasons —?

FRAU M.    She — merely asked me. There are no new reasons that alter things. But her asking, begging me rather — to make what is incomprehensible absolutely necessary. Our silence is necessary — and our deception.

STEFAN    But surely we can't keep that up? The stone —

FRAU M.    No. Don't worry, Stefan. Trust me, Stefan. This turmoil is too much for me, all these twists and turns. Promise me, Stefan —— promise me, Stefan, for my peace of mind, for I already have my mind on higher things and peace of mind is a blessing: be on your guard! Keep the secret that even the stone will not betray. What happened, happened many weeks earlier. Heinrich was delirious at the time. How could he remember clearly and exactly. That is what I shall prove to him, as immutably as it is engraved in the stone.

STEFAN  How you've taken it to heart! I promise you I will never tell him anything but what he has heard from you.

FRAU M.  And what he will hear is: Weeks before her death — and he got the date wrong. Yes?

STEFAN  That way Heinrich's most treasured memory is safe.

FRAU M.  And a blessing on this house!

STEFAN *in front of the small table.*  Where is the photograph?

FRAU M.  I — I hid it away. Since the child cannot be here, his likeness should not remind you of that every time you look at it.

STEFAN *smiling and passing his hand over the flowers.*  And in its place you put these gorgeous flowers?

FRAU M.  Yes, Stefan.

STEFAN  Is Agnete back —?

FRAU M.  She's upstairs.

STEFAN  Then she can tell me how the child —

FRAU M. *quickly.*  Visit him yourself. He will be pleased, though he has all he wants, as Agnete says. He's happily playing with his train-set. But he will soon forget that when he sees you.

STEFAN  I'll take a cab to the house.

FRAU M.  You don't need anyone to accompany you. Do you know where Fräulein Feustel is staying?

STEFAN  She told me, in case she was needed before this evening.

FRAU M.  Let her go away. What we have to act out here makes greater demands than most people have to face. We need to focus all our strength. *She has accompanied Stefan to the door.*

*Exit Stefan.*

*Frau M. turns towards the French windows, right. She peers out through the panes. Then she opens the glass door and waves hesitantly. In anticipation she steps back. Heinrich — in new, light-coloured, civilian clothes — appears on the threshold, hesitates.*

FRAU M. *goes to him, puts her arm around his shoulder and ushers him in, shutting the door behind him. She takes both his hands.*   You are home, Heinrich. Even if much has changed — and one disappointment seems almost unbearable — it is home.

HEINRICH *remains motionless.*

FRAU M.   You're numb, but you must come alive again, Heinrich. Feel your heart beating. Follow your inner voice — don't shut yourself off from what life compels: it bids us live.

HEINRICH *remains frozen, as before.*

FRAU M.   No words of mine can express what needs saying. Who am I to comfort you? What presumption to think I had such power — nobody has. There is only one consolation: she loved you.

HEINRICH *draws a deep breath.*

FRAU M. *leads him to the sofa and sits down in an easy-chair beside him.*

HEINRICH *slowly begins — as if to himself.*   So we crossed the border — and I was back. All those years — wiped out — and everything that happened in them. You would think they must have left their mark, indelibly. Like scars, to remind you of the wounds. Yet it was all gone, over and done with. Nothing left to feel bitter about. I walked through the streets of that border town like a boy let off school — overjoyed. Some great festive occasion you hadn't expected and your heart's singing and you're ready to jump up and down with excitement and wave your arms around like flags. I wrote out the telegram and noticed that I wasn't used to writing any more, and I laughed. Then I bought this suit — I wouldn't accept any dark colour. I even teased the shop assistant: my dear sir, I'm not going to a funeral — I've just come back from being buried. But enough of that. Siberia will have to get along without me. Even the most beautiful place has scant attraction if you're forced to admire it under duress. That was my farewell to what had been — and the train carried me off — almost too quickly — into a rosy future, blotting out all the past. I wanted to bask in that feeling of expectation flooding over me until I was totally intoxicated, and I revelled in conjuring up images that then all seemed so pale and inadequate I could only discard them. The present will transcend them all — I shall see her in person — she will have long since received my telegram — will have known I was coming and will not have slept all night, just as I did not sleep. —— *Holding back his emotion.* And there she stood, where I had seen her standing a thousand times in my imagination. I saw her as soon as the train pulled in and I leaned out of the window. With Stefan — naturally. Stefan — old friend, faithful friend. They have both come to meet me. What a reception. A wonderful dress — rose-patterned — or is it poppies? I can't quite make it out yet. And below her hat, her face must be bathed in a gentle rosy light — for the hat is reddish and seems to let the sun through. If only I could see her face — Stefan mustn't mind if I don't pay him much attention. Don't be an idiot, Stefan — it wasn't for you I decided not to die — that was Lena's doing, Lena who compelled me, when she —— *He stops — shakes his head and continues more calmly.* Then the misunderstanding was cleared up — Stefan cleared up much else besides. He needn't have said any more. Why did he? Can my brain take in any more? *He presses his clenched fists to his brow and sits bent over.*

FRAU M.    Stefan had to explain why you were coming here. That the sisters' house no longer existed. That it was years since Lena ——

HEINRICH *groans.*    Years —!

FRAU M.    It had to remain a secret.

HEINRICH    And I did not die. I lived for this day with a fervency that gave me the strength to defy death!

FRAU M.    Should one not also live to keep a memory of the dead alive? Is true mourning not a resurrection — breaking open the dark enclosure of the grave?

HEINRICH    When mourning weighs too heavily — does it not drag even those who resist down to the grave?

FRAU M.    Life will not abandon you yet, Heinrich.

HEINRICH *looks up.*    Haven't I had my fair share?

FRAU M.    A great deal — but not all there is.

HEINRICH    The dregs?

FRAU M.   Does the great wide world not open before you, waiting to be conquered?

HEINRICH   Stale — flat — unprofitable. When chaos looms, some things one remembers even more clearly. A shape, a sound, a radiance — and a voice that cried out: *Heinrich*. That rescued me from the realm of shades. A human cry had revived me — but also left me in a daze, as if anaesthetized. Can there be anything more marvellous than to feel oneself blissfully happy — in a daze?

FRAU M.   And that bliss was what you experienced?

HEINRICH *emphatically*.   It was! — What more has life to offer? What source could it possibly draw on, after I drained the cup it offered me — that Lena offered me? — And that I drank — from Lena's lips. — And our lips did not part. *Continues, more to himself, steadily and calmly.* I lay ill. Poisoned by the swamps. The invisible enemy in the air — the noxious vapour that knocked me out. I collapsed — as we marched. I passed out. One last step in the dense fog and suddenly there was no ground under my feet and my whole body was falling into some infernal crater, into soft lava and sulphurous fumes. I was sinking — plunging downwards — until I ended in a bed in the field hospital. Though I didn't yet know it was a field hospital — a manor house, deserted because of the war. All around me yawning depths and steep escarpments. The primordial desolation left by an earthquake that had shattered houses and mountains and oceans with a thunderous, deafening roar. Then the noise had stopped — I sensed I would be heard if I cried out for help. That I would be pulled out of my hole in the ground — for that's what it had shrunk to — before the crumbling blood-red clay of the walls cracked and crashed down on me. But it had to be quick. Such a death would be too horrible. I was fully conscious the whole time, only as if blinded. With my eyes tight shut, I could still see everything with my inner eye exactly as it was. If I had opened my eyes, nothing would have changed. I could not be mistaken — a mistake would have meant death. —— To save me from the bottomless pit — about to collapse at any moment — I called for her — she would come if only she heard my cry. I cried out incessantly, at the top of my voice — so that she should hear my cry through forests and across vast plains. And she heard it, and set off. Not once does she pause to rest, she takes both the highways and the byways to save time. Her strength is unflagging. She won't be too late. I just must keep calling so she doesn't miss the trench I'm lying in. There's great danger I will be buried alive. I'm pressing back against the earth wall to stop it crumbling — my arms are already tiring — dry grey sand is trickling through my fingers — if she doesn't come now —— And at the edge of the pit, above me, there appears someone I don't recognize who says down to me: she has arrived — and disappears. I lift the mountain of stone already crushing my chest, and prepare to assist in the rescue operation that will cost her an enormous effort. But then she manages to lift me up quite easily: she simply calls my name and touches me lightly — and restores me to life —— to a life that did not exist before —— radiant —— suffused with love ———— *Pause.* Then it was dawn — the nurse came in and was surprised I didn't recognize her. Now you will get better, she said with a smile. I will die — was my answer. She merely laughed. But I insisted and told her why: the outside world no longer corresponds to what I see in my mind. She asked: what was not real? — That Lena came and saved me. — But she was here, the nurse exclaimed — she only left you an hour ago! — I started up from the pillows and shouted out: so it was all true!? The church — the altar — the songs of praise — the feast? Even the feast and the going away and —?! She stared at me, baffled — she didn't understand. How could I explain! — So I merely asked her: what day was it yesterday? For I must set this day apart from all others — it is my special holy day! — So she told me, and I learnt it by heart and knew I would never forget it. *Pause. He looks at Frau M.* It was the day Lena became my wife. The wedding took place in a desolate manor house. That night a snow storm raged outside the windows. And it was wartime. The war that reclaimed me. I refused to take leave. I wanted to help complete the war effort without delay, for that would secure the happiness I had attained —— and I received the wounds that delivered me into enemy hands. *With emphasis.* And once again I did not die. For how could I die while someone was still alive who had bound herself to me, body and soul — as Lena did to me that night after she had come to me through all the horrors and terrors of winter. *He suddenly buries his face in his hands, deeply bowed.*

FRAU M.     —————— Don't lose heart, Heinrich.

HEINRICH *softly.*     That was a betrayal.

FRAU M.     Betrayal?

HEINRICH     What happened that night should never have been uttered without the other's permission.

FRAU M. *gives him a long look. Then says calmly.*     I knew already.

HEINRICH *looking up.*     From Lena?

FRAU M.     She told me — when she came back.

HEINRICH     But why did she —?

FRAU M.   She was very happy and she wanted to tell others. Don't you understand that?

HEINRICH    Why did she leave next morning?

FRAU M.   Heinrich — she was already suffering when she started out on her journey. How she contracted it — it started with a cough we didn't pay much attention to — that was certainly not the real reason she became so seriously ill. She was worrying her heart out — that coughing fit would soon have passed, but you were preying on her mind, Heinrich, night and day. For when the doctor wrote that she should come, that it would be helpful — indeed almost essential for your recovery — she no longer attached any importance to her health and forgot how the journey would endanger it. *With emphasis.* She ignored it — Lena wanted to go, whatever the cost to her own life, and was iron-willed in carrying it out. She arrived in time. — When she fled before dawn the next day — it was with the journey back in mind. It was a long way and a very difficult way and her strength was giving out. She had to hurry to get to the pure mountain air as soon as possible. She could not stay any longer — overwhelmed by the temptation: to be a woman in love. It was either: leave at once or never!

HEINRICH *after a pause.*    And in the mountains?

FRAU M.   It was already too late. One fine, clear, sunny day, at noon, she passed away. She simply did not wake up — without suffering — without any sense of dying.

HEINRICH    —— And her grave?

FRAU M.   An evergreen mound in the mountain cemetery.

HEINRICH *silently drops his eyes.*

FRAU M. *watches him attentively.*

HEINRICH *finally, in a flat voice.*    When did she die?

FRAU M.   Four weeks after your special holy day.

HEINRICH *sighs.*    In March then, when spring is in the air. How hard that makes leave-taking.

FRAU M.   She didn't need to feel that.

HEINRICH   Don't you feel the sun already that much hotter in March?

FRAU M.   She was no longer alive in March.

HEINRICH   But she died a month after —?

FRAU M.   Exactly four weeks after. It had just turned February.

HEINRICH   Just turned February — but that's when she was with me!

FRAU M. *firmly.*   In February she was in her grave. Her travels were at an end.

HEINRICH *agitated.*   Her travels were at an end, and yet —! *Bursts out.* Who casts doubt on that day of all days? The living? The dead? Are the shades consorting with the living in some dance of death? Am I a shade? Or flesh and blood?

FRAU M.   You live on — she is no more. The stone she rests under will disclose the truth. It was deepest winter — January — when Lena was united with you. —————

HEINRICH *at a complete loss.*   Did my letters survive?

FRAU M.   No.

HEINRICH   Were none delivered?

FRAU M.   I received them all, and I burned them all. No one should ever read what Lena had confided to me alone.

HEINRICH   You read my letters?

FRAU M.   Every one, to see if you could bear to hear the distressing news.

HEINRICH   And the date I celebrated in each one. What was the date?

FRAU M.   One that did not deserve to be celebrated. It was dreadful to see you commemorating the very day that robbed you of everything.

HEINRICH *slumps — numbly.*   So that too was a misunderstanding. First the one, then the other. At the beginning and at the end. Like two poles rammed into the ground with a wire strung between them. And I step out gaily along the wire — unshakable, confident — as if it were a broad highway. Yet it is only a narrow, swaying wire after all. One false step and down you plunge, it's inevitable. I only need to feel the slightest bit apprehensive — or for it to occur to me that there is possibly nothing waiting for me here — that the woman on the platform is not Lena — can never be Lena —— that it is all a misunderstanding —— everything —— everything ——————

FRAU M.   I did not want to shake the wire, Heinrich. It was not your fate to perish, but to return. And you have survived. That was meant to be — you can be sure of it. I was merely the instrument when I decided to remain silent. Did your letters not tell me as much? That you could live since she was alive? For the sake of that day? — Which your mind, still dazed by the fever, then projected into a later time as the mist slowly cleared. Your first day, when you had fully come to your senses, can only have been ecstatic, so that all that is beautiful and good in life must surely have happened on that day. And yet — it was only a dream. Reality puts a different date on it.

HEINRICH *calmly.*   I freely accept that. I recognize that reality is all-powerful. And like all great things, beyond our comprehension. I didn't choke to death in the mud, I didn't pine away. So I live on. But for what? Is that not just another misunderstanding? Like everything else?

FRAU M. *does not interrupt his silence as he stares blankly.*

HEINRICH *finally turns to face her.*   —— Agnete?

FRAU M.   Became Stefan's wife.

HEINRICH   I heard him say so. Only I could not reply. They married soon after Lena's death.

FRAU M.   Agnete was very lonely without Lena.

HEINRICH   The thought that Stefan might want her as his wife —

FRAU M.   But he's always loved her.

HEINRICH   I'm surprised he wasn't too shy to propose. Wasn't he inhibited by his eye condition?

FRAU M.   I was their go-between. I don't regret it. This house is blessed with a wonderful sense of harmony that took root amid the havoc of war, and so it has remained.

HEINRICH   —— And there is a child.

FRAU M.   A son.

HEINRICH *repeats slowly.*   A son ———— *After a pause.* Where is he?

FRAU M.   With relations for the time being — until Agnete can look after him again properly. He is noisy and unruly and she has no time for him right now. As Lena's sister — she wants to try to take your mind off things.

HEINRICH   I scarcely remember what Agnete looks like. When I went off to war, the last thing I remember was her giving me flowers. That's all. — Flowers like these ones. From the garden. I really only saw the flowers, not Agnete. — Can I see her now?

FRAU M.   I'll call her. She'll be pleased you still remember her flowers. She brought these ones in, too. *With an effort she rises from the easy-chair. Then, summoning up all her strength, goes resolutely to the door, left. Exit.*

*Heinrich has risen from the leather sofa. Stands looking helpless. Then stares absent-mindedly at the flowers. His gaze shifts to the French windows — he goes over and looks out.*
*Enter Agnete, left. Remains standing at the door.*
*Heinrich turns slowly on hearing the sound. Takes some hesitant steps, stops — looking at Agnete.*
*Agnete awaits his first words, motionless.*

HEINRICH *at last.*   Is it really you — Agnete?

AGNETE   Don't you recognize me?

HEINRICH   Seeing you here —

AGNETE   Where else should I be?

HEINRICH *passes a hand over his brow.*   So it's not just a figment — stories from the past that you might forget.

AGNETE *comes closer.*    It's not like it once was, Heinrich.

HEINRICH    So there once was something — else? And nothing remains?

AGNETE    What do you mean?

HEINRICH    A house with two sisters. The elder one was my fiancée. Has the whole house gone?

AGNETE    There are strangers living there now — long since.

HEINRICH    What would they have thought of me if I had turned up unexpectedly after years, asking for Lena? How I would have stared at them if I had been turned away with the words: we don't know if she is alive or dead. That was my intention — just to turn up. But then I thought better of it and sent a telegram. To Lena. Who opened the telegram?

AGNETE *hesitates.*    Stefan — or Stefan's mother.

HEINRICH    Then they showed it to you?

AGNETE    Yes — I got a shock.

HEINRICH    They should have kept it from you.

AGNETE    Why — keep it from me?

HEINRICH    Then no one could have asked them to bring me here — and make it all too clear to me what I'd lost. *He sinks into an easy-chair and buries his face in his hands.*

AGNETE *taken aback, looks down at him in silence.*

HEINRICH *looking up at her.*    That is not a reproach. Forgive me, if that is how it sounded. I would rather have remained missing, presumed dead, and have lived in hope for the rest of my life — and even endured those shattered dreams more patiently — if my memory had not been so cruelly awakened. To see you standing there — someone life has granted — in the midst of the mad destruction — what it might have given back to me — my heart's desire — life with Lena. How it all started, and abruptly ended —— *he stares blankly.*

AGNETE    Lena died with your name on her lips.

HEINRICH    It was her name I must have whispered a thousand times at death's door, and conjuring it up prevented me from dying. Then she came — through crackling frost and driving snow — and I was healed. *Bursts out.* She should not have come with the promise of life, only to flee again!

AGNETE *feeling her way.*    Did she flee?

HEINRICH    Into eternal silence — silent as the mountains around her grave.

AGNETE    She is at rest there, Heinrich. Amid the glories of the earth. The same earth that bears us too. There is little to divide the living from the dead. We should hold their memory dear and never let go. They want to live on, so we must too. I lost my sister. I thought I could never have feelings again for another living person. It was as if I were frozen. I returned from her grave to the empty house — *With rising passion.* — and I can only explain what finally happened then as a sort of inspiration: I was not meant to give up — it was a mercy I was led first through the darkest labyrinth, with no end in sight, but which suddenly cleared and opened up, and I emerged as if liberated from my heart-sick anguish and lonely seclusion, to which I was not meant to succumb. But it is only through suffering that you are shown the way back to other people. Making sense of why you had to suffer gives you that right. Then it is not lying. Then you can live with others.

HEINRICH    You lied?

AGNETE *evasively.*    Everyone here has. Said nothing — and lied — to you, Heinrich. We had to. Our tongues were tied — we could never have spoken. Who could have given us the right to speak when that would have been life-threatening?

HEINRICH    Does anyone know when their life is threatened, Agnete?

AGNETE    When someone appears at the last minute — as it were, out of the fog that had so far enveloped them. And it was the last minute, terrifyingly so.

HEINRICH    You found Stefan.

AGNETE    Stefan was the one.

HEINRICH    When will the fog clear for me?

AGNETE *respects his silence.*

HEINRICH ———— So you got married soon after you were left alone?

AGNETE   Yes, soon.

HEINRICH   ———— Was the child born soon after?

AGNETE   Within the first year.

HEINRICH *to himself.*   It could have happened — in the same year — and now it would be ———— *Pulling himself together.* Who does it look like?

AGNETE *quickly.*   Stefan, I'm sure.

HEINRICH *alarmed.*   Stefan? — Is there not a danger it might have the same eye complaint?

AGNETE *happily.*   No — its eyes are sharp and strong and shining.

HEINRICH   ———— You've taken it away. So that it's not here as long as I am here.

AGNETE   It's so boisterous, it would take up all my time. I wanted to be there for you.

HEINRICH *rises and walks up and down. Then goes to her.*   I'm afraid of this child, Agnete. You mustn't show it to me. I must never run into it in the house — in the garden. Laughing — romping around — it would turn my blood cold. For it is not mine — and yet, if the hammer blow of fate had not struck and snuffed out the torch, newly lit, it might have been ——. You cannot understand. But you must see that the sight of this child — because it is her sister's child — horrifies me. Let that suffice — and let me implore you: even though separation from your child is a great sacrifice — bear it. For my sake! *He takes her hands and holds them clasped within his.*

AGNETE *softly.*   It is not the greatest one.

HEINRICH   Have you made greater ones?

AGNETE *looks him full in the face.*   No, Heinrich —— it was no sacrifice.

# ACT TWO

*Morning.*
*The French windows on to the terrace are wide open. The awning raised, so that sunlight floods the room.*
*Frau M. is sitting meditatively in a corner of the sofa.*
*Stefan is selecting books from the bookshelves, reading the titles through a magnifying glass.*

STEFAN *after a pause.*   Why don't you go on ahead? It will take me a little longer to find the volume. You can already be sitting in the garden. The air and the sunlight will refresh you.

FRAU M. *does not move.*

STEFAN *noticing.*   Are you worried about something, mother?

FRAU M.   Yes, Stefan — I am worried.

STEFAN *puts down book and magnifying glass and goes to the sofa.*   What is it?

FRAU M.   Heinrich's behaviour.

STEFAN *silence. Then.*   He is a silent — invisible house guest.

FRAU M. *sighs.*   Every time I see him, I'm shocked. Night thoughts seem to be haunting him more and more, and he can't shake them off in the course of the day. His eyes are sunken, as if —— *She pauses.*

STEFAN   He's not sleeping. He paces around his room above — Agnete has already moved into the nursery so she doesn't have to hear the incessant sound of his footsteps.

FRAU M.   Our old order of things has been disturbed. It will only return when Heinrich's attitude changes.

STEFAN   What could change it? His grief is overwhelming — and nothing has been able to distract him. Our every attempt failed. No conversation that caught his attention was ever completed — in the middle of a sentence he would break off and steadfastly remain silent, then shut himself off in his room.

FRAU M.   With his thoughts elsewhere. ————

STEFAN   The way he was when he returned from town recently.

FRAU M.   Trembling, white as a sheet.

STEFAN   He was scared stiff. We were walking through the streets. Suddenly he must have remembered something that literally stunned him. He had my arm to guide me and was shaking it and then he gasped out: *Turn around — turn around at once — let's go home — there are ghosts here — quick, Stefan — run!* I didn't know you could be so terrified.

FRAU M.   Since then he hasn't once left the house.

STEFAN   There was no persuading him. ————

FRAU M.   Now he even avoids the garden. Doesn't look at the flowers or breathe in the fresh morning air. Surely everyone has a right to his share in the abiding glories of nature. Duty dictates that we help him overcome his fears as he tries to find his way. We must not stop trying. We would be failing in our duty if we did not try to reclaim Heinrich for life, every morning afresh and more resolutely than the one before.

STEFAN   I'll go up and try and persuade him to sit outside with us. I'll say it will make us happy if he will. We want to keep him close, now that he has so almost miraculously been returned to us. We are eager and impatient. That's what I shall tell him. He won't be able to refuse. — Is Agnete coming soon?

FRAU M. *rising.*   It depends when she leaves the child. She rushes off at dawn — and comes and goes. It's unpredictable. — So both of you come then. I'll move the chair into the sun for Heinrich. *Exit through French windows.*

*Stefan returns to the bookshelves and replaces the books he had taken out. Then goes to door, left, and opens it.*
*Heinrich enters.*

STEFAN *surprised.* I was just coming to you — mother wanted to ask you something ——. But now you are here, that is no longer necessary. Let's go to her at once. She is reading for me. What would you like to listen to? Plutarch, maybe? The depiction of great destinies — both illustrious and notorious. Is it not amazing that things fixed in time past reach out into the continuous present? We participate in what is dead and gone as if the present had brought it forth. Does man change so little? Is that a defect or an advantage? Let's talk about it. Outside?

HEINRICH *has gone to the right and closed the French windows.*

STEFAN Are you closing the windows because you want to stay here?

HEINRICH Yes, Stefan.

STEFAN Mother expects you in the garden. I promised her I would bring you. She's happy every time she can make sure you are not just a delusion that she has dreamt up. She wakes up worrying — then sees you — and the worry is gone. Don't leave her worrying. Come and sit with us.

HEINRICH *sits down in an armchair beside the fireplace and remains silent.*

STEFAN She's concerned about you. I am too. And Agnete. We cannot let you shut yourself away — not from the light and warmth of such a glorious spring morning — an almost unheard-of run of fine days. That is surely not without significance. It holds out a promise. It's meant for you. To encourage you. Let yourself go. Put your dark brooding behind you, a bright and colourful world awaits. A radiance — one you can perceive more fully than is granted to me.

HEINRICH *shakes his head.*

STEFAN Not here. The sun cannot surge through here. You even close the windows, so its healing rays cannot penetrate. Healing every breast that suffers but still wants to be cured. Just as your blood keeps pounding, though it seems to turn cold and freeze in your veins. Yours too, Heinrich. The momentum is unstoppable: to become once more part of the great, moving pageant of life. Are you not already here ? Have you not escaped the darkest depths — and will you not soon see a new radiant dawn?

HEINRICH I came — to talk to you.

STEFAN *struck by his matter-of-fact tone — sits down in the armchair facing him.* Talk about what, Heinrich?

HEINRICH    I want to finish it.

STEFAN    Finish — what?

HEINRICH    With what you call — *Makes a vague gesture.* I've stopped calling it that long since. How can you give such a name to a condition so totally alien to everything known as life ——

STEFAN *in a hushed warning.*    Heinrich —!

HEINRICH *looking up.*    It's come to that, Stefan. Believe me, I'm no coward. But there are defeats one does not recover from. Visible — invisible — and the invisible ones are perhaps the bloodiest. I've fought on, covered in wounds, and did not die.

STEFAN    Remember that!

HEINRICH    That. And everything else. It's not a decision I've rushed into — like jumping from a bridge because there is a rushing river below — and if it were not for river and bridge one wouldn't have jumped. I've come to it from a quite different angle. I refuse to be taken unawares. I've already decided how it is to be done. —— First I calculated. Added and subtracted — multiplied. Like at school. It came out as a minus, Stefan.

STEFAN    You'll find there's a mistake in your calculation.

HEINRICH    What mistake? Am I enchanted by being back home? Does my heart leap at the sight of every desecration that —

STEFAN    Things will improve here, too. Are you not a guarantee of that? Your survival?

HEINRICH    Survived again. Then survived some more. There's always that consolation — *Bursts out.* Then finally it was only a lie that had survived — at the cost of a misunderstanding — that, too, one had to survive — until everything was in a whirl and there was no knowing what was true and what false. Oblivion, extinction is the only escape.

STEFAN    It was a lie that rescued you.

HEINRICH    Stefan — I know I would not be sitting here otherwise. In such a case a lie is not a lie — but, otherwise, it is. Or, say, not a lie but a white lie. A white lie is not a lie — That is eminently reasonable and indisputable. Except, I get a headache thinking about it. *He presses his hands to his temples.*

STEFAN    Lack of sleep means you are not thinking straight. Words have a depth of meaning which they lose if they are merely reeled off. We give them meaning. We are words.

HEINRICH    And deeds?

STEFAN *After much thought.*    Your deed — my word: together, do they not make a whole?

HEINRICH    Neither is complete. Both easily wounded, imperfect. So even less blame attaches to a deed that seals off once and for all whatever gap exists between life and death. Then no more life — or no more death? What has become of me then — wise Stefan?

STEFAN    Death is not life — life is not death. That is the only wisdom.

HEINRICH    You are fortunate, Stefan. You have an answer to everything. It's good to say one's last words to a very happy man. Something like joie de vivre rubs off — and one dies more easily. I thank you. It is the greatest service a friend could render. *He stretches out his hand.*

STEFAN    I take it only to hold you back.

HEINRICH    In that you will not succeed, though in much else. What you are confronting here is irrevocable. My resolve is absolute — and was from the start — the moment you said the word — on the platform, after that ludicrous misunderstanding had been cleared up. I couldn't see her face under the big hat. —

STEFAN    Can't you shake off these harrowing images that torment you?

HEINRICH    I want to — that's why I'm taking leave of this life. It's the only way. They are all I can see — I can't suppress them. They are totally overpowering. Because they are so glorious. Because my most glorious experiences were with her!

STEFAN    You loved Lena.

HEINRICH   Love — Stefan — love ——

STEFAN   Because it remained only a betrothal — and was destined to be an eternal betrothal — you refuse to call it a perfect love.

HEINRICH *smiles inscrutably.*   Destined to be an eternal betrothal ——

STEFAN   Of all your afflictions, the most unbearable: unrealizable hopes. ——

————

*Silence.*

STEFAN *again forceful and resolute.*   You see, I can follow you — into the realm of grief you were forced to inhabit. Almost to the end of the dark path you pursued — driven by wild, tormenting visions your memory conjured up from bloodless wraiths. But even you do not reach the end. There is still a final step you cannot take. No more than a step, perhaps — but still too far. You cannot take it. The law of life dictates, compels one to turn back, not to take the ultimate step. It compels you, too!

HEINRICH *places his hands across his chest.*   I do not hear the call.

STEFAN   It does not come from within. You cannot persuade yourself. I am charged — by the power of friendship and our mutual dependence, one upon another — to lead you back from the edge of the precipice, from death's awful embrace, into the sunlit uplands of life.

HEINRICH   And what do I see there?

STEFAN   Other people. Not the crowds — you are still tormented by the noise of milling crowds. Let them pass — do not become part of the stream, not yet. You have every right to rest. Do so — and you will see life opening up again all around you. Learn to hope again. Hope is life. And love, love for the living, that can be yours again.

HEINRICH *sinks his head.*   If only ————

STEFAN   It must, Heinrich. The black cloud is already dissolving — you can see the possibility of a happy return. Someone will be there — someone waiting for you. Someone who does not know when you will come, yet is already full of it. A bond is already being woven between you in anticipation. Don't sever it and create more suffering.

HEINRICH *looks up.* Even if I wanted — if I had the willpower to break down the numbness that terrible blow inflicted —

STEFAN What's stopping you ?

HEINRICH I must not.

STEFAN *taken aback, remains silent.*

HEINRICH I must not, Stefan. Something is stopping me, a feeling of guilt. There is something I must answer for, all I can do is wipe it out. In the manner I described. A life for a life. Atonement.

STEFAN And you feel guilty of — what?

HEINRICH I caused Lena's death

STEFAN *starts back in his chair.*

HEINRICH Yes, yes — I have blood on my hands, I am a murderer. I have robbed another human being of life and what makes life worth living. What else do you call someone who summons a person to her doom in order to escape alive himself?

STEFAN How can you come to that conclusion?

HEINRICH Is it so hard to understand?

STEFAN Unfathomable.

HEINRICH You decide, then, if your judgement would be different from mine. —— When I was lying in the hospital with fever — I called out for Lena, feverishly. Only she could save me from my stricken state. I implored the doctor — for he heard my feverish appeals — to demand that she come. My insistence on seeing her must have sounded so horrifying — as the doctor described it — that she did indeed set off — although it was a long and terrible journey. Martyrdom for an already ailing body. She ignored her suffering and brought me nothing but her whole being in all its richness — and I did not die. — — Just think, it was winter. Harsher than any we know here. An east wind howling in from the steppes, whipping up the snow — and Lena facing its icy blasts. Lena, who should be convalescing. Who coughs and feels the cold terribly and is constantly at risk even if exposed to the evening air. She needed to look after herself and take things easy — as your mother told me. *Emphatically.* Then she would have nipped the first signs of her illness in the bud. And I prevented that. By my wild entreaties for her to come! ———— Her life-force soon gave out, her light all but extinguished by the icy storms. It flickered on a little, weeks only, then she descended into the dark. ———— The dark you want to reclaim me from — into which I banished her. May I, then — tell me — may I who caused that to happen — dance on her grave?!

STEFAN *ever more absorbed in what he has been hearing, now rises from the armchair and steps back.*

HEINRICH    Now you stand up. Now you walk away. Now even you shudder! — Yes, Stefan, you can be a murderer without hiding behind a bush and throttling your victim with your bare hands. There are other ways — but they are also tantamount to murder. Sometimes there are mitigating circumstances. In my case, as I acknowledge — negligence. Granted. But towards whom? Towards the very person who should have been able to depend upon me more than anyone to protect her — me, who would sooner die — a slow and painful or a sudden death — rather than endanger her. I did it — I committed murder — I pass sentence on myself.

STEFAN *paces up and down — controlling his emotion with difficulty.*

HEINRICH    I'm going away. Today. Into the mountains. To the cemetery there. On her grave I'll — see it through. —— *Takes a letter from his pocket.* This letter gives you power of disposal over whatever is mine. It's all yours. Keep it or give it away as you think fit. My signature has been witnessed — it won't present any difficulties. I'm nonetheless grateful to you. Don't say anything. Take it. *Has risen and makes to give Stefan the letter.*

STEFAN *claps his hands behind his back. Then after a pause and visible effort.* You must not give me this letter.

HEINRICH    Why may I not give it to you?

STEFAN    Because — it makes me a murderer if I accept it.

HEINRICH    Who would you be murdering?

STEFAN    You.

HEINRICH *drops his hand holding the letter and looks enquiringly at Stefan.*

STEFAN *fights down the final obstacle holding him back from speaking. From the French windows, through which he had been peering into the sunlit garden — as if seeking advice from there — he returns to the middle of the room. More as if to himself.* I have a right to speak out — and ignore a promise I made, since it would be dangerous to remain silent. We hadn't thought of that — that silence could be guilty of threatening a human life. *Looks up.* You think the reason life debars you from any kind of happiness is because you demanded a sacrifice from Lena to which she then succumbed —— but Lena did not make that sacrifice. — ——— When you cried out for help, as you put it — when in the delirium of fever your doctor — a good doctor, he must have been — heard what alone might prevent your condition worsening: namely, the presence of the person so repeatedly invoked — well, she was no longer capable of taking even the first step of the journey. Lena was no longer alive. She was lying surrounded by mountains and as cold as the snow on their peaks. —— Was that something you could be told? Should the doctor have been informed, and bury you under an avalanche of words — cold and hard, from the mouth of a stranger. —— A blighted hope, implacably cruel, yes, but should not a familiar voice break the news in more compassionate, gentler tones? —— A messenger was found — Lena's sister. It was Agnete who was to tell you of Lena's death. —————— When she found you — clinging to life by no more than a thread that the slightest tremor would have torn — let alone the grim news that would have been like an earthquake — the messenger withheld her deadly tidings and told you Lena was alive. ——— — That was all Agnete told us initially. That she had kept silent. When we asked her what excuse she had given for Lena's absence — all she said was that she had managed to calm the patient. The main thing was that he should believe Lena was alive. And proof that he did so believe was his renewed courage to go on living — that was what it was vital to sustain. And he was told nothing — until now. —— Finally, Agnete did admit something she had never mentioned before. She probably only recalled the details after you had got in touch. Apparently you did not recognize her at the time — and, for you, she was Lena. —————— It was so important to her that that illusion should never be shattered that she made us swear — in a formal oath! — never to reveal it —— and to invent another date, weeks later, as the day Lena died — since you had such a clear recollection of the day Lena came to you. After all, you mentioned it in every letter you wrote. ————— In order not to flout Agnete's will, mother deceived you about the date. She attributed the mistake to you — you had got it wrong when you were still in a state of delirium — but the date engraved on the stone would not lie. You would read it — and know that she was already at rest, that her soul had already made its final journey. —— But it was not you who had caused her death — other powers were at work — you are innocent. —————— So, why did Agnete want to keep this secret? —— What she wanted was surely to create an image of her sister as a shining example — someone who, though at death's door, struggles through blizzards and across the icy steppes to find you, and when she does, saves you, only to succumb herself, having sacrificed herself for love. ———— That is a beautiful image to retain in one's mind. But you want to die. So I was obliged to erase it. ———— You cannot blame Agnete. This lie caused Agnete much distress. It threw her into a state of utter confusion when she learned you were coming. But the fact that you could come back at all — that you owe to her and her alone. So her deception is excusable. —————— Can you not forgive her?

HEINRICH *who has not interrupted Stefan with a single sound — a single breath — continues staring at him as if spellbound and turned to stone. He remains silent.*

STEFAN    Will you not go to Agnete and tell her: I understand everything. Even if the truth still hurts — she is forgiven; for now I can live again. Will you not lift the load that is weighing her down? For her sake?

HEINRICH *remains silent and motionless.*

STEFAN    Do it for my sake, then. She is my wife.

HEINRICH *Sighs deeply.*

STEFAN    Shall I tell her that all is now clear? — That you found out and do not condemn her?

HEINRICH *groans.*    You don't know — what you are saying.

STEFAN *looks at him enquiringly.*

HEINRICH *begins to pace up rapidly and down.*

STEFAN *watching him.*    Is it so distressing? — Would you have preferred to depart with the beautiful image intact — rather than stay here, disillusioned?

HEINRICH *halts — passes a hand over brow and temples.*

STEFAN    How can the truth so transform you?

HEINRICH *almost hastily.*    Am I transformed?

STEFAN    First you are flushed, then you turn pale — I've never seen the like of it.

HEINRICH   It's so close in here. Can air be close?

STEFAN   In a figurative sense, certainly.

HEINRICH *hand on throat — stammers.*   In a figurative sense ——

STEFAN   Can you laugh about it?

HEINRICH   I'm laughing — no, I certainly can't laugh — but then I do laugh. But no, I mustn't!

STEFAN   Something's going on —

HEINRICH   One thing is going on! *He grips Stefan's arm.*

STEFAN   What is it?

HEINRICH   I want to keep that beautiful image in my mind!

STEFAN *happily.*   In order to live?

HEINRICH   In order — not to kill!

STEFAN   Who?

HEINRICH   You, Stefan!

STEFAN *shrugs in a gesture of incomprehension.*

HEINRICH   And there must be silence — shackled with seven seals. Woe to anyone raising more questions or indulging in loose talk. I mean it, Stefan! You have told me nothing — you will never disclose to anyone that you've revealed the secret. Promise me that — and I promise you I'll go on living till my ancient lungs breathe their last!

STEFAN   Your life is the important thing.

HEINRICH   Important, Stefan, important? In this situation no one knows what is important. You don't know — so how can I know?

STEFAN   Come to the garden — Plutarch shall teach us both.

HEINRICH    No, Stefan, send me your mother in from the garden. She might be able to teach me — someone must —

STEFAN    Plutarch!

HEINRICH    Your mother, Stefan. I must hear it from a mother —

STEFAN    She will come, Heinrich. Later the two of you come out to me.

HEINRICH    Later —— later —— later ————

*Exit Stefan through French windows.*
*Heinrich's gaze follows him as if he were an apparition. He does not change his stance until Frau M. enters.*
*Enter Frau M. hurriedly, right.*

FRAU M.    Stefan tells me that — to my great joy — you were very animated when you finished your talk. Almost unrecognizable, he said, as if given a new lease of life. Stefan is delighted. I don't know what you talked about — only that he welcomed the effect it had. But you wanted to see me —

HEINRICH *does not move.*

FRAU M. *closes the French windows and goes over to Heinrich.*    You were under a spell that made you lose all interest in life, but I knew that one day the spell would be broken. That day has arrived, Heinrich. It's no sacrilege to say, in advance: praise be. The darkness has lifted, there is no concealing it. *Stops short.* You don't say a word. Yet you sent for me — why did you send for me, Heinrich?

HEINRICH *puts his hand on her arm and leads her to the leather sofa. He sits down in an easy-chair. Softly.*    Was that Stefan who just left?

FRAU M.    Stefan, who you were talking to —

HEINRICH    That really was him, in the flesh?

FRAU M.    Of course it was Stefan. How could there be any doubt?

HEINRICH    What certainty can there be — when everything is questionable? A misunderstanding can turn a person into someone quite different.

FRAU M. *anxiously.*    Did your talk tire you?

HEINRICH *looking up.* Talk? — So it did happen — it wasn't just a ghost. Spectral figures come and go. Figures ———— *He stares blankly.*

FRAU M. Was it so unusual, what you were talking about?

HEINRICH *again addressing her.* Is it normal to talk about murder?

FRAU M. Good Heavens, Heinrich. What murder?

HEINRICH One that almost happened — that was prevented at the last minute.

FRAU M. When? Who was to be murdered?

HEINRICH Me.

FRAU M. Who — but it's senseless even to ask — who planned it?

HEINRICH You did — and Stefan stopped it happening.

FRAU M. Heinrich!

HEINRICH *breathing heavily.* Yes — he revealed all. I forced him to break his oath. Because I had condemned myself — for the wrong reason — and he had to prevent me carrying it out. I did not need to follow Lena's example, whose death I had allegedly brought about. On the steppes, in the snow and the ice — that Lena had never been exposed to! — It was Stefan, wasn't it, who came and told me everything?

FRAU M. *remains speechless.*

HEINRICH Or will you now try to persuade me that what happened today — praise be! — happened yesterday, or can only happen tomorrow for it can't have happened today?

FRAU M. Heinrich, please say no more!

HEINRICH Say no more — say no more —— Why should I say no more? —— How can I say no more? Did I not summon you to sit here while I speak? Who should I — blab to? Stefan?

FRAU M. Don't put it into words, even now!

HEINRICH  That would be tantamount to strangling me, and I've only just been saved — from suicide a moment ago, and back then from succumbing to a burning fever and delirium! — Is it really true I didn't cause Lena's death? If I did, I'd hide in the nearest thicket and blow my brains out — or rather my guilty soul out of its body — then it, at least, would be as pure as the earth itself. — I didn't entice anyone to face the deadly terrors of the steppes?

FRAU M. *calmly.*   No one can reproach you.

HEINRICH   If I hold out my hand — will you take it, is it unsullied?

FRAU M. *takes it.*   Unblemished.

HEINRICH   Absolved — cleansed — all behind me. —— Released from the dungeon. Into the pure morning air. I can breathe — like a bird beating its wings! *Paces up and down in long steps.*

FRAU M. *after watching him for some time in silence — emphatically — resolutely.* Today is the day you finally recovered, Heinrich. Now you have a new lease on life, you must seek it out and live it to the full.

HEINRICH *absorbed in his pacing.*   Seek it out — seek it out. And where does it lie, that island where things happen in the ocean of time? The only oasis in a desert sea? *He returns to the easy-chair and sits hunched and brooding.* One thing I come back to again and again — and it takes the shape of a long, low manor house, and a snowstorm howling around it, one winter night that knows no end. A snowstorm on a winter night. —— I don't recall any daytime — it was not the light of day that streamed in, transfiguring the night like sunrise upon sunrise. —— It was from the night itself that life came forth. If you seek life, seek the night, and woe to you if the night rejects you — if the room remains shrouded in darkness — if a door does not open: and from the threshold a cry ring out, a promise of salvation —— someone bestowing favour —— *Fervently.* Agnete! —————————

FRAU M. *startled — then composed.*   You mustn't say her name like that.

HEINRICH *looks up.*   Why not? — Was it not Agnete?

FRAU M.   It was Agnete.

HEINRICH   And this time nothing can drive her away?

FRAU M.    Nothing.

HEINRICH *rises again — leans against the mantelpiece for support.*    Must one not then interpret these signs — when nature brings together two of her creatures in such a miraculous way? Must one not act without delay and follow the tangled paths that all lead — somewhere. Where is that — somewhere? Is it — *Gazes around* — here? *To Frau M.* Can it be here?

FRAU M. *apprehensively.*    What does that question mean, Heinrich?

HEINRICH    Was I still asking questions?

FRAU M.    You were asking me.

HEINRICH    I was only expressing amazement: that nothing had changed here — that the roof hadn't lifted off — the walls hadn't collapsed — overwhelmed by some gigantic primordial power. — Questions — where the answers are known in advance? Echoes before you make a sound? — Aren't they proof of unshakeable validity? Evidence — that stands the test of time? Better than any documents?

FRAU M.    Evidence of what, Heinrich?

HEINRICH    Of my marriage to Agnete!

FRAU M. *raises her hands as if fending off a blow.*    No!

HEINRICH *pays no attention.*    A great unbroken arch stretches from there to here. One end there, touching the earth, the other here. A rainbow bridge you can cross, secure, high above countries and blood-stained fields and smoke and —ruins. And cross it I did — sanctioned and spared by destiny. Since a dead woman cannot walk, it sent a living one. Too many died, but their dying breaths breathed life into her. Life! — What right transcends the right to life?

FRAU M.    Don't create confusion, Heinrich!

HEINRICH    I'm shedding light on what has been obscured. My claim is based on more than any written agreement. From the most desolate solitude, from the perils of war and the injuries it inflicted, I finally emerged into daylight as if from a pit polluted with bestial creatures and noxious gases. And I see, with rapture, what I thought I would never see again: a face bending over mine — a face I could not distinguish from another, for to do so would have spelt my doom — ah, the wisdom of Providence! — So what call now for delay?

FRAU M.   You must not claim Agnete!

HEINRICH   Must not?

FRAU M.   Not from Stefan. Stefan's love for Agnete has brought him an indispensable happiness. He needs it like birds need to fly. Deprived of that, they drag their wings feebly along the ground. If you want to cripple what is best in Stefan — what is perhaps unique, then — *She stops.*

HEINRICH   But Stefan can look back on so many years of happiness and fulfilment, while I only caught a glimpse of happiness before it disappeared again. He has drunk his fill — I scarcely took a sip.

FRAU M.   Stefan suffers too.

HEINRICH   What does he suffer from?

FRAU M.   He suffers too — even if he does not feel it or know why.

HEINRICH   Then it's a mild form of suffering. And does the pain not wear off? What other thorn in the flesh remains — when he sees his child?

FRAU M. *remains silent.*

HEINRICH   His own flesh and blood — does that not extinguish any pain that might still oppress him?

FRAU M. *sits as if exhausted.*

HEINRICH *has been pacing up and down. Now he quickly returns to Frau M.*   I'm not in a position to say anything to Stefan. I am a guest in this house — a guest does not upset the domestic peace. I would be guilty of ungratefulness. I do not want to put asunder what — others — have joined together. Who arranged it? Was it not your will that brought them together? Did you not speak highly of your achievement — as soon as I arrived? I remember — just as I can always remember if people do not deliberately sow confusion.

FRAU M. *sighs.*

HEINRICH    It was not an achievement to be proud of. Premature. You should have been more patient. Providence had prepared a better plan. Now you must arrange for it to come about. Stefan should give up his claim — on your instruction, which he has already followed once. When he courted Agnete. Was he not obedient?

FRAU M. *shakes her head.*

HEINRICH    Did you not send him to Agnete?

FRAU M.    I arranged nothing — and can undo nothing either. It was Agnete who came and asked for Stefan.

HEINRICH *astonished.*    Another lie?

FRAU M.    The lie that gave rise to all the others — that Agnete needed to find a home for her child.

HEINRICH *goes rigid.*

FRAU M.    ————— Is it now your wish that I should —— disclose Agnete's lie?

HEINRICH *falteringly.*    If that is the truth ——

FRAU M.    Which I discovered when she removed the child from the house before you arrived — to prevent her becoming even more confused.

HEINRICH    The child ——

FRAU M. *firmly.*    Does it not call for your silence? Since everything that is being done is being done for the sake of the child, which is flourishing?

HEINRICH *dazed.*    Where —— is the child?

FRAU M. *carefully.*    Not here.

HEINRICH    Not here —— Then where?

FRAU M.    It's being looked after by acquaintances of Agnete.

HEINRICH    Acquaintances —— Close acquaintances?

FRAU M.   Would one entrust it to them otherwise?

HEINRICH   Close acquaintances ——

FRAU M.   Agnete is there most of the time herself.

HEINRICH *lost in thought.*   Agnete could stay with him —— she should not come here any more ————

FRAU M. *in suspense, pays close attention to his words — rises from sofa.*   I will go to Agnete. Is that what you want me to tell her?

HEINRICH *still preoccupied.*   But I would need to know —— where I ————

FRAU M.   Think things through while I'm with Agnete and the child.

HEINRICH   I've already thought things through ————

FRAU M.   Then I'll go at once. *Exit, left, making as little noise as possible.*

*Heinrich pays no attention to Frau M.'s departure. He stands motionless a few moments longer — then sits down in a corner of the sofa and, almost mechanically, takes the letter from his pocket, slowly tears it into ever smaller pieces, which he first piles up on the little metal table — then stuffs into his pocket. — Then, as decisions form in his mind, he raises his head with a jerk — looks around — jumps up — quickly goes to the French windows, which he shuts. He takes rapid steps to the sliding door to rear — opens it and enters the study — sits down at the desk — searches for paper and pen, and begins to write.*

*Enter Agnete, left. She smooths her hair and notices the open door to rear — sees Heinrich. Not wanting to draw attention to herself, she crosses the room to the French windows. She carefully presses down the handle — the windows remain shut. She tries again, rattles more firmly: the panes of glass clink a little.*
*Heinrich raises his head and looks at Agnete.*
*Agnete holds his gaze, somewhat embarrassed. Heinrich crumples up the piece of paper on which he was writing and puts it in his pocket. Then he emerges from the study, closing the sliding door behind him.*

AGNETE   I didn't want to disturb you — you looked so busy, writing. The French windows wouldn't open — they must be locked from outside. I'll go out round the house. *Makes to leave, left.*

HEINRICH *very calmly.* The key here has been turned.

AGNETE   You've locked yourself in to be sure you wouldn't be disturbed — and I come running in and rattling the glass. Don't be angry. Please go on writing.

HEINRICH   This letter can only be finished later. I couldn't finish it here while Stefan — *He breaks off.*

AGNETE *surprised.* Where is Stefan? Isn't he in the garden?

HEINRICH   He's sitting under the lime-trees. He loves the shade there. The broad leaves ward off the light when it's too glaring. Like too many sharp arrows.

AGNETE   Has this letter got something to do with Stefan?

HEINRICH   Most of it.

AGNETE   Why most of it?

HEINRICH   Because it's to him.

AGNETE *smiling.* You sit here writing a letter to Stefan, while he sits outside?

HEINRICH   I wanted to say goodbye.

AGNETE   You're — leaving?

HEINRICH   I've made up my mind — to travel.

AGNETE   And you don't want to tell him — in person?

HEINRICH   Perhaps one should —

AGNETE   You must. He would be most distressed if you left just like that. Stefan is very attached to you. We all have to make allowances for Stefan. We mustn't hurt Stefan.

HEINRICH   Let me speak out then —— and block off that escape route. My plan was to flee, Agnete.

AGNETE   You wanted to flee? Flee — from this house? From the town and its surroundings, full of memories but now empty?

HEINRICH   The plan was much more far-reaching. I wanted to flee into a boundless, silent realm, one that bids you welcome — even after an act of violence. You open the gate — and silence closes round you. No more accusations — no more blame. You have paid the penalty — by condemning yourself!

AGNETE   I wish I could understand —

HEINRICH   You could get Stefan to explain it to you — he demonstrated to me most eloquently how mistaken my initial plan was. He was adept at providing proof and weakening my resolve. Stefan gave no thought to the consequences — for himself.

AGNETE   What is it Stefan could explain —— without thinking of the consequences?

HEINRICH   How, without knowing it, and with an innocence I find staggering, he gave up the right to — possess you.

AGNETE *recoils.*

HEINRICH *behind an armchair.*   It's a strange tale — do you want to hear it? Like so many things that had their roots in the war — some dreadful, some miraculous — it all began in the thick of it, with battles raging all around. And with scorching heat erupting from a hellish hotbed of fever — breathe that in, and you were soon in a stupor, hovering between life and death, with everything in the balance — what way would the scales tip? Now one way, now the other, the darkness prevailing or the light, day after gruelling day, a wild desire vying with hopeless exhaustion. Life or death, which would it be? —— And it happened — just as the decision could be put off no longer — that another nameless presence added its weight, and the scales came down triumphantly on the side of life — until night was put to flight and a new living day dawned. ———————

AGNETE *forcing a smile.*   So that's what happened?

HEINRICH *smiling.*   What happened, Agnete?

AGNETE   Nothing, Heinrich.

HEINRICH   Nothing, Agnete, nothing. Nothing that matters. All blown away by the winds of time, swallowed up in the eternal flux and nothing to say it had ever been. All trace buried in the desert sands. As I was too, cocooned and ignorant of the caravan path that leads us through the desert, home from our ceaseless, desolate wanderings — Was I not on the wrong track, in need of rescue — a child leading me by the hand and bid welcome by a child's voice? —— Does my child not expect me, Agnete?

AGNETE *as if paralysed.*   Who told you that?

HEINRICH   Stefan's mother — she had no choice. It was inevitable she could hold nothing back. Stefan had already revealed too much — the weapon was in my hand and aimed at my heart — to stop it beating, just as I had stopped Lena's beating — when, ill as she was, she made her pilgrimage to me, and never recovered from it. I wanted to settle my debt — but there was no debt. Stefan had exonerated me — and what he said seemed to fill the room with flocks of wild birds, and the beating of their wings blocked out any other words. —— And I told him to send me his mother as the only one who could calm the pounding of my blood — and allow me to put my demands into words: namely, that she release you, extricate you — for me — just as she had once bound you to him. And that exposed the lie that had only just been concocted. It had not been arranged by her — and she could not dissolve it. It was you, Agnete, you who had willed it and brought it about. ————

AGNETE *hoarsely.*   I had no will, Heinrich. — Had I had the choice, I would not have flinched from looking death in the face. But I could not drag down another life with me.

HEINRICH   Do you need any justification?

AGNETE   Before whom? Who will demand that?

HEINRICH   No one shall reproach you. Here I stand to vouch for that.

AGNETE *falteringly.*   Then — Stefan should be told?

HEINRICH   How can I justify taking you from him?

AGNETE   For the sake of the child —?

HEINRICH   More than that, Agnete — for your sake! *He has come close to her and attempts to draw her gaze.*

AGNETE *slowly fastens her gaze on him. Hesitantly.* For my sake? *With the utmost modesty.* Do you love me then?

HEINRICH Agnete!

AGNETE You have only loved me since today. That is not very long.

HEINRICH Have you loved me longer?

AGNETE How could I not have loved you always?

HEINRICH *gazes at her intently.* The sound of your voice!

AGNETE To think you could forget it after once hearing it.

HEINRICH It penetrated the very depths of my soul — and there it lay until it was reawakened today.

AGNETE Aren't you at all disappointed?

HEINRICH Why should I be disappointed?

AGNETE I was afraid that —— *She falters.*

HEINRICH What made you afraid?

AGNETE *without ceasing to smile.* Everything, Heinrich. I was afraid from the very start. I was afraid until a moment ago.

HEINRICH When did it start?

AGNETE As I was rushing to bring you the message, when you were almost at your wits' end. You had uttered a cry for help — can such a thing go unheard? Inconceivable — no such empty space exists. Someone will hear it and run out of the house and follow the sound of such a cry. I ran, Heinrich, I ran as fast as was in my power to run. I ran with your image before my eyes. That blotted out the other world, with all its clamour and talk and faces. To all of that I was deaf and blind. But within, I could see a thousandfold. I could see you — your face tense with anticipation — your lips pale and bloodless from too much crying out. And to this image I spoke: I'm on my way, Heinrich. Do not lose heart or stop longing, for I'm drawing ever nearer. Fighting against savage winds and black snow — dense and impenetrable as the night — but I shall not tire. I shall not be too tired when I reach my goal. That I promise. — So many words of love I sent on ahead to you, you could not but love me when I arrived.

HEINRICH *in wonderment.* The voice I heard — like some constant, mysterious singing in my head — it was your voice?

AGNETE I knew you were listening. I knew you would not let me call out in vain. For I, too, was calling for help. I needed protecting — from loneliness, and the terrible howling of wolves. I was alone in an alien land — some of the rivers had no bridges and uprooted trees blocked the paths through the forests. And I saw war. — I fled, and forgot the message I was bringing. It had left my mind, all I could think of was finding refuge — and I rushed to your arms, that opened to receive me.

HEINRICH And I was so thrilled, I sank into an enchanted daze.

AGNETE And it was night — a night of muffled whispers.

HEINRICH Then morning — and in even more of a daze I asked the nurse — Why did you flee?

AGNETE *softly.* I had deceived you, Heinrich. I knew I loved you —— but if you could love me, I've only just asked you.

HEINRICH Are you pretending you — forced me to?

AGNETE I deceived you —— I did not want to give up the deception. ———
——— *Continues to smile the same smile.* But you pay a penalty for deception. Soon I had worries enough. First it was a wonderful surprise. Only gradually did I realize I would have to protect what I had conceived. I would need to find a safe refuge for the treasure in my womb. Could you provide it? You were so far away — and far from knowing the truth. The truth would certainly have killed you. It only becomes bearable when it is spoken. As I speak now. As you stand before me. Is it bearable now?

HEINRICH More than that. It buoys me up, higher and higher.

AGNETE Then, you might have despised me. You might have pitied me. Or protested vehemently and demanded proof. Proof that I could not give you in writing. It was all very complicated. I didn't know what to do. But then cunning takes over. I had already outwitted you, why could I not ensnare Stefan as well?

I did ensnare Stefan — and the child was born under this roof. There was no more uncertainty surrounding it.

HEINRICH    I could not have protected it then.

AGNETE    Nor could you protect me from the fear that you might return.

HEINRICH    Was I meant to die in action?

AGNETE    You were only meant never to know that —— *She looks at him.*

HEINRICH    Not know what, Agnete?

AGNETE    — that when I saw you again — I could only love you again, as I always have loved only you.

HEINRICH    Why should I never know that?

AGNETE    Because I would be hurt if you didn't love me.

HEINRICH    Too little — never enough!

AGNETE    You must love me! *She wraps her arms around his neck and kisses him on the mouth. — Then nestles her head against his chest.* Now I have found my refuge. Journey's end. A journey though all those years — and a fog of lies that never lifted. Now you are here — and love me. No need to hide behind lies — only the truth is beautiful. A glorious sunrise over the world. Is it our world?

HEINRICH *steps back — excited.*    The world, Agnete, the world — is a great ship, sinking. It was no match for the rocks — it ran against them, its bow ripped open, smashed to pieces. A boat is lowered from the wreck and pushes out through the crashing breakers — thrashing around madly in the foaming spray — and yet — — *He breaks off and draws Agnete beside him on the sofa, holding both her hands tightly.* How to escape? With wife and child?

AGNETE    Did you not want to flee?

HEINRICH    My mind was set on flight. I had already made arrangements. I wrote to Stefan. My demand was clear and based on the past. What happened later was a misunderstanding. This time he was on the receiving end. No one can escape the turbulence of the times unscathed. One must be steadfast — and endure suffering. As I had suffered! — Now I claimed my rights and would have asserted them against all objections — against you too, Agnete!

AGNETE    Did you want to abduct me?

HEINRICH    You and the child. My mind was set on abduction. I was already planning the whole adventure — how to entice you into a waiting carriage, then leaving it to the driver — whom I'd bribed — to whisk us off somewhere. While I smothered your cries — I would have smothered them with kisses.

AGNETE    And I would have cried out, Heinrich — for kisses!

HEINRICH    Now I don't need to waylay you.

AGNETE    And I've already kissed you.

HEINRICH *strokes her hands.*    Agnete! — Now Stefan's mother can ——— *He smiles mischievously.*

AGNETE    What about Stefan's mother?

HEINRICH    She guessed what I was thinking — after she told me everything. It must have been all too easy to read the effect it had in my face. My brain was already feverishly at work forging plans, involving violence. At that point she crept out — to forestall me. To warn you against getting into a coach with me, waiting to disappear round the corner.

AGNETE    I'm sure she would have tricked me into not showing myself any more.

HEINRICH    She's an expert at trickery. But finally her own tongue betrayed her. She had to confess everything! — Now she's too late coming. You're here. Did you not run into her as she stormed off through the streets — to save what still could be saved?

AGNETE    I came back into town along the ramparts.

HEINRICH    The old town wall — my secret place!

AGNETE    Where we used to play. The embankments and ditches like hills and valleys — and the tremendous fun you could have in the moat!

HEINRICH *subdued.*    And now my son is romping there too — in my footsteps, the cycle begins again, even better —— what reason to be disconsolate? — *Again animated.* I'll talk to Stefan. I've dismissed all thought of abduction. I won't steal out of the house leaving only a letter of explanation. Didn't you take the decision yourself? You weren't overpowered —— forced to flee?

AGNETE    I wanted to go with you.

HEINRICH    Then there is nothing wrong with it. He cannot oppose it — I did not use force. Has he any right to hold you back?

AGNETE    How could he want to — if you ask him for me?

HEINRICH    More than anything that might move him into letting you go would be for you to ask him. That's all he needs hear — he needn't know any more. He'll never know what drew us together from the very beginning. Just ask. Say you want to leave him and follow me. Can love not grow wildly, out of nowhere — like a sudden shaft of light?

AGNETE    You ask him, Heinrich. You say that.

HEINRICH    How easy it is to speak when there is only one thing that needs saying. I'm not afraid to speak to Stefan any more! ————

AGNETE    And then we go away? — Far away?

HEINRICH *has risen.*    Far away from here, Agnete.

AGNETE    Where?

HEINRICH    A different continent, one that will not bring back so many memories. Others have gone ahead — I was to follow. There was an old letter — I read it just now as I was going through the things I had to settle. There are two brothers. One stayed behind on his estate — the other emigrated to Chile and invites me to join him. There is work there — work I would enjoy — a new start and a new life. If it appeals, his brother can tell me exactly where he is and how he is faring. — Shall I ask him?

AGNETE    We didn't have a honeymoon last time either.

HEINRICH   It mustn't be postponed any longer. Seas and shores I shall show you, as unknown to us as happiness has been. — Will you stay here? Or come with me? I must make that telephone call. I'll do it in town.

AGNETE   You go and make enquiries.

HEINRICH   If this is to be our goal, then let us take the plunge. The sooner, the better. *Exit quickly, left.*

*Agnete sits as if lost in reverie.*

*Stefan appears behind the French windows — tries without success to open them. Only by knocking on the glass can he attract Agnete's attention.*
*Agnete rises and — clearly uninvolved in all she does and says — goes to the French windows and turns the key.*

STEFAN *entering.*   When did you get back?

AGNETE *in a peculiarly impassive voice.*   Just now.

STEFAN   Did you not meet mother?

AGNETE   No.

STEFAN   Nor Heinrich?

AGNETE   No.

STEFAN   Then you must have thought we had gone, when you didn't hear any voices from the garden — and locked up?

AGNETE   Yes.

STEFAN   There's a different explanation for why I was alone in the garden. Listen, Agnete, this will hearten you as well. I do believe that this morning has seen the most welcome change. Heinrich is no longer the same person who wouldn't listen or talk to us here yesterday. After the conversation I had with him, he wanted to see Mother. Now they have both gone off — it helps to say what has to be said walking in the fresh air. And since it began so promisingly, Mother didn't even tell me before setting off, so as not to endanger Heinrich's full recovery. Is that not wonderful, Agnete?

AGNETE   Everything is wonderful.

STEFAN   And with serious consequences too, Agnete. Just think: Heinrich has been relieved of his sadness — and with it, his over-sensitiveness. The child would no longer disturb him. The happiness it spreads would even help him. It would be easier for him to laugh with the child, since it is not as inhibited as we are. Isn't that reason enough for you to bring back the child?

AGNETE *who clearly did not follow what Stefan said, continues to muse on something else.*

STEFAN *likewise remains silent and listens in the direction of the door, left. — Now with animation.*   You must think about it. It would be to everyone's advantage if the child returned. — That must be Mother on the phone. She will be longing to give me the news. I've must go. *Exit left.*

*Agnete — as if obeying some inner compulsion — goes to the chest in which she had locked away the photograph. She opens the chest and takes it out.*
*Enter Stefan, slowly.*

STEFAN *crest-fallen.*   Mother is not with Heinrich. She is alone with the child. And she is not leaving the child — until everything has been cleared up. ——
What does she mean? —— She says she is staying to protect it —— Do you understand that? —— *Noticing the photograph in her hands.* You were going to put up the photograph already? —— Is it not too soon? ———————

AGNETE *clasps the photograph tight to her breast and smiles inscrutably.*

# ACT THREE

~

*The afternoon of the same day.*
*The sliding door to the rear is open. Stefan is sitting at the desk, arranging things before starting work again.*
*He takes books and papers from the drawers and spreads them over the desk.*
*Enter Heinrich, left. On seeing Stefan, he carefully shuts the door. Then he goes behind an armchair and gazes at Stefan.*

STEFAN *putting down the magnifying glass he uses for reading, looks around.*   Is anyone there?

HEINRICH *approaching the sliding door.*   When I came in I was astonished to see you at your desk. That's the first time I've seen you there since I've been here.

STEFAN   You're not disturbing me. Come in. I haven't started work again yet. I'm just getting ready. I need my secretary before I can start. Fräulein Feustel is particularly suited for the post. She becomes completely absorbed in someone else's thinking. I'm constantly aware of how dedicated she is. It amounts to self-sacrifice, and that makes me happy. Can anyone render a greater service ? To us, or to a project?

HEINRICH *remains on the threshold.*   If the project is worthy of the sacrifice.

STEFAN *smiles.*   You think me presumptuous? It may sound like that, but don't expect me to apologize and demand less service and less sacrifice. It's fully justified. *Almost mysteriously.* As will be shown as soon as I am able to give voice to what is still an echo in my mind. For that there are certain requisites, and these are not lacking. *Again openly.* Above all Fräulein Feustel, who is as instrumental as my right hand.

HEINRICH   Are you expecting her — today already?

STEFAN   She should arrive this evening. I sent her a telegram. So the work that was interrupted can begin again first thing tomorrow.

HEINRICH   Why was it interrupted?

STEFAN *evasively.*   I gave Fräulein Feustel leave. She went to her brother's and will come back rested and refreshed after her stay in the country. — Wouldn't you like to spend some time in the garden before it gets chilly? It would be rash to leave it any later — you've hardly been out in the air since you arrived. Be careful, Heinrich, take it easy until you've gradually built up your resistance. Won't you go?

HEINRICH   Can we have a talk, Stefan.

STEFAN   Now?

HEINRICH   Yes. It can't be put off.

STEFAN   Then there is nothing more important. I'll come over. *He rises — comes out of the study and slides the door closed.*

HEINRICH *steps back against the fireplace.*

STEFAN *sits down in an armchair. After a pause.*   Is there still something we didn't discuss this morning?

HEINRICH *hesitates.*   After our talk I spoke with your mother.

STEFAN   I know. I sent her in. Afterwards she left the house at once and hasn't been back.

HEINRICH   Isn't that odd?

STEFAN   Not after her telephone call, when I had put the right construction on what she proposed to do. She is anxious about the child, she sees it too little, and she pictures the mental and physical damage it might suffer if she doesn't protect it. Actually, she wants to protect herself against her own anxieties. It's in the blood, Heinrich, that feeling. It flows from generation to generation. We all experience it and have to deal with it. —— Do you see things any differently?

HEINRICH   There was another conversation.

STEFAN   Which you had?

HEINRICH   Yes, Stefan.

STEFAN   Then it was with Agnete.

HEINRICH   You haven't see Agnete since?

STEFAN   She's locked herself in the child's room upstairs and was not to be disturbed as she wanted to sleep.

HEINRICH   She's keeping out of sight.

STEFAN   If that's on account of your talk together — then I know what you talked about.

HEINRICH *smiles.*   You can guess?

STEFAN   It can only be the one thing: that you told her what you had heard from me — before some question came up that forced her to confess of her own accord. Is that it?

HEINRICH   That and —

STEFAN   Nothing else. Shame — at the extent of her lies — and the exhaustion that sets in when a danger is past and the worst is over — that's what caused the state she's in — one she hasn't come to terms with yet. She wants to be left alone. And to sleep. A dreamless sleep she will wake from feeling liberated and relieved of her earlier anxieties. She will restore everything here to the way it was before.

HEINRICH   Are you certain?

STEFAN   I feel sure. After I told you the whole truth, I knew instinctively that what we had to keep obscure — to create this fog of evasion, though with the best intentions — would all become clear again. That what had become distorted like shadows — where the trivial appears hugely important, and what is important becomes insignificant — would regain its true character, and we would be able to breathe again and life would open up before us once more. For that is the reality — that we can now talk about what is past without trembling. We speak of it, and it is erased. How important words sometimes are, however much they are disparaged. We can put our trust in the future. As I did today when I got ready to start work again. I could not resist the impulse. Is that not a sign that I can have high hopes of finishing it — with help at hand to lend the utmost support? ————

HEINRICH *after a pause.*   You are lulling yourself into a false sense of security, Stefan. Things will not return to how they were before.

STEFAN *looks up at him enquiringly.*

HEINRICH    You say Agnete will restore everything to the way it was. — Agnete will merely make things more complicated than before.

STEFAN    What do you mean? More complicated?

HEINRICH    She's been here until now.

STEFAN    She still is.

HEINRICH    Now she too will leave.

STEFAN    To go where?

HEINRICH    Where I plan to start a new life.

STEFAN    Agnete wants to go with you?

HEINRICH    She and I have decided — it's settled.

STEFAN *remains silent. He sits somewhat hunched and with eyes cast down.*

HEINRICH    —————— Would you like me to explain? —— How that can happen in a single day? From a first exchange of words in the morning to a mutual understanding and decision to leave before evening?

STEFAN *shaking his head.*    It didn't just happen in one day.

HEINRICH *taken aback.*    Earlier, then —? How could that be, Stefan?

STEFAN    The knot had been tied earlier, Heinrich, without your knowledge.

HEINRICH    When, earlier?

STEFAN    When you were lying in the field hospital, and Agnete visited you.

HEINRICH    But I've only just learnt that. At the time, I made no distinction.

STEFAN    But you learnt today that it was Agnete who had undertaken the arduous journey to find you.

HEINRICH   That was graphically depicted — by you, and your mother.

STEFAN   And would not our depiction have roused your passion?

HEINRICH *with a sigh of relief.*   Yes — your depiction made me see things more clearly.

STEFAN   And so you now saw Agnete in a more passionate light. Do you not owe your very presence here to her? You could not but be shaken when you learnt the full truth. The person who reminded you of all that had been — yet who also pointed the way to the future. You could not resist the temptation. Nor could a stronger person have resisted — someone with greater respect for friendship. —— And so you wooed Agnete. I'm not offended, nor angry. You could do no other. —— *Pause.* Does Agnete love you very much?

HEINRICH   Would she follow me otherwise?

STEFAN   Her decision is not so deeply rooted in the past as yours. Hers is not an empty life — the empty life that you recoil from. She has a home here. She possesses a great deal — I mean, in human terms — that she will have to give up. —— And that all decided in a matter of hours?

HEINRICH   It was inevitable from the start, Stefan!

STEFAN   Was she driven by a feeling of guilt towards you? That she must live out the dream she had conjured up: that she must become Lena, as she had once claimed to be. Was that her motivation?

HEINRICH   It's too late for brooding and disputing.

STEFAN *looking up.*   She must love you. *Very calmly.* One cannot defy that law. One must face the truth. When feeling compels, one has no choice but to obey. Only those who lie are punished, and unsparingly. Agnete cannot lie. When she came to me, she was — lonely. She was in need of protection. That I could provide. That made me very happy. Only someone who has reconciled himself to a life of renunciation can be happy, Heinrich — in the broadest sense of the word. As I had. I was already far removed from life — and she called me back. It was a kindness she bestowed upon me. I've never thought of it as anything else. And I have learnt to be even more grateful: for a gift from her that opened up a whole inner world for me, as if it were a secret, hidden key. ———— Should I hold her back? When it is you who stir her senses? She must feel such a wave of happiness, her blood must be pounding so joyfully, that this one day — that

began like any other — has undone all that had seemed unshakably secure. ——
I foresaw this might happen. One cannot keep both. Not when the one thing is
so absolutely imperative — then one must be prepared to sacrifice. Have no
qualms about accepting this sacrifice. Do not pity me. *He leans back in the
armchair and lapses into silence.*

HEINRICH *watches him with rapt attention.*

STEFAN *after a pause, beginning afresh.*    Where are you taking Agnete? *When
Heinrich does not answer.* You have not yet been able to decide where?

HEINRICH *with self-control.*    That has also been decided.

STEFAN    Are you keeping it from me? Why?

HEINRICH    We are going to Chile.

STEFAN    Are there better opportunities for you there?

HEINRICH    The only ones, Stefan. I must make a fresh start. Here I am
confronted at every turn with wreckage. Like whole forests uprooted in a storm.
Obstacles I cannot surmount. I cannot shift them — I must fill these lungs with
good sea air before I set foot ashore again and use my new-found strength.

STEFAN    Will you find work that fulfils you?

HEINRICH    If I seize the opportunity I've been offered, I'll be active, in the
saddle, from sun-up to sundown. It's no sinecure — you have to earn your wages,
though my taskmaster is a good friend. I rang his brother today — he's staying
behind here — and he advised me to set off quickly. There's no shortage of work
in Chile, just the opposite, and anyone willing to pitch in is more than welcome.
Good prospects for me, are they not?

STEFAN    What is the climate like?

HEINRICH    Southern — hot.

STEFAN    Agnete would get used to it?

HEINRICH    Nothing to worry about.

STEFAN    Being with you will build up her resistance.

HEINRICH    She'll be the happiest person alive, Stefan — believe me!

STEFAN    What worries could there be? Think if the child were with her and its strength sapped by the unaccustomed, debilitating climate. It will thrive here — safe and sound under this roof, as ever. You can be sure of that, Heinrich, you and Agnete. ——————

HEINRICH *paces agitatedly up and down in front of the fireplace. Stops behind armchair. The words come with difficulty.*    You spoke forcefully — convincingly — about how sacrifice must extend even to self-sacrifice.

STEFAN *in agreement.*    If the object is a worthy one.

HEINRICH *almost heatedly.*    And if a mother does not want to be separated from her child — is that a worthy object?

STEFAN    The highest. Why do you ask?

HEINRICH    Stefan — Agnete is taking the child!

STEFAN *starts up in his chair.*

HEINRICH *imploringly.*    Stefan — make the sacrifice! — The highest sacrifice, as you called it.

STEFAN    The highest sacrifice, Heinrich — I couldn't make the highest sacrifice if I let the child go.

HEINRICH    What do you mean?

STEFAN    I would be unfaithful to my work. I could no longer carry out what I am wedded to — with priest-like devotion, Heinrich!

HEINRICH    And what is that?

STEFAN    That is a question I struggle to answer. Once, in a vain quest, without direction, I went astray — in a stony, desolate wilderness. Think of it like this: I was climbing ever higher, along the topmost mountain tracks, among boulders and scree, where the air is thin and you are left gasping for breath. And you go on, for it gets even higher, you go on only because there is something higher still than what you have already attained. You feel more and more giddy, all clarity gone — and pale as a sheet you stagger towards the edge of the chasm you would finally plunge into, smashing your brains out at the bottom of the void.

HEINRICH   The void opened up?

STEFAN   I already felt its icy blast from the murky depths below as I approached — searching like a blind man, a man possessed, an obsessive researcher confronting the unknown, the unknowable, staggering over yawning crevasses to the edge of the abyss —— When a voice called out to me. It was not like the loud warning that pulls you up short, and you are saved. It was only a weak sound — yet it made my blood race more than any cry. It was a child calling. Calling me. And I heard it. For it was my child.

HEINRICH *presses his clenched fists to his lips.*

STEFAN   I heard the voice of my own blood, Heinrich. It wanted to speak out and it spoke with a different tongue, but it was my tongue too. So I could understand. And I greedily opened my ears to the new sound. It was a command, an exhortation, reminding me that I had a child: to put an end to the arid sifting of desert sand, and to look to how the life of the mind must engage with being fully human. And that is what I have done — embarked on the path towards real being. But I would have lost my way again were it not for the encouragement of the child, leading me on like a guide with an inextinguishable torch — towards the ultimate goal, one that tolerates no weakening — that demands rigorous, unflagging dedication — life itself!

HEINRICH *heatedly.*   Does life need that kind of — revelation?

STEFAN   Yes, Heinrich. Error flares up all around us, engulfs us. We must safeguard life and cherish it.

HEINRICH   Are you sure you are not mistaken?

STEFAN   How can I be mistaken?

HEINRICH   If what you are building on is not, after all, a fundamental error!

STEFAN   When it is life itself that I feel, how can I be in error?

HEINRICH   Do you feel it so intensely?

STEFAN   I have a son.

HEINRICH *remains silent.*

STEFAN   You cast doubt on this feeling, but I can substantiate it. And why shouldn't you doubt? It is something you have never experienced.

HEINRICH   Stefan — Stefan, you can never prove it!

STEFAN   Conclusively — and you will be convinced. When you arrived the child was taken away. Lest it distress you. Agnete insisted. Her mind was made up, and we submitted. Mother and I. With the child gone, the house was dead. As if the very air I breathe had been sucked out of the door with it. My mind was blank. My goal obscured. Without my little guide. I stopped working and dismissed Fräulein Feustel — that was the reason I gave her time off. —— Is that not proof that what the child means to me — and my obligation to it — are so tightly intertwined that only a sword could cut the knot? And then blood would flow, life turn to death — the void that we should turn our back on while we can. ————

HEINRICH *maintaining self-control with difficulty.*   Deny Agnete, then. You are within your rights to do so. — But let me appeal to you: give me the child.

STEFAN *astonished.*   Deny the mother, yet submit to you?

HEINRICH   I beg you. Don't turn me down.

STEFAN   What fervour! Has Agnete driven you to this?

HEINRICH   I needed no prompting from Agnete.

STEFAN   You demand the child of your own free will?

HEINRICH   I do, Stefan. I am resolved.

STEFAN *rising from the armchair.*   You?

HEINRICH   Don't ask and don't resist.

STEFAN   So you are —?

HEINRICH   What, Stefan?

STEFAN   You are the enemy I must fight?

HEINRICH   You want to fight over —?

STEFAN *emphatically.*   My son!

HEINRICH *suppressing a loud exclamation.*   Your son —————!

STEFAN *with a calm gesture.*   I have explained what I am defending. To give him up is to give up life itself. So I must defend myself. We must fight a duel, Heinrich. Perhaps you still doubt whether my feeling is genuine. Put it to the test. Words did not suffice. Let us fight for the child.

HEINRICH   With what weapons?

STEFAN   The weapons men use to resolve a feud. The best place will be between those deserted towers on the ramparts. We won't be disturbed there. We shall exchange shots until one of us falls.

HEINRICH *stammers.*   It would be — tantamount to murder.

STEFAN   Shall I not be armed too? Let me fire the first shot.

HEINRICH   You can scarcely see far enough to ——

STEFAN   I issued the challenge. Are you refusing to take it up? You, an officer!

HEINRICH   — Stefan — if you knew the truth ——

STEFAN   It shall be determined by weapons. The decision must be conclusive. Whether life awards me custody of my son, or rejects my claim as unjustified.

HEINRICH   Not by weapons ——

STEFAN   By weapons, Heinrich. I could not convince you any other way. Now blood shall seal the judgement. — Will you see to the weapons? — Good. — Then I shall fetch the child.

HEINRICH   Why fetch the child now?

STEFAN   It must be given over to the victor at once.

HEINRICH   You want it to ——?

STEFAN   Lead me out through the garden. A cab will take me there and back. Don't forget what you must do. The affair must be settled today. *He goes ahead of Heinrich to the right — opens the French windows — exit.*

HEINRICH *follows him. Exit.*

*Agnete — in a loose, light-blue dress with stole — enters, left. Her far-away expression has been replaced by a flickering anxiety. She moves around more quickly, though for the moment aimlessly. Then she stands still, passing a hand over her forehead as if to dispel disturbing thoughts. Finally her attention is arrested as she looks though the open French windows. She sighs and steps aside. Heinrich returns, right, his head sunk, his hands pressed to his temples so that he does not see Agnete. He moves quickly to the left, as if pursued.*

AGNETE *suppressed exclamation.*   Heinrich!

HEINRICH *lets go of door handle — turns quickly.* Agnete! *He goes to her.*   I was about to wake you. *Gazes at her.* Were you wakened by the —. *Dismayed.* You look upset.

AGNETE   By a dream I had to shake off — that weighed on me so oppressively I was numb and hadn't the strength to resist while I was still asleep.

HEINRICH   Was it such a vivid dream?

AGNETE   Am I not still dreaming?

HEINRICH   How can you be when you are talking to me?

AGNETE   In my dream I saw you walk past me — as you did just now when you came in and didn't see me.

HEINRICH   I had my hands almost covering my eyes — how could I see you straight away?

AGNETE   Why did you cover your eyes, Heinrich — so you could not see me?

HEINRICH   Why are you so impassioned, Agnete?

AGNETE   I'm still shaken by my dream. It spilled over into reality and makes my head swim. Yes, it's you standing in front of me — and you who came from afar in my dream and didn't see me and only looked up and stopped when I cried out. It was my own cry that woke me, and I had to repeat it, just as loudly and urgently at the last minute, otherwise you would have been irretrievably swallowed up in — the void.

HEINRICH   Was I not coming to find you? That's why I wasn't looking.

AGNETE   Not in the dream. In the dream I had to cry out before it noticed me. *Explaining.* The child. For you were also the child.

HEINRICH   Did your dream mix up the two?

AGNETE   Yes — at a distance it was the little child. As it came nearer, it grew to your size and finally it had your face too, but your face was also its face, there was only one person. And I had to watch my own grown-up child walking past me as if I were a stranger. That's when I cried out. Did you hear it?

HEINRICH   It echoed to the bottom of my heart! Let us sit down and talk. *He shuts the French windows, leads Agnete to the sofa, and pulls up an easy-chair for himself.* Let's examine your dream and interpret it. It might well be that we would not otherwise discover what destiny has in store for us.

AGNETE   Don't you know, Heinrich?

HEINRICH   I was so sure of it all day long — this wonderful day — that I left one thing to the last, after all the preparations: my talk with Stefan.

AGNETE   And now you have had it?

HEINRICH   As clear as could be — quite unequivocal.

AGNETE   He understood you and me? That we love each other?

HEINRICH   He produced elaborate theories to account for how it had happened. And when he had explained it to his own satisfaction, he even counted it a blessing that you had been with him such a generous span of years. He was deeply grateful and rose far above the pain of losing you. You have to admire that, Agnete.

AGNETE   I am grateful, too. If only I can find the right words to tell him so.

HEINRICH   But will he listen?

AGNETE   Why would he not listen?

HEINRICH *stares blankly.*

AGNETE   Has Stefan left the house? Is he not coming back as long as we are here?

HEINRICH   I took him to find a cab. He's going to bring back the child.

AGNETE   Is that what you arranged?

HEINRICH   More than that: that we should go to the ramparts and fight for the child. Whoever falls —— *Looking up.* Who will fall?

AGNETE   Fight for the child?

HEINRICH   That was his horrifying proposal. He wants to go face to face with pistols, half blind though he is, and wait for me to shoot after he has shot in the air. I would be his murderer — and after the murder we rob him of his child!

AGNETE *instinctively objecting.*   It is not his child!

HEINRICH   Will you tell him?

AGNETE   To save his life!

HEINRICH   Except that it would totally destroy him if he were to learn the truth. He would still find some way to take his own life. Is the duel he insists we fight not proof enough that he no longer wants to live?

AGNETE   How can he feel so passionately about the child?

HEINRICH   He feels there is some mysterious bond between them. When he talks, you are powerless to interrupt and destroy the illusion. I couldn't say a word. I do believe the roof would have collapsed on top of me and blacked out the whole world in a cloud of mortar and dust. There would never have been radiant light again. It is not just his life that would be destroyed, it is what he alone can see in his mind's eye, his luminous, sacred, visionary goal. ——————

AGNETE   He must live — for the sake of his work.

HEINRICH    If he is to continue his life-enhancing work, he must not be haunted by the chill of death. And that's what would haunt him without the child's warm laughter carrying through — *He looks towards the study door* — to where he sits immersed in his task, totally engaged, straining every nerve to finish it. How does he go about it? What are those puzzles it is his task to solve? Will he ever be free of the obligation put upon him? Can he step out of the magic circle before he has plumbed its mysteries — mysteries we sense will fulfil us and empower us all? — Have we any right to put obstacles in Stefan's way? ——————

AGNETE *in astonishment.*    You mean to submit, then? You've resigned yourself?

HEINRICH *has risen, agitated, and paces up and down.*    I don't want to be a murderer. I don't want to kill Stefan. I want to repay him in equal measure for what he did for me. He held me back when I was on the edge, he told me the truth — shall I repay him with a lie? I shall say nothing. It is his child. He must not be deprived of it. It must always be here — and help Stefan. Otherwise he will lose his way and all those who look to him for guidance will be led astray — into an empty, stony wilderness ——————

AGNETE    —— We leave it behind?

HEINRICH *going to her — taking her hands in his.*    Agnete — you must get over it, I must get over it. I am paying off my debt to Stefan, for I owe it to his goodness that I am still alive, that he didn't allow me to put an end to it all. — What an easy solution that would have been for him — nor would he have ever had to lose you. —— *Becoming more animated.* You too, Agnete, pay off your debt. Put an end to the guilt that is weighing you down, too.

AGNETE    Guilt ——

HEINRICH    When you presented him with the child. It wasn't his, yet you let him take it to his heart as if it were his own flesh and blood, the miraculous manifestation of his will! — Can you deny it?

AGNETE    After giving him so much — can I still be guilty?

HEINRICH    Not any more. Provided you don't take anything back. It's too late for that. You can't rob him, snuff out the light the child brought and leave him in darkness. We must make the sacrifice — or we won't deserve what awaits us.

AGNETE    And what is that — that demands such a sacrifice?

HEINRICH   The future — our future. That's all that matters, Agnete. We bid farewell to sadness, unfurl the sails, and straight away the wind catches them, billows them out, and we're off — no looking back, as the land disappears under the horizon, for ever. Forget it all, Agnete — can you forget?

AGNETE   If that's what it takes — to live.

HEINRICH   Perhaps we must keep our eyes tight shut. Or look only at each other, unceasingly. Then from the depths of our souls there will arise an island — and we are saved from the shipwreck, escape the raging torrents that try to drag us down, and put ashore, victorious! Look at me, Agnete. What can separate us again — what can threaten us?

AGNETE *looks up at him.*

HEINRICH   It was a long, tortuous road and we've come much too far for us not to see where it was leading. Do you see it any differently?

AGNETE *remains silent.*

HEINRICH   What are you thinking?

AGNETE *very softly.*   The child ————

HEINRICH *stares at her.*

AGNETE *almost timidly.*   I conceived the child —————

HEINRICH *remains frozen.*

AGNETE *as if spellbound.*   Was it too far — for me to conceive it with you?

HEINRICH *shakes her gently.*   Are you dreaming, Agnete? A new dream? Let it pass. We still haven't interpreted the old one. I think I understand it now. It's comforting. You saw me in the distance, and it was the child. But as I came closer I grew, and all my gestures and facial expressions were unmistakably those of Heinrich. I was pressing my temples, just as I was when I came in here in reality. In both cases you called out to me as I passed by, and I stopped as if I had been expecting it — this sudden cry. In the dream and in reality. Did your cry not bring me up short, as it went on and on? Its passionate urgency — was it not directed at me?

AGNETE   You?

HEINRICH   Who else?

AGNETE   You, yes — but not just you. The child, too.

HEINRICH   It was still far off — I was coming closer. It was me you recognized.

AGNETE   You looked like the child.

HEINRICH   Am I so similar?

AGNETE *smiles.*   If I look at you closely, and let my gaze stretch away into the future — I can see no difference.

HEINRICH   You don't know who it was you called out to?!

AGNETE   I don't know — yet. —————————

HEINRICH *steps back and looks around uncertainly. His gaze falls on the French windows.*   Stefan! —— Stefan is back! —— He doesn't have the child!

AGNETE *has risen and also looks out through the French windows.*   —— Why has Stefan come back?

HEINRICH   He's stopped. Something must have occurred to him — something very important, for him to turn and go away. —— Can you still see him? He's disappeared into the shadow of the trees.

AGNETE   Gone to fetch the child?

HEINRICH   I don't know, Agnete. But one thing I realized when I saw him approaching.

AGNETE   What?

HEINRICH   If he had been leading the child by the hand — I would have rushed out and seized it away from him. I would have forgotten everything I swore and my heart would have opened up — like a crater under enormous pressure. And the lava of my words would have choked him, killed him stone dead. And I would have taken the child and stepped over his body and gone off to wherever there are no people to recognize me. Doesn't the murderer go into hiding with his booty?

AGNETE *resisting.* The child must never be exposed to such turmoil.

HEINRICH That's what I want to protect it from. I must never see the child. The warning was all too clear — Stefan appearing by himself in the garden — it was meant to stop me acting, as I would have — instinctively. Now every step I must take is preordained. You tell him, tell him I've already decided the outcome of the duel. You did not want your child to be fought over. Is it mine? He's in the dark about so much, he could only wonder why I was defending a right you had already relinquished. Will you tell him that?

AGNETE That you had already left — so as not to see the child?

HEINRICH I want to keep my promise inviolable. By fleeing temptation. And flight it is, Agnete. Flight brooks no delay. We must flee this very instant. No more putting it off. Are you ready?

AGNETE I must kiss the child first.

HEINRICH Kiss it in my name, too. But hurry. —— What are you thinking?

AGNETE Might I be denied this kiss?

HEINRICH Who could forbid it?

AGNETE Why did Stefan turn back again?

HEINRICH He has gone to fetch the child now. As is fitting. Am I not giving way to him? Providence has decreed!

AGNETE *inscrutably.* But if she remains implacable?

HEINRICH Who?

AGNETE I could not leave without this kiss. —————

HEINRICH *in consternation.* Agnete —— are you wavering?

AGNETE Heinrich — hope and believe I shall be acquitted! *She turns towards the French windows.*

HEINRICH   By whom?

AGNETE *lost in thought.*   By ——

HEINRICH *following her gaze.*   By Stefan?

AGNETE *as if feeling a sudden chill.*   He's come alone.

HEINRICH *with a surge of anger.*   Stefan, whom I reprieved — whom I could destroy with a single word ——?

AGNETE *softly.*   Not Stefan.

HEINRICH   Then who, Agnete?

AGNETE *murmers.*   Who —?

HEINRICH   Who is the judge? Who is condemning — who is acquitting?

AGNETE *stares blankly.*

HEINRICH   I don't want to meet him here. There's nothing more to quarrel about or to settle. What can separate us now? What unknown power? Is there such a power? — Find an answer — I can't. *Exit quickly, left.*

AGNETE *stands transfixed.*

*Enter Stefan, right.*

STEFAN *with feeling.*   Agnete?

AGNETE *looks at him.*

STEFAN   When did you get up? You've been asleep all day long. A deep sleep?

AGNETE   I had deep dreams, Stefan.

STEFAN *tentatively.*   You were expecting me just now?

AGNETE   You —— and the child, since you were going to fetch it.

STEFAN   You know about that?

AGNETE *remains silent.*

STEFAN   Was it Heinrich —? Where is Heinrich?

AGNETE   Not on the ramparts. — Nor will he be. — He doesn't want to kill you — just as you held him back from death.

STEFAN *almost softly.*   That's my reward? — He's leaving me the child?

AGNETE *clearly.*   He's leaving you your child. ————

STEFAN *sits down in an armchair.*   I didn't want to force him to renounce it. I was serious about fighting him. I would have taken good aim. I would have asked him to call out "Here" and shot at the sound. My ear is a reliable guide. I hear targets as sharply as others see them. I would have been at no disadvantage in the duel. I could have won. But he stepped aside and did not load the weapons. — Should he not have acknowledged — since I told him so clearly — that I am a worthy opponent and his match?

AGNETE *sits down in the middle of the sofa.*   Nothing would make him alter his decision.

STEFAN   The deeper reason is that I was forced to insist it was of vital concern, a matter of life and death, and he didn't close his ears to my entreaty. Is that not what prompted him?

AGNETE *in a firm voice.*   There was never any other reason.

STEFAN   Why do you say that with such emphasis?

AGNETE   To give credit to Heinrich, who overcame his —.

STEFAN   Overcame what?

AGNETE *remains silent.*

STEFAN   I know what, Agnete: his instinctive defence of your right — the most basic natural right of a mother to the child she has borne.

AGNETE *draws a deep breath.*

STEFAN   He was fighting for you — and would have followed me to the ramparts and shed his blood. Did the child really mean so much to him that he would give his life to protect it?

AGNETE   He did it — for my sake.

STEFAN   Because he loves you. That was inevitable, even though it was only today he truly saw you. Though it didn't only happen today. It began on that winter night, in that desolate place, when you changed your identity for another's. How could he not but be enthralled, reunited here with the one who links past and present across an abyss of suffering and death?

AGNETE   Yes — that explains it.

STEFAN   In a single day a new life has opened up for you, Agnete. A day that points you in a new direction. You were overwhelmed by his advances — and you did not resist. *In deep thought.* Nor should you resist.

AGNETE   Why did I find resistance impossible?

STEFAN *rises — moves back and forth in front of fireplace — leans against the mantelpiece. Calmly.*   You were never able to love me the way you love Heinrich. You came to me after much deliberation. I can see it in my mind's eye. You hesitated many times before you crossed the threshold — when you could see no other way. Reason prevailed.

AGNETE *sits upright with her palms resting on the sofa.*

STEFAN   You mustn't misunderstand what I am about to say. We won't be exchanging many more words. But let one thing be fixed in your memory, something that has revealed itself to me more clearly now that you love Heinrich: namely, the child.

AGNETE *almost moaning.*   What are you saying, Stefan?

STEFAN   Its mystery, and its mysterious significance for me. When it was born in this house, a charge was laid upon me that I have obeyed ever since. It was that word and deed should no longer be separated, that the unity of creation be consummated, boldly and fully. I understood the direction my work must take, and I pursued it. The work progressed, its conception was indebted to a child. The question was whether that origin was strong enough — whether the work would one day confirm it was through its living embodiment, in its quintessential core. ———— I no longer have any doubts. For if your blood throbs at the thought of Heinrich, it also pulses through the child: the child is flesh of your flesh — it will not destroy the beautiful, audacious living thing that has been created in its image — my work! ——————————

AGNETE *with difficulty.*   Trust the child: it won't disappoint you.

STEFAN *softly.*   I'm grateful to you for loving Heinrich. *More distinctly.* Strange as it may sound — but in a deeper sense — that alone makes sense of what has happened.

AGNETE   Can you explain that?

STEFAN   The birth of this son was predestined — it imposed a duty, not just on me — to add fuel to the sacrificial pyre, that its flames might burn higher than any fire has ever burned. For great sacrifices there have been — and only the heat of the sacrificial fire brings warmth to the world.

AGNETE   What is my sacrifice, Stefan? Whom does it warm?

STEFAN   That is the most unfathomable question. My insight is dimmed. I cannot focus through the fog — it is impenetrable. Blurred by a bad dream.

AGNETE   A dream?

STEFAN   Yes.

AGNETE   What happened in this dream?

STEFAN   It was after I left the house, Agnete. I had to close my eyes in the glare of the sun, and time and space were transformed. Where were we? On a plateau, rising out of a rugged landscape and seemingly inaccessible on all sides, we were received by an assembly of people. We had been expected. Every eye was turned on us. There was a general murmuring that announced our presence to those standing further away. We stepped into the middle of a circle that closed around us. Encircled us — the child and you and me. Then you responded to the feverish frenzy of the crowd — though no one said a word — and lifted the child and held it up for all to see, and they were quiet and awestruck. Then there broke out a tumultuous rejoicing and the rapture was directed at the child. —— But you were suddenly overcome with exhaustion. You lurched and the child fell — fell on the hard ground, and there was a thunderous roar as if the earth had split asunder. The crowd howled and scattered and fled, not stopping at the edge of the plateau, until their flight ended at the bottom of the abyss. —— All around me was empty. I could not see you. Only the child was still there. I knelt down to it. There was no injury to its body — but it was blind. A terrible blow! All my fervent hopes were destroyed: the inherited seeds of promise would never come to fruition, never be fulfilled. ——————

AGNETE *to herself.*   Because I had let go of it ——————

STEFAN *more softly.*   These are dreams we speak of.

AGNETE *shaking her head.*   I haven't yet made my sacrifice ———

STEFAN   Dreams must give way to reality.

AGNETE   But I also had a dream, a bad one — I dreamt he no longer saw me.

STEFAN   Who do you mean?

AGNETE   He walked blindly past me — that's why he was blind —— it was him ————

STEFAN *listens in wonderment.*

AGNETE *looking up.*   Where is the child?

STEFAN   Not far away, Agnete. But — *He stops short.*

AGNETE   Who is reluctant — to leave it with me?

STEFAN   She wants to wait until the most important thing has been decided here — I don't understand why. What is the most important thing?

AGNETE   Did she not tell you, when you turned back again?

STEFAN   What she said was even more mysterious when I told her that the two of us — Heinrich and myself — were about to settle the matter decisively. It cannot be decided between the two of you, she said — the presence of the one who must decide is urgently required.

AGNETE   She won't let me kiss the child?

STEFAN   Why should she shield it from you?

AGNETE   Is she that afraid?

STEFAN   She has a will of iron, I know of none stronger.

AGNETE   She loves you so much?

STEFAN   What do you mean?

AGNETE   She will understand — tell her that I love my child no less — and if it were possible to surpass the extent of her love — I would succeed! ———— Go to her — she's waiting for that message!

STEFAN *hesitates briefly, then leaves.*

AGNETE *stands motionless. Slowly the tension of her stance and gestures, occasioned by her decision, eases. She leans against the arm of a chair as if exhausted. Then she fixes her attention on the door, left, and in anticipation half raises her arms.*

*Heinrich — in a light travelling coat — enters quickly, left.*

AGNETE *goes to him with outstretched arms.*   Heinrich! *She kisses him repeatedly on mouth and cheeks.*

HEINRICH *between her kisses.*   I heard the sound of footsteps on the gravel —— I saw him hurrying through the garden —— was that the final parting?

AGNETE *kisses him again.*

HEINRICH   So let us go. There are dangers lying in wait for us here that could engulf us. A sudden cry, and we could be undone — and who could escape the chaos alive? Take pity on man and child — the quicker we go, the more compassion we show. Let us go!

AGNETE *hangs on his neck, silently.*

HEINRICH   No reaction? Can you not —— *Attentively.* Don't you want to?

AGNETE *remains silent and motionless.*

HEINRICH *profoundly astonished.*   So that wasn't farewell?!

AGNETE *lifts her face to him.*

HEINRICH   Are your tears your answer, is it so terrible that words fail you?

AGNETE *still with difficulty.*   It should not be terrible.

HEINRICH *heatedly.*   You're not coming, Agnete — is it for Stefan's sake?

AGNETE   It's for your child's sake I'm not coming!

HEINRICH   Is it more powerful?

AGNETE   More powerful, Heinrich — for I conceived it with you and presented it to Stefan: and everything now is gloriously complete! I can hold it up for the world to see and my arms do not wilt. Who dares challenge that? You, Heinrich? You, who once gladdened my heart? — Though you did not know it!

HEINRICH   Nor did Stefan know it!

AGNETE *in glowing terms.*   Neither you nor Stefan should lay sole claim to the son that was born. Neither of you. It has been entrusted to me and I shall watch over it. Over your child, for Stefan — Stefan's child, for you. And so the miracle comes to pass! — What guilt is there in that?

HEINRICH *steps back — looks at her.*   If anyone were to accuse you, I would rip out his tongue and choke such blasphemy!

AGNETE *almost crying out.*   Do you absolve me — of deceiving you — and Stefan?

HEINRICH   Let me bear witness by whatever is sacred.

AGNETE   What do you swear by?

HEINRICH   By the first rays of the sun, which shine on you as they set in my new world!

AGNETE   That is the light from your sacrificial flame!

HEINRICH   When was it first kindled? Long ago. The spark that lit this fire flashed from the thunderclouds of war. What can extinguish it? No stormy wind. The flame gives warmth — draw close to it: amid snow and ice we create life and with our bodies we shield its first breaths. *He draws her to him and kisses her mouth. — Then releasing her.* The sun — don't forget — when it becomes visible to you, it has gone from me — but it will come again to me. Will you tell him to hold the sun sacred — it rises victorious over both him and me — does that not unite us in the same victory? — Will you tell him?

AGNETE    I shall tell him of the sun's victory!

HEINRICH *pointing to the French windows.*    It lit up your day. Now, wrapped in its purple victor's mantle, it bids farewell. I shall follow it to a new battlefield and bear witness to its eternal victory! *Exit, left.*

*Agnete — who has also turned towards the French windows — remains motionless. She then moves closer to them.*
*Stefan returns.*

STEFAN    I told her, just as you instructed. It had the most profound effect. Now she could bring you the child, she declared, overcome with joy. It no longer needed her protection, you had removed the dangers that might have threatened it. Were there dangers?

AGNETE *looks past him into the garden.*

STEFAN *after a pause.*    She was quite carried away and gave me reason to build up my hopes quite inordinately. *He hesitates.* That you would not go away —— that Heinrich had left.

AGNETE *draws closer still to the French windows.*

STEFAN *deeply moved.*    It was for the child's sake — I know — that he willed himself to do it. He should not have given way to me. I would have submitted to the law. But he discovered a higher law that reconfigures all rights. Can that law remain hidden any longer?

AGNETE *now stands on the threshold of the French windows.*

STEFAN *peers out.*    There it comes, running into the garden. Do you hear it? You can see it already. I can only hear its footsteps. Your eyes already enfold it. ———— Now I can see its face shining. ———— Is it not wonderful that I cannot distinguish between it and Heinrich? As if it has been transfigured by the greatest power: the power of love? —— Was it a miraculous birth? Is this son no longer my child? Did Heinrich also mould him with his stronger hands? ——

Will it not now be led by the two of us? —— Our son? —— Is anything more radiant with promise? —— Is that promise not already fulfilled?

AGNETE *has sunk to her knees and stretched out her arms in anticipation. With the utmost passion.*    I gave birth to — this son!

*The sun — now a fiery red ball — throws its rays on the kneeling woman, who appears to be bathed in a cloud of sparkling radiance.*

# The Gordian Egg

## (*Das gordische Ei*, 1941)

### A Comedy

# CHARACTERS

Abel Oberon, writer
Marjory, his daughter
Moberly, his publisher
Eileen, Moberly's daughter
Fenton Wing, student
Frank Hunter, student
Tobin, Oberon's butler
Mrs Hittington, landlady


*Time: the present. Place: London*

# ACT ONE

*The drawing-room in the London villa of the famous writer, Abel Oberon. Later, when the electric light is turned on, the bright, spacious room is seen to contain opulent furniture and rugs from many different epochs. There are stone and bronze sculptures, but only one oil painting, hung on the back wall above the fireplace. It is of Abel Oberon himself, life-size, in evening dress, with the sash of an order across his shirt-front. On the wall, left, a short staircase with a Renaissance balustrade leads up to a door likewise decorated with ornate carvings. To the left of the fireplace, a sliding door: on luminous Japanese lacquer, writhing dragons with darting tongues are vividly depicted in gold. Arranged in a semi-circle around the fireplace are various seating arrangements, little tables, cushions. The whole of the back wall consists of three high windows which are also doors, opening on to the terrace and the garden beyond. All three are shut, for it is night, and were it not for the full moon and the dim moonlight permeating the drawn net curtains, nothing of the following scene would be visible. It mostly takes place near the middle French window, where there are armchairs and a sofa, and begins, after a period of complete silence, with a key being cautiously turned in the lock of the French window.*
*It is Abel Oberon, letting himself in to his villa. Dressed in a heavy overcoat and cap, and still holding a suitcase, he emerges from behind the net curtains, holds them apart and beckons to someone outside to enter — but as silently as possible. Enter Marjory Oberon, also in travelling clothes and holding a leather bag. She is hesitant, puzzled.*
*Abel Oberon disappears again behind the net curtain, which has fallen back, so that only his moving shadow can be seen. He bends down as if searching for something on the floor.*

MARJORY *steps close to the curtains and says in a normal voice.*    Are you looking for something?

OBERON's *shadow rises at once and hisses.*    Sh! Keep your voice down. Yes, I'm trying to find the key. It fell on the floor. But speak softly. *The shadow continues its search.*

MARJORY *in a whisper.*    You won't find it. It's too dark. I'll turn on the light. *She turns into the room to look for the light switch.*

OBERON *immediately pops out from behind the net curtain.*   No! No light. Stop.
Don't even try — *Marjory looks at him questioningly.* I've found the key. Here it
is. I'll lock up again. *Before disappearing behind the curtains he turns round again.*
Don't move.

*Marjory stands still, watching the shadow lock the French window.*
*Abel Oberon finally emerges from behind the curtains, but his attitude remains*
*cautious.*

OBERON   The cases — not on the floor — on the chairs — that won't make a
noise. *Stops short, head to one side, listening for a noise from below.* Did you hear
something?

MARJORY   Maybe Tobin has woken up.

OBERON   Did you hear Tobin?

MARJORY   I heard nothing. You said you heard something —

OBERON   Not Tobin. How could you hear Tobin when Tobin is not — *He sighs.*
Let's sit down. I mean — if that's permitted. If I'm justified in inviting you to sit
down.

MARJORY   Who's to stop you?

OBERON   Do you get the impression — that I still live here?

MARJORY   That you live in your own house —?

OBERON   Give me an answer. I'm not sure — that's why I ask. *He sits down on*
*the sofa.*

MARJORY *sinks into an armchair.*   Yes, I have my doubts, too. After what I've
just seen — the way we crept in — through the garden — the cab had to stop
three houses away — we slink along the wall in the shadows — you pull your cap
down over your eyes — it's still there!

OBERON *pulls it off. He has grey hair.*   Did anyone see me?

MARJORY *laughs.*   Are you afraid the police might arrest you for breaking into
your own house?

OBERON   It might looks like that — but it might just be that.

MARJORY   You mean that none of this belongs to you yet? That you have to pinch it all first?

OBERON *nods — gravely.*   And it might be too late for that.

MARJORY *remains silent. Then concerned.*   The trip has tired you out — those little trains rattling along, and the dim lighting. Let's have some light now. Then I'll wake Tobin. He'll run you a bath, and after your bath —

OBERON   Stay where you are — don't try to turn the light on.

MARJORY   There, you've said it again — try? What sort of expression is that?

OBERON   You'll soon see. For the moment, moonlight is all we need to talk by, beaming down from way up there since time immemorial — until judgement is passed: light — or no light.

MARJORY   Shouldn't Tobin run a bath first?

OBERON   Is there still a Tobin?

MARJORY   No Tobin? I'm sure he heard us long ago and is getting dressed. I bet you anything. I'll call for him.

OBERON   First the light — then you might change your mind.

MARJORY *taken aback.*   Is that a warning? What should I expect?

OBERON   No light, no Tobin. More to the point: no house in London. At best, some shack in Scotland. The shack we've just left. How long were we there?

MARJORY   Quite a few months.

OBERON   And winter, to boot. It was winter, wasn't it?

MARJORY   With its raging storms, then deadly hush.

OBERON   Why was Abel Oberon not in Madrid for that festival of his plays? Why was he staying in some Scottish fishing village where it gets dark in the afternoon — and not here in the limelight, with the curtain going up every night in more than a dozen London theatres?

MARJORY   There was no new play of yours in the offing, no rehearsal they needed you to supervise. That was the reason for your trip.

OBERON   The trip around the world that I announced — the trip that finished even before the harbour was in sight. Half-way there, we turned and headed north. Next day: journey's end. And no one picked up the trail and made the world-shattering discovery that Abel Oberon was not circumnavigating the globe — on a luxury liner in a first-class cabin. No, he was in a fisherman's shack where you bang your head on the ceiling and trip over the sunken floor-boards. What did you think I was up to there? Why slink off and keep it a secret where I was, so the Post Office couldn't find out and forward mail? Why give myself a different name so no one could blow my cover? Come on, don't hold back, none of your usual sweet talk when I do things that strike you as odd.

MARJORY   You never do anything that —

OBERON   Oh yes, I do — I'm moody — quickly offended — blame others when it's my fault — I'm irritable — on edge. Especially of late, on edge — *breaking off*. But enough of that. First tell me: why do you think I fled from London? Was it all a mystery?

MARJORY   I think I understood at once — you wanted peace and quiet to be able to work.

OBERON *sighs.*   Work ——

MARJORY   Well, no theatre needed you to be here — not even Burbage, who has sole performance rights — but still, you would never have had a moment's peace in London to get on with your new play. All those invitations! Imagine a reception at Lady X's where she can't introduce you to her guests? — Unthinkable! A sandwich without filling. Name a single event of any importance that you're not invited to. And you can't say no. You're a figure-head. Abel Oberon represents Art. That's as much a fact of London society as four o'clock tea. You could no more withdraw from your responsibilities, above all here in your own house, than you could ban afternoon tea.

OBERON   That's what Moberly said, too ——

MARJORY   Anyone who has been invited here never stops talking about it. It's considered a great honour to have been in these rooms — the finest in London, people say. I've often seen them shyly looking up at your portrait above the fireplace as if it were presumptuous to be so close to the shrine. *Dismissing his gesture.* It is my shrine. If there was one thing missing in that fisherman's shack, it was this portrait. Apart from that, I was quite content. And proud to share the solitude with you, thinking of what it might bring forth.

OBERON   And did the sacred monster produce anything? Did you see him absorbed in his work?

MARJORY   You put nothing down on paper.

OBERON   Did you write it down for me?

MARJORY   You dictated nothing for me to write down.

OBERON   So what was the upshot?

MARJORY   As yet nothing visible. It is still gestating. Everything you absorbed, standing on the cliffs for hours on end, watching the waves beat against the rocks, the thunderstorms and the scudding clouds. You had to see your fill. Let everything you experienced sink in. That's what you were after up there — and now you're here, you will give it shape and form. This is the only place you can do that. The setting is indispensable. You've all the space you need and you're surrounded by works of art. That's why you came back. There, no one was permitted to disturb you since you were preoccupied with the new work, just as now you avoid bright lights and won't wake Tobin. We crept in like thieves in the night and have to stay invisible. For how long? When do you ring Moberly and present him with the manuscript? Then there's Burbage, waiting for it at the theatre. Waiting for Abel Oberon's *Tragedy of the Cliffs.*

OBERON *slowly.*   Abel Oberon's tragedy ——

MARJORY   Am I right?

OBERON *shakes his head.*   Not entirely. There's not enough material for a tragedy.

MARJORY   But it must be terribly serious. The grey north is not exactly conducive to laughter.

OBERON    The material's at fault if no real sense of terror develops.

MARJORY    And what is the material?

OBERON    The material is — me.

MARJORY *Stares at him uncomprehendingly.*

OBERON    Well, isn't it? Do you see me as a King Lear figure? On the blasted heath, in the wind and rain, lamenting his lost happiness? I'm not at all like Lear. I've not lost my Cordelia. I can't imagine a more faithful daughter than you, Marjory. I could never doubt your faithfulness, as Lear doubted Cordelia. That was the real source of his unhappiness. Abdicating the throne was simply preordained — things like that happen time and again. Provided you don't end up totally abandoned and bereft, a fisherman's shack under the cliffs might be all you need.

MARJORY    Do you feel — abandoned?

OBERON    It's not a feeling — it's the current account of my situation, as explained by Moberly.

MARJORY    Current account — explained by Moberly — your best friend —?

OBERON    And my publisher! — Quite a depressing meeting that was, with Moberly the publisher, in his office, one morning last autumn. He'd asked to see me — it sounded innocuous. Probably about the new edition of my Complete Works — something we'd long been planning — we'd discussed it here, round the fireplace — of course, the outlay would be considerable and I fully understood why he was hesitating — but now he would have done all the calculations and it was time for action. And that was why he had summoned me — in the gloomy half-light of the dawn — a time I hate — I don't even want to die in the dawn.

MARJORY    Don't talk of dying. Abel Oberon will never die.

OBERON    That's what I thought, too, on my way there. Moberly is about to make me immortal with a classic edition. I tot up the number of volumes — fifteen, twenty — if nothing is omitted, twenty-five.

MARJORY    Every line you've ever written must be preserved!

OBERON   Oh, there are some ephemera, things anyone could have written.

MARJORY   No — it's all unmistakably the product of your head and your hand.

OBERON   The hand didn't always exert itself, sometimes it only produced a scribble.

MARJORY   You can't mistake the imprint of your art. Not if you can tell a peacock from a turkey. You couldn't even trick a blind man into thinking blue was yellow: your art is so unmistakably blue, everything else is yellow.

OBERON   You don't think I wrote too much?

MARJORY   Too little!

OBERON   That's what Moberly thought, too.

MARJORY   He said that — in spite of twenty-five volumes?

OBERON   Too little — compared with my expenses.

MARJORY *stares at him. Then hesitantly.*   Do you — spend too much?

OBERON   More than I bring in. More than Moberly is willing to advance. I've reached the limit — I'm not just overdrawn, my account has been frozen. —— That was a grim morning when I fell from clouds of glory and twenty-five gilded volumes — and landed with a jolt that still hurts my head, so I can't string two thoughts together into a half-way lucid sentence. And I really did rack my brains — up there, on the cliffs.

MARJORY   Has Moberly been making demands?

OBERON *mockingly.*   Demands —

MARJORY   I'm sorry, that's too blunt a word. One doesn't make demands on Abel Oberon. Of course not. He intimated that he would like a new play from you for Burbage to put on?

OBERON   He had his hands round my throat, threatening to throttle me if I wasn't gone from London within three days, and not to show my face again until he had received my manuscript — completed in total isolation — and confirmed that he had received it.

MARJORY  He said that?

OBERON  And more. He threatened to seize my house and distrain all my chattels on the third day if I didn't do as he said.

MARJORY  So — you did what he wanted?

OBERON  Not in the way he meant. I left on the third day all right — but not to some desolate spot, as he wanted. I took my leave, telling him — and the papers — I was off on a luxury cruise around the world.

MARJORY  But then you've made an enemy of him.

OBERON  I couldn't stop myself — just as he couldn't stop himself positively yelling at me that he wasn't going to dish out any more, and what he'd already dished out he wanted back. 'My money, I need it — for more worthwhile projects. I can't afford any more nectar for the Olympian gods to knock back at their endless garden parties and revels. I'm a mere mortal publisher and have to live off my hard-earned pounds' — his extortionate profits, more like! And all the while he was bobbing up and down around me like a weasel — a man-size weasel, that's how he struck me — and any moment he'll attack me, sink his teeth into my neck and drink my blood dry! And he only didn't because then he would never have got his money back.

MARJORY  Maybe he's in financial difficulties. It's been so long since you produced —

OBERON  Then it was doubly stupid of him to provoke me. He should have flattered me, appealed to my pride. I know I'm vain. I don't pretend I'm not. I'm even in awe of my own name sometimes — it's instinctive. As if I weren't always Abel Oberon, but only admitted to possession on special occasions, as it were — otherwise merely the guardian of the name, to protect it from abuse. Can you understand that?

MARJORY  It is my shrine — and there is the image. *She points to the picture above the fireplace.*

OBERON  Moberly should have showed more respect. If he had had the sense to convince me he was dying to see an encyclopaedic edition of my works in twenty-five volumes, but that it desperately needed one more piece from me to finish off the sequence — then I would have buckled down at once and buried myself away from all the hubbub of town in some remote hidey-hole.

MARJORY    Which you did do — in that shack under the cliffs.

OBERON    Yes, for I wanted to work — but I couldn't. I couldn't shake off Moberly. He stood behind me like some spectre every time I sat down. He was by my side every time I strode along the beach. His voice was in the wind and the spray, urging me on, haunting me — he ruined everything. First the seeds of an idea, and then when I tried to start writing it down. I felt hollow — as if dispossessed by someone calling himself Abel Oberon, but who was miles away, in London — since genius knows no bounds and is at no one's beck and call, but free, unshackled. I was Moberly's prisoner, and he was tightening the screws. Threatening — if I showed my face in London before I had written confirmation that he had received my manuscript —

MARJORY    And now you've come with no manuscript —

OBERON    It would be too late anyway, even if I had.

MARJORY    Moberly wouldn't accept it?

OBERON    It would be too late to placate him — to stop him taking his revenge for my trip round the world.

MARJORY    So you think he really did —?

OBERON    What's to stop him? Just think — I mocked him — then totally disappeared and lay low — as if I had accepted the inevitable outcome.

MARJORY    You saw it coming and still did nothing?

OBERON    I closed my eyes to it. I was too cowardly, Marjory. I couldn't stop it happening. The only salvation — a manuscript for Moberly — was beyond me. Disaster beckoned. I couldn't prevent it. ————

MARJORY *after a pause.*    Why did you come back here?

OBERON    Why does the criminal return to the scene of his crime? He's drawn back, as if by some terrible spell. Maybe it's just childish curiosity — to see what it's like now and remember how it once was.

MARJORY *looking around.*    But nothing has changed here.

OBERON *following her glance.*    It's all as we left it.

MARJORY *has risen. Beside a small table near the fireplace.*   Look, there's —

OBERON   Don't touch a thing! It doesn't belong to us.

MARJORY   I could swear it's the powder compact I was missing in the shack under the cliffs.

OBERON   Don't swear and don't shout. There may be light sleepers in the house.

MARJORY   If he were living here your voice would have wakened him — you haven't kept it down in the slightest.

OBERON   Then there's no one living here. That's even worse. It wasn't sold. I owe Moberly even more.

MARJORY *in one corner.*   Here's your Scottish scarf — the one you were missing in Scotland.

OBERON   It's not my scarf.

MARJORY   Have a look.

OBERON   It's too dark.

MARJORY   I'll switch on the light.

OBERON   There's no light.

MARJORY   Why wouldn't there be light?

OBERON   When a house is empty, the light supply is the first thing switched off. An infallible sign that you no longer own a single stone of the whole proud edifice.

MARJORY *at the switch beside the sliding door.*   Shall I try?

OBERON   Nothing will happen.

MARJORY   I'll try. Just this once. *She turns the switch: some bulbs light up.* Hello, what's this!

OBERON   A glimmer. They've left that on in case there are burglars.

MARJORY   Let's try again. Second time. *More lights come on.* Still just a glimmer?

OBERON   Some defect in the supply, obviously. Technology isn't perfect.

MARJORY   Third time — they're all on now.

OBERON   Total illumination. Truly like a dream — if I hadn't seen it myself.

MARJORY *beside him.*   As if we'd been out for a ramble since morning — and had just got back. Doesn't it seem like that to you?

OBERON   Uncanny. — What are you doing?

MARJORY   Illuminating the shrine.

*The life-size portrait of Oberon, in a frame which itself lights up, is illuminated by a spotlight.*

OBERON *looking at it.*   Untouched —— not torn down and shamefully desecrated by some rough scoundrel ————

MARJORY *beside him.*   Who would dare?

OBERON   Who painted it?

MARJORY   Someone with the same name as you.

OBERON *gesturing towards the picture.*   The two of us — you and me — it's a proud name we bear. Let us guard it — as if it were indeed a shrine. *They remain in rapt contemplation of the illuminated portrait.*

*The lacquered sliding door to the rear opens abruptly: Tobin — in a short, fitted, double-breasted, black coat and bowler hat — is on the threshold.*

TOBIN *exclaims.*   Oh ——

OBERON *also surprised.*   Tobin —

TOBIN   Mr Oberon, sir!

MARJORY *also surprised.*   Tobin —

TOBIN   Miss Marjory! *Whips off bowler sideways with a distinctive flourish.*

OBERON   Don't be too startled, Tobin. It was only a powder compact that Miss Marjory had forgotten — and my Scottish scarf. Just things for personal use that we are fetching. We came in inconspicuously through the garden, and now we have the compact and the scarf, we'll leave —

TOBIN *slides the door shut behind him.*   You can't leave now.

OBERON   You're right, Tobin — first I must put out the light that I took the liberty of turning on.

TOBIN   I saw the light from a distance and ran as fast as I could.

OBERON   Did you suspect burglars?

TOBIN   I knew it was you at once.

OBERON   So you needn't have hurried. We've got all we need, and we're going —

TOBIN *planting himself in front of Oberon.*   You mustn't go yet.

OBERON *to Marjory.*   That sounds like a warning.

TOBIN   All the staff are gone! ————

OBERON *despondently.*   I knew it, Tobin. I thought as much. One thing after the other — it's inexorable. The ship sinks — the rats flee. And the wages were in arrears. Tomorrow, the first thing I'll do — since it's the middle of the night now ——

MARJORY *vehemently.*   Tell them all that Abel Oberon never owes anything to those who render him service!

TOBIN *imperturbably.*   You will have to owe in this case ————

OBERON *timidly.*   Tobin — are things that bad?

TOBIN   I had no way of reporting everything that occurred here. I didn't know where to send letters to. Though I did write them — that lessened the strain — otherwise I might have got carried away and ——

OBERON    And what, Tobin?

TOBIN    — and struck a woman!

OBERON    Why? And who was the woman?

TOBIN    The cook — for complaining. And she had the nerve to stand before the court and lodge her complaint wearing what looked like a saucepan on her head — that you could boil an egg in if it hadn't been made of straw — such a vulgar, ludicrous sight — I was tempted to knock it off.

OBERON    And what was the judge's ruling — on the complaint, not the hat?

TOBIN    As I anticipated.

OBERON    Namely?

TOBIN    That you should pay this person what she claimed was her due after deserting her post in the kitchen.

OBERON    If someone leaves because she hasn't been paid, that doesn't make her a deserter, Tobin. I wasn't in a position to send you anything.

TOBIN    You were far away — and she was a deserter. She wanted to get married and had arranged the wedding for ten days before the end of the month. That was the point at issue. I refused to pay her for the whole month, as she demanded. Not if you get married, I told her. I will, and I must, she replied. And what compelled her to give up her job ten days early? My husband is a sailor and his ship sails from London on the first. He won't be back for a year — surely ten days of married life are not too much to ask for. So I said: very well — I still had hopes of keeping her — marry, then — let nature take its loathsome course — but when your husband has gone, you will return to the kitchen. To this, she turns a deaf ear: her husband wouldn't hear of it. Hear of *what*? — I expostulate. To me staying on where there's another man. Meaning me. At this I merely looked her up and down, and turned away without another word. The creature's rank arrogance was simply intolerable, the gulf between us too great for any further exchange. I simply indicated that she would pay for leaving the kitchen in the lurch. For she knew how to cook. If the term is applicable to such trifling matters, then she, too, was an artist. She had an unerring instinct for transforming raw ingredients — though without smothering them — into the most amazing concoctions. That's the art of cooking — and she had it at her finger tips. If she had been only a little less proficient at roasting and braising, I would not have disputed the ten days' pay. Here you are, my dear — I would have said, without a hint of reproach or disappointment — now go and sign up with your seaman for life — or like the Patient Griselda, when he comes by once a year and drops anchor —! But this one would have been setting a precedent for the future, and I dug my heels in. All for a few shillings. Which she didn't get. And which she won't get. You'll just have to owe her!

OBERON *passes a hand over his brow.* The whole quarrel was over a few shillings —?

TOBIN   Over a principle, Mr Oberon. Whether it is permissible to abandon talents one possesses and which others do not possess, and on a whim scatter them to all four winds — like desert sand, where nothing grows.

OBERON   A seaman needs to eat as well.

TOBIN   And all the time he is away? Shouldn't she be cooking then? Should she renounce her art just because he is jealous? And deprive us of the rarest delicacies?

OBERON   The husband is jealous.

TOBIN   Then — by God — the man has to ——

OBERON   Has to — what, Tobin?

TOBIN   To disappear, once and for all. *Shrugs.* But I'm not the one to do it.

OBERON   I'll have to pay up, then.

TOBIN *brandishing his bowler imploringly.* No, not the cook — and not the maid either, for what she refused to take! *Twists his bowler to one side with the same distinctive flourish.*

MARJORY *tentatively.* Did she refuse because she saw things had become — difficult?

TOBIN   She was the difficult one. Even after one week she was fretting, oblivious to the demands of simple decency, even if it didn't come naturally. Finally, with a show of strength I wouldn't have credited her with, the delicate little thing rose up against the void.

MARJORY    The void?

TOBIN    The void when there is nothing to do. For there wasn't anything to do any more — nothing at all, however trifling. No day-to-day tasks, no festivities. The house had come to a standstill. None of us needed to lift a hand — we had time on our hands. And she just wasn't up to it. She needed to be doing things. I pointed out that no service is required when the master is away, which was the case. Did she expect instructions to be sent from foreign parts just to relieve her enforced idleness? I urged her to moderate an impulse that can easily get out of hand. Otherwise she would come to typify that wretched, rampant thirst for action that's like getting stuck in a thorn bush, unable to go forward or back. But she wouldn't be told, preach at her as I might, she merely stamped her foot and cut me short. Then she started moaning, but still I didn't give up. I went to her room where she had taken to her bed — sick from doing nothing, as she claimed. She really was pale and her hand feverishly hot. That led to some deep and heart-felt words from me. *Use the time*, I said, *use the time that you may never have again as long as you live, to be completely idle — the greatest imaginable challenge. Prove yourself — be brave, do nothing.* It was not without some effect, though it didn't last. The end came as expected. But before that she held out for a while — having stipulated that she should receive no wages for doing nothing. To this I agreed — I didn't want to burden her with more than she could bear. She was young, after all, and if you've been well brought up, you know how to control yourself. But no sooner had I started to entertain great hopes than they were dashed. One morning she didn't appear — I went upstairs, prepared not be surprised at a relapse — and found her room empty. I never did find out where she went. Probably out to the marshlands, where there's hard work aplenty, digging turf — which she'll do better than any man. But she wasn't up to not being active — even when she wasn't being paid for it. Paying her would be the greatest insult. So you'll just have to owe her, too.

MARJORY *to Oberon.*    That's fortunate — that the girl went without making a fuss.

OBERON *breathes a sigh of relief.*    Even cheaper than the cook — and she would have been content with a few shillings.

TOBIN    How embarrassing if she were to —

OBERON *dismissing the possibility.*    Never again —— *Hesitates.* But Tobin is still here. Tobin, who stayed to the bitter end — who wouldn't budge — who blocks my path because he is justly concerned —— Can we put off the biggest worries until tomorrow?

TOBIN    It perhaps is time, Mr Oberon —

OBERON *sharply*.    I reproach myself, Tobin, I don't need anyone else telling me —

MARJORY *placatingly*.    Let me talk to him. *To Tobin.* Tobin — everything that's happened happened with the best of intentions — almost unwittingly. The trip around the world that people might reproach us for — well, we never ———— *Jokingly.* After all, we could depend on you, here. You've always been so devoted to us and taken care of affairs that sometimes, unfortunately, could not be handled in any other way. What's the most important news?

TOBIN    I've engaged a chef.

OBERON *finding his voice again*.    You've engaged a — what?

TOBIN    After the aforementioned bitter experience, I decided on a male chef. If I may endorse what you said so aptly a moment ago —*Never again*. Never again a female in the kitchen, plagued by an uncontrollable matrimonial urge. Culinary standards would inevitably suffer. In the end — did you not notice? — some of dishes she prepared scarcely passed muster. I would have had to cast a belated cloud over her married bliss. — The new chef is a widower, and as far as I am aware, childless. As he put it himself, he has seen life with all its ingredients, and put it behind him. His last position was a particularly unfortunate experience. A house in decline. Outwardly still glittering as before, but inwardly rotten and hollow. As is sadly often the case in such instances, wages are long overdue. Promises are not kept. Much too late to change things — the whole fraudulent edifice collapses, burying master and servants alike under the rubble. The chef was even more deeply implicated, having lent the master his savings, and thus lost them. He longed for a position in an honest, respectable household. One day he turned up here — I don't know how he knew there was a vacancy in the kitchen — news of what goes on here seems to spread like wildfire. In any case, he applied for the position, like a sinner desperate to find refuge in a house, like this one, built on firm foundations — the chef was well informed! Since his testimonials were excellent, and confirmed by my own scrupulous researches, I decided to take him on. — He is somewhat more expensive than the cook — but more durable.

OBERON *bucking up*.    We must have him here at once —

TOBIN    It's already taken care of. I anticipated this eventuality and stipulated that he should be standing by, day and night, whatever the weather — even if it means coming through the thickest fog — for when you might return without warning. That's no more than proper, for I've been paying his wages for the last three months.

OBERON  Paying an expensive chef for three months —?

TOBIN  The new maid is also in place. She's staying with relatives — and waiting at the end of a telephone. I shall call her to come at once. As you'll see, she is distinctly unpolished. This was a deliberate choice to avoid a recurrence of the collapse of resistance when faced with nothing to do. I'm sure she will quickly and uncomplainingly come to terms with any lack of activity, of whatever duration. She has the necessary phlegmatic disposition, which naturally must not be allowed to degenerate into lethargy or inertia. A virtue becomes a drawback if unfettered. Consequently, I sent her to a domestic training school to acquire some rudimentary skills, where she failed the first course but passed the second with flying colours. *To Marjory.* You probably don't need to…

[…]

OBERON  You will have to cover the expense, and I —— *Putting on his cap —* to Marjory. Let's go, Marjory.

TOBIN  For each step, I took Mr Moberly's advice.

OBERON *as if struck by lightning.*  What?!

TOBIN  Mr Moberly — no one else. — Had I needed money for anything that might smack of extravagance, I had only to turn to him, but in his opinion nothing was squandered. On the contrary, he encouraged me, urged me on. *But surely,* he said, every Monday morning when he invited me to his office — *surely there are still bills to be paid.* I had to bring them — and he settled them. He came here and inspected the house from top to bottom to see if any damage had occurred in one or other of the empty rooms. In particular, he was constantly concerned about the possibility of damp. He had the boiler inspected and upgraded — and I had to turn up the heating until it was sweltering. *It will overheat,* I warned. *Leave it on hot,* he insisted, *it's just the right heat. The right heat? Just what our Maestro needs when he gets back. And we must read his every wish — indeed anticipate it, lest in his anger he strike us down with a deadly glance.* — He was indefatigable in both word and deed, was Mr Moberly.

OBERON  Yes — it is warm here — *He takes off his coat. Tobin takes it. To Marjory.* Do you understand that?

TOBIN   I have endeavoured —

OBERON   I don't mean you.

TOBIN   Oh — excuse me.

OBERON   Whatever can have induced Moberly to —?

MARJORY   Maybe you've got him wrong?

OBERON   I know Moberly. After our quarrel — and yet ———— *He sits down in an armchair and ponders. Then, not finding an explanation, for the sake of something to say, to Tobin.* You said you had gone out. Where were you, Tobin?

TOBIN *brightening.*   At the theatre.

OBERON   The theatre? You go to the theatre?

TOBIN   Every evening.

OBERON   That's rather a lot, Tobin. Perhaps excessive?

TOBIN   It's never too much.

OBERON   What's on?

TOBIN   There's only one thing worth seeing.

OBERON   And what is it you go and see over and over again?

TOBIN   The same thing.

OBERON   Is it one of Burbage's productions?

TOBIN   No — Fenwick's.

OBERON   So what has Fenwick put on?

TOBIN   Your new play! ————

OBERON *spins round and stares at him.*   My ——

MARJORY   Your ——

OBERON *and* MARJORY *simultaneously.*   —— new play??

TOBIN *stands holding Oberon and Marjory's coats and caps.*   In a production that makes your heart sing. More like one of Burbage's than Fenwick's. I never once felt: Burbage would have done this better or that better. Fenwick is simply unbeatable. With top stars in all the minor roles — ensemble acting of the highest order. And every repeat performance — and I've seen them all, nearly a hundred and fifty — in no way inferior to the last. The storm of applause, like on the first night, seems unending. It's *the* talking point in London — and I'm not alone in saying so: it would be a boon if another theatre could stage it as well, and relieve the daily grind of the population at large who are missing out because of the huge crowds flocking to see it. It acts like a tonic — it gladdens the heart. What greater gift can there be?! — *Oberon and Marjory steadfastly maintain their shocked silence.* Oh, forgive me for offering my own thoughts on the work — they are of course quite inappropriate in the presence of the creator himself. I got carried away — I beg your pardon. ———— All praise and honour to Fenwick, too. I'm still full of what I saw. I had to speak out. ———— I awaited this moment partly with eager anticipation, partly with great apprehension. Your return restricts the freedom I hitherto enjoyed of an evening. May I therefore be so bold as to request leave to go to the theatre twice a week — in exchange for giving up my day off. ———— *As no answer is forthcoming, he bows and leaves through the sliding door.*

OBERON *slowly recovering from his astonishment — to Marjory.*   Did you hear what I heard — that I —?

MARJORY *equally disbelieving.*   That it was Fenwick ——?

OBERON   Fenwick, you say? So the name was mentioned?

MARJORY   And in conjunction with your new play —

OBERON   Which Moberly would never have given to Fenwick —

MARJORY   Only to Burbage —

OBERON   Who could not have received it since I haven't written it! —— *Ponders.* Does Tobin not give the impression of being bereft of his senses?

MARJORY   But everything he said seemed eminently sensible.

OBERON    His words, yes — but that curious sideways gesture with his hat? Didn't you notice?

MARJORY    He'll have picked that up recently.

OBERON    Where from? Who twirls his hat like that? — It's a symptom of some — derangement. Confusion in the old grey matter. Bats in the belfry. And he gets things mixed up — Burbage is Fenwick and Moberly gives Fenwick what he hasn't got —

MARJORY    But Moberly has paid for everything here.

OBERON *more calmly.*    Still, everything has changed. *Pause, then open-mouthed.* It surely couldn't be —— *He stops short.*

MARJORY    You look horror-stricken —

OBERON    Somebody else ——

MARJORY    Somebody else what?

OBERON    —— While I buried myself away in Scotland, some — villain — here in London has been getting up to the most outrageous skulduggery ————

MARJORY    But that's absurd —

OBERON    No more absurd than Tobin's charade with his hat ————

*Enter Tobin on the staircase, left, now in a striped livery jacket, with a tray piled high with letters and cards. He crosses the room and sets it down on a table in front of the fireplace.*

OBERON    Tobin!

TOBIN *turns to him.*

OBERON    When you raised your hat, you used a certain — movement. Before I say what I think, tell me where you got it from. Who uses that sort of greeting?

TOBIN *beaming.*    Everyone in London now.

OBERON    Copying one of the royal family?

TOBIN    No, not the royal family.

OBERON    Who then?

TOBIN    It from your play! —— It never fails, when two people greet one another with this flourish — it's only a detail, but everyone recognizes the allusion to the play — it's made it famous throughout London. —— *In a matter-of-fact tone.* This is the post that accumulated after the opening night. I regret I was unable to forward it. *Exit through the lacquered door.*

*Oberon and Marjory wait until Tobin has closed the sliding door behind him, then go over to the tray.*

OBERON    Not the letters or the telegrams — I have to see it in print. Where are the reviews?

MARJORY *digging through the pile.*    Here they are.

OBERON *unfolds one and reads. Then shakes his head.*    It's true! —— By Abel Oberon ———— *He hands her the review.* You read the title — I can't say it.

MARJORY *reads and looks up at him open-eyed.*

OBERON    Is your tongue tied, too?

MARJORY    It does sound rather odd.

OBERON    Odd or not — *Seizing the review from her hand. He crumples it and throws it on the floor.* I wish I could smash it and stamp on it. You can do that to eggs.

MARJORY *pensively.*    What can it mean: *The Gordian Egg?*

OBERON    That's for Moberly to explain — how this play has materialized out of my posthumous literary remains!

MARJORY *taken aback.*    But you're still alive.

OBERON    Not for Moberly. For Moberly I've rung down the curtain — profitably so, for him — the profit coming from my literary estate. Now do you understand?

MARJORY   He thinks you're dead?

OBERON   Jumped overboard, driven by despair — in some watery waste teeming with sharks. And they'll tear me to shreds, down to the last bone. But that shark Moberly will still be feeding off me after I'm gone. He'll find he's mistaken if he thinks I'm a tasty morsel. I'll soon cure him of the delusion that dead men don't talk. They can — in a voice like thunder. Like the last trump on Judgement Day. Lightning is all the more terrible at night-time. — Are you through to him?

MARJORY *holding the telephone to her ear — nods.*

OBERON   No answer? — No wonder. He'll drop the phone like a hot brick when he hears who's ringing. In future it won't be so easy to get hold of him — we'll have to set traps to catch him, with his infinite cunning — Is that him now?

MARJORY *whispers.*   No — Eileen.

OBERON   Ask her where her father is — I want him now.

MARJORY *on the phone.*   Eileen ———— *She cannot speak as she is forced to listen. Softly to Oberon.* She recognized my voice straight away.

OBERON   And didn't hang up?

MARJORY   I can't stop her talking — she goes on and on.

OBERON   Of course — she won't know. Demand to talk to her father.

MARJORY *tries to get a word in edgeways.*   And where shall I say we are?

[...]

MARJORY *hesitates.*   Maybe it was Fenwick —?

OBERON *flares up.*   Fenwick! — Fenwick, that bungler, has the audacity to take some trash of his own and ————!

MARJORY *scornfully.*   Can Fenwick write?

OBERON   He's the villain — it must be him! And what he's written doesn't actually matter, thanks to the glittering performance and first-rate actors. Even the trivial becomes important in the mouth of a great actor. Mere clay turns to gold — that's the alchemy of the stage. You can puff an egg up to the size of a balloon if you have the magic wand — a name that guarantees the value of the product. Take a bite — it tastes good!

MARJORY    Who could fall for that?

OBERON    Ask Tobin. How do people greet each other in London now when they meet? A la Fenwick — up to now — like this. *Gestures.* But come tomorrow, people will take good care to avoid demonstrating they've been made a fool of. End of the madhouse — at my behest the play comes off. I'll have Fenwick in court and made an example of. It'll cost him three times over what he made by swindling, using my name.

*Tobin opens the lacquered door. Eileen Moberly rushes in — still wearing her evening wrap.*

[…]

MOBERLY    […] no less than the light that Prometheus brought to man. And one gives thanks by using it — and thanks you by laughing — as happens night after night. Aren't you pleased with us, Divine One?

OBERON *not taking Moberly's hand.*    I'm in the dark —

MOBERLY    I was sure you had turned your back on us. The insult was a rash one, offence was taken — divine wrath! — and the punishment was extreme. But is all now forgiven?

OBERON    There's nothing you —

MOBERLY    Eileen, you back me up, beg for forgiveness for your father's sins. He was a sacrilegious fool. But he has repented. His daughter implores you. Can there be no reconciliation?

OBERON *to Eileen.*    I'm forgetting my manners — *shakes her hand.*

MOBERLY *clasps his hands around theirs.*    A shaft of divine favour, dispelling our darkness — we seize upon it! Let peace reign between Moberly and Maestro Oberon. — May we sit?

MARJORY    Do.

MOBERLY *and the others sit down in the armchairs around the fireplace.* The same old setting — *Looks up.* — and — ah! — the portrait in its full glory. Now when are you going to step into the spotlight yourself — to the storm of applause that has been waiting so long for that moment? When —

MARJORY *interrupting.*   We've just got back from a long trip and it's possible —

EILEEN   Tell us about the trip. You never even dropped us a line — if you hadn't been spotted from time to time —

MOBERLY   We might have thought there had been an accident.

MARJORY   Who spotted us?

EILEEN *to Moberly.*   Who was telling us recently that Abel Oberon and his daughter —

MOBERLY   At Lady Witherspoon's — they were all talking about it.

EILEEN   About where Abel Oberon was staying. He had been caught sight of. Oh yes, the secret was out — cover blown.

MARJORY *hesitantly.*   Where —

OBERON *likewise.*   — were we spotted?

MOBERLY   At the Raja of Jodhpur's court.

EILEEN *since Oberon and Marjory are struck dumb.*   There was even talk that the young prince — but that's all nonsense, of course. People talk just for the sake of it. But do tell me: was he very much in love?

MOBERLY   That's private. How can you —

EILEEN   But it's all been and gone. She's back here now. A flirtation is not a broken heart. Love can drive you mad, as I know. Is that the impression she gives? *To Marjory.* So, tell us: what was it like, in the palace or on the top of an elephant, when the two of you —

MOBERLY   There'll be time enough tomorrow for herds of elephants and all the marvels of a magical world we can only dream about — *To Oberon.* but that you experienced — so, of course, old, grey London and its theatres were soon forgotten.

OBERON *with a dismissive gesture.*   Nothing was forgotten —

MOBERLY   Except for me. You consigned me to the depths of oblivion — not a sound, not a sign, for you I was dead. You killed me — that morning in my office when I told you how the accounts stood. What possessed me?! I didn't see what was staring me in the face. Why didn't you say a word? Even a gesture would have been enough — *Points to his chest.*

OBERON   The gesture I couldn't —

MOBERLY   No, you couldn't even point — I'd paralysed your arm before it could move — with my accounts. I had no option. All my hopes had come to nothing — and there was a lot of money riding on them — a lot. One failure after another, as if people had simply stopped reading. I was left with enough books to fill a cathedral to the top of the dome. My money turned into paper — but worthless paper with printing on it. I was drowning in a sea of printer's ink. If only I could have kept the paper and the ink apart, I wouldn't have had sleepless nights. An insomniac — someone who runs the gauntlet through worries of his own making, and each one lays on the lash, round and round in endless torture. One such night the end seemed nigh — but then salvation beckoned: Abel Oberon. He's the one who can save you — and must save you. Must! For he's the one who took advantage of you —

EILEEN *interrupting him.*   Which you put it in no uncertain terms —

MOBERLY *to her.*   I behaved abominably — but all is now forgiven. I brandished the account-book as if it were an axe and someone was attacking me. Or maybe I was the brigand: Your money or your life! And that meant the life of the mind, the creative mind. I was giving orders to the Maestro to get on with it and create — the cheek of it — me lecturing the Maestro! And literally sending him into exile. London was out of bounds — forbidden fruit — unaffordable. I threatened to close the house and sell off the contents to recoup my losses — if he didn't take himself off to some secluded spot, far from the madding crowd, within three days, and only return with my permission — after I had acknowledged receipt of the masterpiece.

EILEEN *laughing, to Marjory.*   And that's my father, whom I must honour!

MOBERLY *to Oberon.*    You despised me and my ravings. A contemptible sight! Intolerable — yes? You can tell me now what names you were secretly calling me. At the time you didn't say a word — merely observed a majestic silence, and that provoked me even more. I was ready to throttle you — I wish I had tried, for then I would have felt what I couldn't see — what was in your coat pocket — the manuscript!

OBERON    What — ?

MOBERLY    Bulging under your jacket — enough to fill a whole evening — five full, rounded acts — not just pigeon eggs — real ostrich eggs. If only I had reached out, I would have known. But you didn't deign to raise a hand to your pocket and take out the longed-awaited item. I wasn't worthy of it. You turned away and went as silently you had come — with the treasure that I had stupidly forfeited.

EILEEN    Quite right, too, Papa!

MOBERLY    How subtly you took your revenge! Masterfully engineered and flawlessly executed. On the third day you let me know that you were keeping to my deadline, but that you were off — not to some remote hideaway, but round the world.

EILEEN *to Marjory.*    You didn't even come and say goodbye.

MOBERLY    Better that way. I might have forgotten myself with the daughter of the man who had made a mock of me while I was burning in hell — *To Oberon.* I didn't know at the time that you only wanted to punish me — that the fire brigade was already on its way to put out the fire: Fenwick. He turned up the day after you had left: *Let's draw up a contract. — What do you want to put on? — Abel Oberon's new play. — Oh, if only there was one! — There is: he's just delivered it!*

MARJORY    Delivered to Fenwick?

MOBERLY    Not in person. You had left the day before.

MARJORY    Then who delivered it?

MOBERLY    A messenger. That's not important. What's important was the realization that I should be ashamed. That I overrated myself — that I am quite dispensable. Burbage, too, for all his belief that he was born to act. The two of us — disposed of at a stroke, while Fenwick, the despised Fenwick, rose up from the depths and demonstrated his genius in a way Burbage never would have with this play.

EILEEN   Burbage lacks the light touch.

MOBERLY   It's easy to say that now that Fenwick has shown the way. But who discovered Fenwick's talent? He deserves all the glory. *To Oberon.* And that, too, belongs to you. You alone recognized it and were courageous enough to give him a chance. And his response to the task you entrusted him with has been exemplary. As you will see — words can barely describe it. When can you attend the theatre? *He picks up the telephone.*

OBERON *restraining him.*   Never —

MOBERLY   You won't be disturbing him. He's just waiting for a call from you.

OBERON   You've told him I'm back?

MOBERLY   Him — and the press. After all, London deserves to know.

OBERON   And Fenwick —

MOBERLY   What, Maestro?

OBERON   — is pleased that I am here?

MOBERLY   He can't wait to throw himself at your feet in gratitude for *The Gordian Egg.* You've made him the happiest of men. He worships you. *To Eileen.* Isn't it touching, the way he talks about the Maestro — and the questions he asks: *You know him better — will he be satisfied? Will he like the way I've mounted his play?* He's longing for you to see it.

EILEEN   He wanted to share a cab with us here just now.

MOBERLY   There's a good reason for that — that's why I want to phone him. The idea is to put the play on simultaneously in another theatre as well. — Don't be shocked. Naturally he won't be able to match the present cast — it is incomparable. But no matter if the cast is weaker, the play can take it. It is indestructible. It is simply — good. Look at the reviews — *Bending down he notices the pile of papers on the carpet.* There's one you've missed. — *Taking it up.* All crumpled up — *Smooths it out.* — of course, the best one would fall under the table — and it turns out to be the crucial one. Your fiercist critic has changed his mind. *The Gordian Egg* he calls: *an unexpected twist in the creative process of one we thought we knew inside out. We didn't. We're still learning. The light touch is astonishing and — something completely new — the gaiety which it radiates. Not laugh-out-loud merriment but sunshine in the soul, a heart-warming affirmation of life. We resolve to be as little aggrieved at the passing of the years as is our protean author, who has discovered the secret of eternal youth.* — Well, just look at you, tanned by the sea and the wind — who could doubt that you have truly rediscovered your youth!

OBERON *somewhat at a loss.* But has no one any doubts ——

MOBERLY   If doubts are measured by success, then everyone has. Quite right, too. That applies to Fenwick even more so — and above all the American Hubbard with the offer he's brought from New York — you can only wonder if you've heard right. But Hubbard isn't just all talk and no action. We were with him in the theatre this evening. At the end, all he did was squeeze my hand. The print-run is astonishing. Hubbard wants the American rights — he'll stage it on Broadway and take it all over the country with his own players. Can you come to breakfast tomorrow? Hubbard will be pleased as Punch to meet you. He wants to — *Breaks off.* But he'll tell you himself. Where shall we have breakfast?

MARJORY *struggles to her feet.* Not tomorrow.

MOBERLY   Why not tomorrow?

MARJORY   Because tomorrow — because today — and tomorrow, and the day after — *To Oberon.* It's all been too much at once — I think you should wait until you can decide properly. *To Moberly.* There are decisions to be made —

EILEEN *rising, to Moberly.* You can put Fenwick off, and Hubbard, too. Tell them the Maestro is back. That's the main thing.

MOBERLY   The writer is at his desk! *To Eileen.* Yes, I'm coming. *To Oberon.* Just one more small thing — and it really is a small thing now: I've begun printing the Collected Works — exquisite format, superb typeface. Even if we don't cover our costs — that's all taken care of in advance. I sleep like a log again — and the next time you come to my office you won't be confronted with an open account-book and some raging monster demanding money. Now I'm the one splashing out — I've already paid for all sorts of things here. *Wagging a threatening finger.* Your debts were bigger than I thought. But I'll say nothing. Let people believe what they want. Now let's forget it. — Incidentally, I personally arranged with Tobin about the heating and the staff —

*Marjory has pressed a bell-button.*
*Tobin slides open the lacquered door.*

EILEEN  We'll send the car round tomorrow for a trial run. After the full moon tonight, tomorrow will be a lovely day. *Exit, waving, with Moberly in tow.*

*Tobin closes the sliding door.*
*Oberon and Marjory remain motionless.*

OBERON *with an effort.*  My hands are tied — I'm at someone's mercy — but whose? *He begins to pace up and down.*

MARJORY  Why are your hands tied?

OBERON  They're tied by my silence.

MARJORY  You had to hear all there was to hear first. But tomorrow —

OBERON *stops short.*  What can I do tomorrow?

MARJORY  Forbid it.

OBERON  Forbid what?

MARJORY  Forbid any further performances.

OBERON  Forbid fearless Fenwick? Who spared no expense? Who staked his all on a single card that turned out to be an unbeatable trump?

MARJORY  But it's cheating.

OBERON  But not by him — nor by Moberly, who can now sleep again and who has already plunged into enterprises that only need to falter to bring down the whole house of Moberly.

MARJORY  But you're surely not going to stand for it —?

OBERON  I must.

MARJORY    No! You've got to protect your name from being misused.

OBERON    I didn't lift a finger, let alone bang on the table and dismiss the whole thing as an illusion. I didn't make the slightest effort to nip it in the bud. I allowed myself to be feted as the one who generated this rich harvest for Fenwick and Moberly.

MARJORY    You shouldn't feel under any obligation to —

OBERON    I'm only thinking of my reputation.

MARJORY    How can that suffer if you expose the truth?

OBERON    Will people believe me — that it is the truth?

MARJORY    What do you mean?

OBERON    That I wasn't aware of the deception? That I hadn't read about what Fenwick was doing in some newspaper while staying with the Raja of Jodhpur? In Jodhpur — where we were spotted!

MARJORY    Those are all just legends. Deny them.

OBERON    Strip away the legends around any great man, and you'll see how soon they start throwing stones at what they previously idolized.

MARJORY    You think they might suspect you were in league with this —?

OBERON    Why else would Abel Oberon hide away in a fisherman's shack? Has he had his fill of London triumphs? Which he always used to bask in. Why the change?

MARJORY    Well — why?

OBERON    Because he didn't dare take the final step — he didn't dare step forward and receive an accolade for work that was not his own. Work that had merely been passed off as his — his own is no longer up to it — it's stale, passé.

MARJORY    But now you have come and are going to speak out?

OBERON    Pricked by conscience. I couldn't stand it any longer. I wasn't strong enough to keep up the pretence. So I let fly: plagiarism! treachery! — However loud I shout, they take no notice. They just whisper: he's been bought — he's allowed his name to be put to it. Then he regretted it — tough! He should have thought of that before.

MARJORY    You must defend your good name in court — nothing can stop you.

OBERON    And the whole of London turns out for the case. Imagine: they catch the blighter — *He stops short, collapses into an armchair.*

MARJORY    Then what?

OBERON    But they won't catch him. He's far too clever — he hasn't claimed a penny from Moberly, though he must know what a smash hit brings in —

MARJORY *is also reduced to silence.*

OBERON *looks up.*    Why has he made no claim? Why hasn't he gone to Moberly and revealed his hoax behind closed doors? A poor devil with some talent who wants his share. It's his work, after all, and he's not after the honour. He's content to sail under my flag. He asks politely and Moberly treats him quite properly. He gives him some money and makes a contract with him for his next opus — but this time under his own name. It could end like a fairy tale where they live happily ever after. They put the devil in a sack and bury him in a bog — the wages of sin —

MARJORY    What's he after, then —?

OBERON    Me, Marjory! — He wants to ruin me, utterly, body and soul. He's a cold, calculating villain. He's got me caught in his web and I can't move. That's what it's come to. Go back to the day after we left. He handed over to Fenwick —

MARJORY    He had it delivered by a messenger.

OBERON    His messenger delivers the book. So he must have been watching our departure very carefully. News of that only appeared in the press two days later. After all, I only posted the letters in the station. Wasn't there someone on the platform — I seem to remember someone watching us. Weren't you suspicious?

MARJORY *shakes her head.*

OBERON    He'll have had better sources. He was informed about my trip — from the beginning. He even knew about the hide-out in Scotland.

MARJORY    How could he?

OBERON    He knew everything. He engineered the whole devilish plot and even knew about the shack up north. What I was doing there — the fact I wasn't doing anything — that I only wanted to keep out of the way and not to reappear for a while — that all suited him perfectly. And he made consummate use of it to devastating effect.

MARJORY    You mean?

OBERON    The glittering prize Fenwick handed him — which in turn allowed Moberly to pay for everything here, thus unwittingly delivering me into the blighter's hands. There's no way out for me.

MARJORY    But when he comes here — can't you —?

OBERON    He will come — to blackmail me. He'll put his hands round my throat and squeeze and I won't be able to do a thing: the plot thickens — it's already developed this far, I can't stop it now without damage. *With emphasis.* Or should I just disappear for ever into the fog swirling round that windy coast, singing its eternal dirges. Is that what I must do — is that what you must do, irrevocably, standing on the threshold of your young life?

MARJORY    You should never have hidden away.

OBERON    Thou shalt not lie — it never turns out well — *Looking up at the portrait.* — and it damages one's name. Put out the light.

MARJORY *switches off the illuminated frame around the picture.*

OBERON    Darker.

MARJORY *switches off the lamps.*

OBERON    Darker.

MARJORY *switches off more lights. Then goes to Oberon, who sits, bent over, in the faint light.*

OBERON *taking her hand.*    Are you still proud of me?

MARJORY    Could I live otherwise?

OBERON *presses her hand to his cheek.*

MARJORY *strokes his greying hair with her other hand.*

# ACT TWO

~

*A spacious though rather low-ceilinged living-room, let out by Mrs Hittington. A window with flower-patterned, muslin curtains stretches along almost the whole of the rear wall, to the right of which rises a narrow, iron spiral staircase. Though modest, the furnishings and ambience are typically English — namely, comfortable and homely. In the middle, a large table on which breakfast is laid out. Near the wall, left, a desk and bookshelves full of books. On the right, another desk surrounded by glass cases on the wall containing collections of butterflies and beetles. The morning sun, finding all is well with the world, has settled comfortably across the flower patterns on the curtains.*

*The occupants of this room are Frank Hunter and Fenton Wing — two amiable, unassuming young men working on their dissertations to round off their studies — and currently having breakfast. That is to say, Fenton Wing talks while Frank Hunter breakfasts — without revealing that he is not paying attention; on the contrary, with every mouthful he nods emphatically, as if Wing's words were a favourite delicacy.*

WING *leaning back in his chair.* That was the nicest dream I've had in a long time. I dreamt about the creation of the world and it was perfectly clear to me that we exist in a state of unimaginable imperfection. At first all was dark, a complete blank. Since I couldn't see, I called out: isn't there any light here? — and waited. I waited a thousand years, then a voice, an immense distance away, answered: this is the first light. And the first star appeared in the heavens. It couldn't dispel the darkness, so I called out: isn't there any more light? A thousand years later the voice rumbled again: this is a new light! — and another star lit up. But the darkness was still too great, and I kept demanding: more light, more light, more light. And each time an answer came after a thousand years, and with it a new star — until there were all the stars there are now. But still I wasn't content. I kept calling out, every thousand years, aiming to dispel the darkness totally. I knew that if only I kept calling, the voice would have to answer and add another star — as long as I didn't weaken and lose hope. So finally I was calling out at the top of my voice, happy to think that I would soon succeed, and watching the dark patches between the stars getting smaller and smaller — until they disappeared completely. Night had ceased to exist. The stars had won. The light formed a great arc like a bronze dome. And there was no sun bathing half the day in gold — we no longer need the sun to take pity on us, for we have eternal light all around!

HUNTER *after a pause — still eating.*   Is that conclusion meant to be understood in a moral sense: that light is perfection?

WING   An unmistakable symbol: Let there be light! And our inner demons — those frightful monsters — take flight. Nothing but light — more light — light eternal!

HUNTER   And I say: more darkness — darkness eternal.

WING *snorts.*   But that's terrible!

HUNTER   It's not terrible. You just mustn't be afraid in the first place. Nor should it spoil your appetite. As it seems to be doing.

WING *going to the table.*   I'll have breakfast — though what you say is a dagger to my heart.

HUNTER   You might get a fright to start with — but when you had made your mind up and decided —

WING   Decided what?

HUNTER   What I decided in my dream — and never regretted. Now eat.

WING   You had a dream as well last night?

HUNTER   Every bit as oppressive as your's, at first. But with a happy end.

WING   Tell me all, and I won't be afraid any more. *He breakfasts, as Hunter had.*

HUNTER *pushing his chair back from the table.*   I was walking through a forest. The tree-trunks were strangely twisted in the pale half-light, with branches only at the top and no foliage. Instead of leaves there were long creepers hanging down from the bare tops almost to the ground. At about head height they ended in a noose, like poor wretches have put around their neck before being hanged. That's not an image I've just thought of. It struck me in the forest and I couldn't get it out of my head. Soon I felt as if these nooses were inviting me to put my head in — and that something would then happen to me — I didn't know what, but I was already tempted. Still I resisted — and then I did it. At once the noose tightened and the creeper pulled me up — the ground fell away below me and I was surely already in the tree-tops, but I kept on rising. Was the tree growing at the same rate? What was the goal? When something so incomprehensible happens, there's always a goal. I was able to think, but not to move. The noose wasn't meant to kill me — only to draw me upwards. To where all was darkness. Where I would never solve the eternal mystery, even if I had avoided the creeper down below.

WING    And what did the mystery turn out to be?

HUNTER    No mystery! No secret at all.

WING    None at all?

HUNTER    None — and yet the secret key to everything.

WING    Everything?

HUNTER    Everything.

WING    How can it be nothing and everything?

HUNTER    When you discover that everything is a mystery, then you've solved the mystery.

WING    That's worse than the sphinx.

HUNTER    Much better. It calls for no human sacrifice.

WING    But then Oedipus appeared and became king.

HUNTER    And, in the end, blind — by his own hand. The bitter fate of one who tries to solve the mystery.

WING    You think it's better to leave things in the dark?

HUNTER    Only if we love life: but not too much light.

*After two short knocks the door, right, is opened quickly by Mrs Hittington — a rather thin woman, dressed for domestic chores — who leaves just as quickly after laying the newspaper on the breakfast table with the words "The paper".*

WING    How did the dream finish?

HUNTER    I woke up.

WING    In reality?

HUNTER    No, in the dream — I woke up and read the paper.

WING    The paper?

HUNTER *lifts up the newspaper that Mrs Hittington has brought.*    Here — the paper. Like this. I opened it and held it —

WING    Don't open it!

HUNTER    Why not?

WING    I can't see you if you do.

HUNTER *leaves the paper folded and merely brandishes it.*    And I had to read everything in it — word for word — from the title to the final full stop, every column, all the politics and robberies and shipping news and weddings and who has left town and who has returned —

WING    Then weren't you dreadfully shocked?

HUNTER    What about?

WING    That your great dream just petered out so feebly.

HUNTER    It was very instructive.

WING    You learned things from the paper? What?

HUNTER    That you could spend all your time reading the paper —

WING *leans across the table and snatches the paper from Hunter's hand.*    That's blasphemy! No more reading the paper today. It's blaspheming against the god of dreams who blessed us both — in a single night.

HUNTER    But I was already reading the paper in my dream. If you want to give up reading the paper —

WING    I do. I will. Out of respect for your dream.

HUNTER    And I will, out of respect for your respect. So, united, we shall lay down the paper and not hanker to know what's in it. *They ceremonially lay the paper down.* Mrs Hittington shall now remove it with the breakfast things. *He knocks twice on the door, right.*

*Enter Mrs Hittington.*

HUNTER *gesturing toward the table.*    Mrs Hittington, the time has come for you to —

MRS HITTINGTON *nods and collects the crockery on a tray. Then lifting the paper.* The paper, too — you haven't read it?

WING *loudly.*    Especially the paper, Mrs Hittington!

*Mrs Hittington starts. Then she puts the paper on the tray as well and carries it out.*

HUNTER    You were shouting. Mrs Hittington will think —

WING    In the first place, nothing at all; in the second, it leaves us as cold as your beetle specimens.

HUNTER *stretching.*    And my butterflies, which are waiting to be sorted. *He sits down at his desk, right.*

WING *going to his desk, left — sighs.*    And my books, which have to be indexed, if not actually read. *Both devote themselves to their work: Hunter bends over his butterfly collection with a magnifying glass — Wing adds titles taken from ancient tomes to his index.*

*Mrs Hittington gives two quick knocks again and enters: she brings the newspaper and lays it open on the table.*

*Hunter and Wing pay no attention.*

MRS HITTINGTON    Since you haven't read the paper, I take it you didn't need to read it?

WING *without looking up.*    No.

MRS HITTINGTON   That's what I thought. Now I understand why you were angry and ordered me to take it away.

WING *as before.*   No — you understand nothing.

MRS HITTINGTON   I've marked something with a cross. It merely expresses my opinion. I didn't want to hold back any longer. Not having said anything doesn't mean I approve. I kept quiet and will continue to keep quiet. But the cross was necessary. It's only a cross — but it should suffice. *Exit, breathing a sigh of relief.*

*Hunter lays down his butterfly case and turns round.*

HUNTER   Did you hear that? What's she blethering about — why has she brought the paper back?

WING *also turns round.*   It seems I have no option but to read the paper this morning —

HUNTER *rises and goes to the table.*   Mrs Hittington wants to draw our attention to something with a cross?

WING *at the table.*   I pick it up — *makes to pick up the paper.*

HUNTER *stopping him.*   The cross is meant to whet our appetite. Let's see what this woman — this Mrs Hittington — thinks is so important that we mustn't miss it — or else that we already knew — hence our dispensing with the damned paper.

WING *reads.*   The King and Queen dined last night with Lord and Lady —

HUNTER   You're reading above the cross — it says below: *Yesterday evening Abel Oberon returned from his trip around the world with his daughter Marjory.*

WING *innocently.*   So?

HUNTER *thoughtfully.*   That's very odd.

WING   The paper announcing it?

HUNTER   No, not that.

WING   The fact he has returned?

HUNTER    Well, he was away.

WING    So what do you think is odd?

HUNTER    That Mrs Hittington has drawn our attention to it. *They both ponder.*

WING *breaks the silence.*    What's her motive?

HUNTER    She's done it in such a — marked — way, as if she's certain —

WING    What?

HUNTER    Well — you know! *Both ponder once more.*

WING    If one thing is impossible —

HUNTER    — it's that. And yet she draws our attention to Abel Oberon , who appears to come right after the king.

WING    Perhaps she meant the king after all?

HUNTER    Then she would have put a cross against him every day, for he's in the paper every day.

WING    You're right: it must be Oberon.

HUNTER *again after a short pause.*    Why should she draw our attention to the announcement?

WING    With a familiarity she's never exhibited before.

HUNTER    And indignation, too — saying she'd kept quiet long enough and now she'd put a cross. A very thick one —

WING    Against the announcement that he'd sailed round the world.

HUNTER    Did you know that?

WING    I'm not in charge of his travel arrangements.

HUNTER    And when he returns to London is of no interest to me. *He folds the paper.* Mrs Hittington can have her paper back, and continue the next exciting instalment of the novel —

WING *putting his hand on the paper.*    Which she hasn't read yet — though she usually falls on it like a ravenous beast.

HUNTER    Because the other thing was more important?

WING    The cross — and us!

HUNTER *sits on the edge of the table, dangling his legs.*    If she's become suspicious — why has she become suspicious? If she is the only person in all of London — Mrs Hittington, landlady to Frank Hunter and Fenton Wing, two perfectly ordinary chaps, indistinguishable from thousands of others in England, who have finished their studies and are preparing for their final exams in entomology and bibliography — are you going to tell me these two — you and me — perfectly ordinary but none the worse for that — have been caught out by Mrs Hittington, and by her alone in all of London —

WING *signalling to him to refrain.*    All of London can hear you shouting. *Motioning to right.* Mrs Hittington is probably listening.

HUNTER    That's how she might have found out — there's no other way.

WING    Oh yes there is, if you're nosy. The landlady's besetting sin — snooping. It's my belief that some of them only become landladies to indulge their craving to mind other people's business. Does Mrs Hittington really have to? She's a nice pension from the Air Force since her husband's crash — trying to hoist a flag-signal on the roof of a hangar and falling on to a plane. She doesn't need the rent.

HUNTER    Think — did you always lock your desk?

WING    Now you're not so sure yourself.

HUNTER    Well?

WING    I always kept the key in my waistcoat pocket.

HUNTER    Well then!

WING   She might have used a duplicate key to open it — the fact it was locked was probably temptation enough —— and then made the unexpected discovery.

HUNTER   She reads novels, not manuscripts.

WING   Why not?

HUNTER   Because it's much harder — being hand-written — and a play at that.

WING   That's just what will have egged her on! What have we here? These two nice, unassuming lodgers that give me almost no trouble and that I see studying all day long — at night, when everyone is asleep, are they secretly — writers? And her imagination lets rip: she has a new Shakespeare living with her, she brings him his breakfast, makes his bed —

HUNTER   But there are two of us.

WING   All the more reason. Shakespeare or Bacon — or both? Who knows for sure? — Only Mrs Hittington — and she knows everything! — She read it scene by scene, as we were writing it, the morning after —

HUNTER   I consider my handwriting illegible.

WING   But she has no idea *what* you wrote.

HUNTER   The issue here is legibility — not content.

WING   Even I don't know what you wrote.

HUNTER   But you say Mrs Hittington knows everything.

WING *shaking his head.*   Don't confuse things, Frank. We've got to keep a clear head. I smell danger in the air. It could be very dangerous if we narrow our argument down to who wrote what. It's exactly fifty-fifty — equal shares, like a piano duet — we wrote it four-handed. You can't say you're the author — I can't say I'm the author — but put both together and you've got something else again, over and above the other two — and it was to promote this that we did what we did. Have we any regrets — excluding Mrs Hittington? None — except for one mistake we could have avoided.

HUNTER   A mistake? That's the first time you've mentioned a mistake.

WING   Perhaps that's too strong a word and it's not worth mentioning.

HUNTER   I really can't think what —

WING   You weren't there — it was the very last thing. Up to that point, everything we did we would do again today no differently.

HUNTER   But never will do again. Don't forget that.

WING   Never.

HUNTER   We keep to what we swore. We're no writers. Even if we were tempted once — and didn't resist the temptation — to turn our backs on dry scientific facts and brew a draught of our own. And pleasantly refreshing it was.

WING   We won't be able to stay together forever, Frank — our subjects are too different — I'll breathe my last in some dusty library — but the hours we spent doing it were hours well spent — when we took the plunge and never looked back.

HUNTER   When I'm in an exalted position, I'll teach my pupils that metamorphosis means each of them can transform themselves. First they crawl like caterpillars, then they turn into fully-fledged butterflies and fly. Each of them in their own different way. If only for a brief span — like a butterfly. As in our case. As I experienced with my friend Fenton, who is now a bent old bookworm.

WING   Only bent, Frank, when I'm oppressed by the secret.

HUNTER   Why should it oppress you?

WING   We loaded our merchandise into someone else's cart.

HUNTER   But hasn't the cart set off? I thought it was well under way — it shows no sign of stopping.

WING   But what if the coachman turns and sees what's in the cart. That's not one of mine, he'll complain — and then —

HUNTER   And then?

WING   He'll instigate enquiries.

HUNTER *laughs.* Searching for you — and me. An intensive search, high and low, on and off the record, telegraph messages and newspaper articles: who is the author? I never wrote a *Gordian Egg*. I will not have my name taken in vain! Let the perpetrator make himself known! Immediately! — Have you read that anywhere? *Slapping the paper.* Here? *Turning the pages.* All you'll find here is: Another performance at Fenwick's, tonight and every night for the foreseeable future — *Looks up.* Has he raised any objection? The Maestro? The great Abel Oberon?

WING   I'm just a bit apprehensive today.

HUNTER   You needn't be any more apprehensive today than any other day. Namely, not at all.

WING   But I am, Frank.

HUNTER   Don't be, Fenton. Forget Mrs Hittington — that's what you said yourself. Our choice of Oberon was inspired — a godsend. We couldn't have found anyone better. We looked at all the others and not one stood up to scrutiny. Only him. We could entrust our little boat to him — he was the right captain. He had so many ships at sea, he couldn't possibly think one of them wasn't part of his fleet — especially if it was seaworthy — a roaring, watertight, success story. After all, *he* has nothing but successes — and whatever is successful must be his.

WING   Yes, that all adds up — he's tacitly acknowledged it.

HUNTER   That was our great good fortune. Think, if we had got involved with some lesser light. How he would have moaned and protested if we'd used his name on the title page. He would have sued us as despicable forgers, we would have defended ourselves — but the play couldn't have established itself for it would never have even reached the stage. As it is, it was read immediately and approved — the name Oberon had simply swept aside all those obstacles that clip an unknown author's wings. There was no delay in staging it, with great actors, and it will still be running — under Abel Oberon's name — when we've long forgotten our own names. — But best not mention death, I suppose?

WING   I was thinking of — money.

HUNTER   Whose money?

WING    There's a lot of money being made when you put on a successful play. It's sold out every night at Fenwick's.

HUNTER    He'll be making a mint, and the writer gets a sizeable cut of that.

WING    Won't that be noticed?

HUNTER    Who by?

WING    The writer.

HUNTER    Abel Oberon?

WING    Even if he's not bothered about the play itself, all that money will surely make him suspicious.

HUNTER    He won't pursue that either, you needn't worry. He's far too rich to know what's his and what isn't. That's even more to our advantage, for all the earnings pouring in are simply added to the pile! — He doesn't do the bookkeeping — his publisher does — Moberly, who published it in such a fine edition. All they do is exchange cheques and receipts. Or not even that — the bank pays Oberon whatever he asks for — and Moberly covers the amount. However much — the sky's the limit — for Oberon has *carte blanche*. A trip round the world today, dinner at Buckingham Palace tomorrow. He has as much wealth as he has honours heaped on him. Abel Oberon!

WING    Yes, that's all clear — all except the cross.

HUNTER *contemptuously.*    Hittington's cross!

WING    Hittington's the one who knows the connection and says nothing — but one day she'll no longer say nothing. Even if she promised today.

HUNTER    You think she might exploit certain facts she knows —

WING    She certainly knows.

HUNTER    — and might go —

WING    She doesn't have to go far. She'll come here.

HUNTER    And demand — what?

WING   Hush-money!

HUNTER *stares at him in shock.*   And if we don't pay?

WING   She'll send an anonymous letter to the concerned party. Saying: Look what Fenwick has put on, why don't you ask who is the author. You'll be amazed.

HUNTER   And hey presto, all is revealed.

WING   He doesn't even have to go and see it.

HUNTER   Then what?

WING   He blows his top, declares a ban: Close it down, Fenwick. The game's up!

HUNTER *paces up and down.*   Before I let that happen — *He stops, clenches his fists.*

WING   You'll strangle Mrs Hittington?

HUNTER   Yes — rather murder someone who doesn't shrink from treachery than deprive thousands of the modicum of pleasure we provided for them — thousands that that two-faced double-dealer should love as her fellow human beings. I could do it in cold blood.

WING   They'd hang you for it.

HUNTER   If you're convinced it's in a good cause — isn't that worth sacrificing your life for? Wasn't that always our guiding principle? Were we trying to make money out of it? That was the first time you mentioned it. We're not after money. We're not writers. We had a spark of inspiration and it caught alight. Now it's burning bright — shall Mrs Hittington put it out, simply because she rummaged around opening our drawers with a duplicate key?

WING   Now you agree with me?

HUNTER   Beyond doubt. That explains the cross. It's a dark and silent threat, signifying: I'm on your trail. Beware. The person whose name you used is back in town. At any moment, when I think the time ripe, I can reveal all — then a thing of beauty disappears — into thin air —

WING   I'm sure she thinks we're making money from it.

HUNTER    All a brain like that can think is that you're lining your pocket. That why she's blackmailing us. The thumbscrews are on — she'll bleed us dry Fenton, and no redress.

WING    The trap is sprung, there's no way out.

HUNTER    We'll have to make her an offer. What can you raise?

WING    I can do without half my allowance, if needs be.

HUNTER    Me, too. — She won't be satisfied with that.

WING    We could pay more when we've got jobs.

HUNTER    Wait a minute. My uncle in Sussex is going to leave me a little hous by a river. I'll never be able to live there. He's ninety-two now and all he does i fish — he can't get around much any more. We'll pledge the house to Mr Hittington, she'll be happy to escape from London — *Breathes a sigh of relief –* and when she's gone, so is the threat, for ever!

WING    Forgive me if I sound a bit callous, Frank, but I could wish your uncl cashed in his chips tonight. At ninety-two that's not asking too much.

HUNTER    Yes — a life for a life. We must get rid of Mrs Hittington. *He knock twice on the door, right.*

*Enter Mrs Hittington.*

HUNTER    Mrs Hittington — *He clears his throat.*

WING *innocently.*    Sore throat again? It's this unhealthy climate. You should b living in a little house in the country.

HUNTER    Ah, Fenton, if only I could. Sit in the sun by a river —

WING    And fish. It's the only way to grow old.

HUNTER    Are you thinking of my uncle in Sussex, who's just turned ninety-two

WING    Ninety-two, Mrs Hittington. The end is near — yet still able to live wit no fear of death!

HUNTER   You live a more natural life in Sussex than here in London, more in harmony with the ebb and flow of the great cycle of being. You're afflicted by anxiety if you live in the city. You die before your time.

WING *with upturned eyes.*   If only one could live like your uncle —!

HUNTER   You're aspiring to things that are beyond your reach.

MRS HITTINGTON *firmly.*   Not beyond your friend's reach, I'd have thought.

HUNTER *taken aback.*   Not beyond his reach?

WING *likewise.*   Not beyond my reach?

MRS HITTINGTON   That would be a fine thing — Mr Oberon living in the lap of luxury, and his secretary with his nose stuck in his books, looking quite peaky, not at all what a nose should look like. Not like Mr Oberon's — bronzed from all those sea breezes — fresher than your London air.

*Hunter and Wing exchange glances.*

MRS HITTINGTON   You might well look at one another — exchange telling glances, wondering what this woman is doing poking her nose into our affairs? You might well look astonished that I didn't simply take the paper and rush off to finish the novel — today was the last instalment and it was getting very exciting. But I resisted the temptation when I brought it, *and* when I took it away.

HUNTER   We wanted to talk to you, too, Mrs Hittington. You marked our paper with —

MRS HITTINGTON   I couldn't stop myself. I did it before I remembered it wasn't my paper. Please forgive me. — Still, if that's the only blemish — if there's not a bigger black mark against justice itself — then you may as well call night everlasting day when there are no shadowy marks at all. But first let Mr Oberon prove it's not true that one man has nothing but sun and another nothing but shadow.

WING   Sun and shadow, Mrs Hittington —?

MRS HITTINGTON   Some things never change. Like rocks in the ground that no one can lift. I know that. And I know that some people move in a different world, which is a wonder to behold when you think of all the disadvantaged people. But they shouldn't leave the disadvantaged destitute. *Pointing at Wing.* You don't have Oberon's advantages. He's so high and mighty you scarcely reach to his waist. He's a giant and you're a dwarf. Even if he deigns to bend down to his underling and say: here's the book, now deliver it — the messenger still deserves his reward.

WING  The messenger's reward —?

MRS HITTINGTON  For delivering it. I'm not saying that's beneath you. Let me make that clear at once. *Raising her voice.* I consider it to be an honour and a privilege that the great writer Abel Oberon gave you his work to take to Fenwick.

WING *flabbergasted.*  But who saw me ——??

MRS HITTINGTON  Potts, of course. Potts took it from you. Potts — the door-keeper at the theatre. Potts is a cousin of my late sister-in-law's brother — and he visits me from time to time, like family do. He recognized you at once when he caught a glimpse of you through the door here. *So his secretary lives with you now? He delivered his lord and master's new play to us recently. It went down well. Mr Wing —* I'd told him your name — *will soon be basking in sunshine. Mr Oberon is not stingy — when he has a hit everyone gets a generous share of the proceeds. You won't see Mr Wing here much longer. He'll soon have his own apartment and get married to some fine lady he's met in Oberon's house. I wouldn't mind being Mr Wing! ——* I didn't tell him that nothing had changed for Mr Wing and that he was still swotting away and couldn't even think of getting married. His lord and master couldn't care less about his servant and swans around the world with his daughter, trying to find her some fabulously rich prince or other. *Jabbing the paper with her thumb.* That's what the cross was meant to indicate. A paper protest, that's all. But not without effect: I haven't seen his play yet, even though it's considered almost immoral not to have seen the egg he laid so — artfully. First let him demonstrate how to be more moral — now that he's back — and share some of his golden treasure: then I'll be moral too, and not avoid his theatricals! *Exit, closing the door noisily behind her.*

*Hunter and Wing stare after her, fixed to the spot.*

HUNTER *bursts out laughing, claps his hands.*  Mrs Hillington, Mrs Hillington!

WING *also laughing.*  We'll have to beg her forgiveness on bended knee!

HUNTER  What a low-down thing to do — suspecting her of rifling through our drawers.

WING   The relief! I could fly!

HUNTER   Winged Mercury!

WING   Oberon's messenger!

HUNTER *twirls around with Wing.*   I can't take it in, take it in, take it in!

WING   And they can't take us in either!

HUNTER   Unimaginable!

WING *letting Hunter go.*   Except for Potts.

HUNTER   What about Potts?

WING   Potts saw me.

HUNTER   So?

WING   That was the mistake I mentioned. We should have sent it by post. Not gone in person. That can be traced. We thought of everything, except for Potts turning up here —

HUNTER   He'll have forgotten all about you.

WING   But he'll come again — he's a relative.

HUNTER   Should we move out?

WING   That would be hard on Mrs Hittington.

HUNTER   And her waiting for some sign of gratitude from Oberon.

WING   We'll have to try and convince her I never was employed by him. I merely took on the job of delivering the parcel. I didn't know what was in it — let alone who had sent it. The real messenger couldn't finish the job. He saw a chance to pass it on to me, and I finished it off. I've no idea who his lord and master was. I refuse to subject myself to any lord and master. I'll not be a slave unless I can order myself around.

HUNTER *by the door, right.*   Are you in the right mood now?

WING   With a vengeance. Just watch me drive all thought of the Winged Messenger out of the Hittington sconce, as if he had never been spotted by that crazy fantasist Potts — *Breaks off.* I'll show the woman the error of her ways. Knock for her to come.

HUNTER *knocks twice.*

*Enter Mrs Hittington.*

MRS HITTINGTON *amiably.*   We almost knocked at the same time.

HUNTER   Did you want to see us?

MRS HITTINGTON   You've a visitor. A lady, asking after Mr Wing.

WING   Asking after — *He looks round at Hunter.*

HUNTER *nods.*   You — that's what Mrs Hittington said.

WING   I've never had a lady asking after me before —

HUNTER *mockingly.*   There's always a first time.

WING   I would have said — I've no secrets from you —

HUNTER   Don't plead the innocent too soon — you're about to be proved wrong.

WING   I know nothing of this lady, Frank — *To Mrs Hittington* — Does she look the sort who —? *Embarrassed gesture towards Hunter.*

MRS HITTINGTON   No, she doesn't, or I would have closed the door in her face.

WING *hopefully.*   Oldish, then?

MRS HITTINGTON   Young and beautiful and refined — I was a bit surprised myself.

WING   Surprised?

MRS HITTINGTON   At her asking after you.

WING   That will be the mistake. Ask her again and —

MRS HITTINGTON   I did ask her — twice.

WING *falls silent. Then tries again.*   And what's her name?

MRS HITTINGTON   Mr Wing — how can I interrogate a lady who chooses to come calling this early so as not to be seen? *To Hunter.* Does Mr Wing think I'm tactless?

HUNTER   Or me, if he thinks I'm staying here — *He turns towards the spiral staircase at the back.*

WING *holds him back.*   Frank — don't go! *To Mrs Hittington.* Tell her I never receive visitors alone — Maybe that will deter her.

HUNTER   So I'm to play the role of bogeyman? Thanks!

MRS HITTINGTON   If I keep her waiting, she'll come in anyway. She doesn't give the impression of being afraid.

HUNTER *to her.*   Mr Wing will see her.

*Exit Mrs Hittington.*

WING   You can't really —?

HUNTER   Leave you to it?

WING   Think me capable of meeting this lady —

HUNTER   Who's not afraid and doesn't need to give her name —

WING   Which would leave me none the wiser!

HUNTER   Fenton — do I look like I'm reproaching you? I'm not. That would be contemptible. You're quite right to keep it from me. There's a principle at stake — much more powerful than is generally supposed. Powerful enough to bring cloud-capped towers crashing down, though they seemed unshakable. Friendship. If this is how it must end, so be it. A stronger power has triumphed. Love. Don't ever let go when you're in its grip. And tell lies. They're only a protective web around the delicate core. Protect that by lying — or you're not worthy of love. You lied well and happiness beckons! — Whistle when she's gone — I'll be upstairs. *He rushes up the spiral staircase out of sight.*

*Wing stands helpless.*
*Mrs Hittington ushers in Marjory Oberon and leaves, closing the door behind her.*

MARJORY *after having a long look at Wing.* Mr — Wing?

WING *very embarrassed.* Yes — Wing —— *Hurriedly.* No — *He breaks off.*

MARJORY Not Mr Wing?

WING Yes — Wing.

MARJORY But you wanted to retract and said no?

WING By no I only meant that Wing — and Wing — *Again stops short.*

MARJORY Are there two Wings up here, then?

WING Only one Wing.

MARJORY And such a unique one that you would be hard put to — *Breaks off.* May I sit? After four or five flights of stairs.

WING I would naturally have come down if I'd known — it's easier running downstairs than up —

MARJORY *caustically.* To confer on the street?

WING Not on the street — in a café —

MARJORY Not in a café either — too much noise when you need to hear every word.

WING *drawing up a chair.* Is this chair —?

MARJORY *disdainfully.* As if this chair was of any importance — *She sits.*

WING You expressed a wish to sit.

MARJORY The least of my wishes. —— You don't know who I am?

WING *sits facing her at the table and shakes his head.*

MARJORY   I don't mean personally. From pictures in magazines. I've been photographed quite a lot — on my own and in company. You weren't tempted to have a glance?

WING *as before, shakes his head.*

MARJORY   It would have been of some use. It would have warned you against taking too big a risk. For then you would have known: Abel Oberon has a daughter. That's me. Marjory Oberon.

WING *stares at her — looks away — lets his eyes wander towards the spiral staircase as if seeking assistance —— and makes an attempt at whistling.*

MARJORY   That's the sound a snake makes when the hunter corners it. Half furious hiss — half mortal fear.

WING *stammers.*   So why are you — hunting?

MARJORY   Because I'm not afraid, Mr Wing — and come looking for my enemy in his hideout before he comes and invades my house.

WING *echoes.*   —— Invades your house?

MARJORY   To ward off the attack you're planning — I launched one first. Without my father knowing — he's asleep. I've sworn to protect that sleep, for the good of mankind — and take up a big stick and chase enemies who threaten him back into their dark corners, even if I am only a woman.

WING   Sleep is as sacred as one's daily bread —

MARJORY   And no one is going to steal a crumb from him either. I would hack off any hand that demands more than — *Falters.* — than it —— *Loudly again.* Even if I had to take an axe!

WING *instinctively drawing his hands back.*   An axe —?

MARJORY   I would be totally ruthless when my father's name is at stake. As Potts has already discovered.

WING *flinches.*   Potts —?

MARJORY    Potts the door-keeper. I got to him before daybreak. Got him out c bed and into the cold porter's office. He was still half asleep, staring at me wit a glazed look on his face — but when he heard what I'd come about, he was wid awake and his eyes were glowing. *The messenger?* He'd had a good look at him He'd be able to tell him from his twin brother, at a glance. After all, he'd brough the manuscript that Fenwick was dying to get his hands on, to be able at lon last to put on something by Abel Oberon — instead of always Burbage, wh didn't always have the magic touch. — Yes, the messenger was unforgettable – so indelibly fixed in his memory that Potts recognized him at once when h glimpsed him through a half-open door. — The trail led straight to Fenton Wing chez Hittington.

WING    I don't remember Potts —

MARJORY    It's only what Potts remembers that's important.

WING *quickly.*    But that's completely one-sided — he could be mistaken.

MARJORY    Mistaken? How?

WING    In thinking I was the messenger.

MARJORY *stops short.*    You didn't deliver the parcel to Potts?

WING    I have so many deliveries.

MARJORY *even more wide-eyed.*    You do?

WING    Connected with my studies. Parcels of books. I am — I will soon be – a librarian. Studies at an end — only the exam now. *With a forced smile.* Quit a slog!

MARJORY *sizes him up, then in a gently mocking tone.*    Even if it has not yet been established that it was you who took it to Potts, there can surely be no doubt tha you wrote the play?

WING    Who wrote the play —

MARJORY    Not Abel Oberon!

WING    Not me!

MARJORY   So who wrote it?

WING   It's hard to say in so many words. It arose —

MARJORY   Like a flower, sown by the wind, with no one to tend it, but still it grows!

WING *beaming.*   Like a flower. That's it, my dear Miss —. That's exactly how. That image expresses it to perfection. A little bit of human assistance, the merest — puff — and the ground the seed sinks into does all the rest. The same creation that created us — one feels humbled.

MARJORY *looks at him closely. Then quietly.*   It may have occurred to me to visit Potts this morning, but I still can't work out what your game is. What's behind it? What are you planning? What do you want from us?

WING   There's no plan — *Lifting the paper.* — just as there's nothing under this paper but the empty table. *Lets the paper fall.* Covered up again now — and what you saw you forget — the empty table you no longer see.

MARJORY *glances at the paper, then looks up at Wing.*   You want to forget that you usurped a name to help you out —

WING   All forgotten already —

MARJORY   So completely forgotten —

WING   Blown away.

MARJORY   — that you marked the arrival of Abel Oberon with a cross? *Prods the notice with her finger.*

WING   This cross —

MARJORY   Is not yours?

WING   No!

MARJORY   Then who marked it?

WING   Mrs Hittington.

MARJORY  The landlady?

WING  Shall I call her?

MARJORY  To tell me that she wrote the play — and sent you scurrying off to Potts with it?

WING *at a loss, falls silent.*

MARJORY *rising.*  No thank you, Mr Wing. Consider this discussion terminated. I dislike having to follow such a zigzag course. I prefer the straight and narrow — straight from Potts to you. Fearlessly — that's the only way to achieve one's goal. You think we're scared? Scared of the arrows you're about to shoot at us? We've a shield to ward them off, untarnished and impregnable. Without a scratch — so the poison you thought would be so deadly will be quite harmless. Consider your attack thwarted. Indeed, it would have been nipped in the bud and never got as far as this charade, if it hadn't been for — *Breaking off.* — But I'll leave that for another judge to decide. I don't consider myself qualified to pass judgement — and sentence. My task was simply to discover the author of this libellous smear — Mr Fenton Wing. The next step —

WING *attempts to speak.*

MARJORY  You don't have to account for yourself to me. I've already heard all your excuses — you needn't try to win time and confuse the issue even more. You've little time left: at five you are to appear before Abel Oberon. He expects you — this afternoon at five. Keep him waiting and you take your life in your hands — first steal his name, then steal his time! *She flings open the door, right, and leaves.*

*Wing wipes his brow, as if dispelling a dream. Then he goes to the spiral staircase and whistles.*
*Hunter appears above and descends, whistling a melody. He heads past Wing towards his desk.*

WING *catches him by the arm.*  I didn't have the strength to whistle sooner.

HUNTER  You know what I think.

WING  You were wrong in this case.

HUNTER  Your visitor — not mine —

WING    It was for you, Frank!

HUNTER    My name was never Wing.

WING    Nor was it always Hunter — nor I always Wing.

HUNTER    What do you mean?

WING    That once we called ourselves something else.

HUNTER    So?

WING    That someone else expects us at five o'clock this afternoon.

HUNTER *stares at him.*

WING *can only shrug.*

# ACT THREE

*Again the drawing-room of Oberon's villa. Those present: Oberon and Marjory —
Oberon in a light-grey suit and very colourful tie — a suit that, while not
exaggerated, aims to convey a youthful impression; Marjory in a discreet cocktail
dress. Both are standing at the fireplace, their eyes fixed on the clock on the
mantelpiece. Oberon even has his hand raised, as if to ward off any interruption.
The clock, flanked by two mythological figures in golden bronze, strikes in a bright,
silvery tone: one — two — three — four — five.*


OBERON *lets his hand fall. Looking at Marjory.*   Five.

MARJORY *firmly.*   He will come.

OBERON   Why are you still convinced?

MARJORY   Cowards can't stand the suspense — they're too weak.

OBERON   It looks as if he can stand it.

MARJORY   I should have told him to come at midday. By now he might have
done a bunk — into the Thames.

OBERON   You really think that's possible?

MARJORY   Anything rather than confront you.

OBERON   It will have dawned on him — after you got to him before daybreak —
that I am not of a mind to deal lightly with him.

MARJORY   I was determined to put an end to the scandal being perpetrated in
your name before another day had passed. I had sworn to find out who it was. I
was up at six —

OBERON   When I'm still fast asleep.

MARJORY   And quite right, too. You shouldn't be troubled with things I could do for you — like going to Potts.

OBERON   A stroke of genius, Marjory — picking up the scent with Potts.

MARJORY   It was the only clue — that there had been a messenger. The door-keeper sees the messenger. The door-keeper might know —

OBERON   And know he did!

MARJORY   So I couldn't miss the forger's lair and could put him on the spot before he had a chance to draw up his plan. The paper was even lying on his table — like a plan of campaign, and your position — that he intended to take by storm — marked on it in heavy pencil strokes as thick as your finger. The storm has been averted before it could break out.

OBERON   Quite right, Marjory. Military images are the only way to describe what you did. You boldly broke through the ranks of the enemy and put him to flight. So decisively that he can't even come and beg for mercy on bended knee. Where is he? It's after five?

MARJORY   Skulking behind Mrs Hittington — he was so embarrassed, the pitiful wretch tried to make out it was her plan.

OBERON   It's no surprise that crooks are so stupid they get hoist with their own petard — like this fellow taking it to Potts rather than sending it by post. But to think others are as stupid as they are — as this Fenton Wing — that was his name, wasn't it?

MARJORY   *contemptuously.*   Whatever he calls himself.

OBERON   Did he deny that as well?

MARJORY   He was going to — said he was Wing but not Wing.

OBERON   Wing but not Wing. Two Wings. One accusing the other — and the one I want to get my hands on doesn't appear. But I mustn't say who it was laid this cuckoo's egg in my unguarded nest. And Fenwick laughs to himself and Moberly laughs to himself and then they slip off and whisper to each other: the sun must have got to him in India — he wants to destroy his big success. And if I persist, they'll force me to produce whoever it was deceived me. And where is

Fenton Wing, who denies it all — at the bottom of the Thames, reduced to silence once and for all?

MARJORY *tonelessly.*   If he keeps silent —

OBERON   As you suggested he might.

MARJORY   He will have thought over the consequences of his action after I left him —

OBERON   And realized what it signified when at first light, on our first day back in London, an emissary comes with the summons to be here this afternoon at five o'clock on the dot — and not to leave before he has confessed before Moberly and Fenwick, who will be called as witnesses, the full extent of his crime, without trying to pin it on me in any shape or form.

MARJORY   Moberly and Fenwick will need to be told first.

OBERON   They will be, Marjory. I'm not afraid of the uproar that's bound to follow. Moberly and his negotiations with America — Fenwick's plan to lease another theatre. The play shall not open in any other theatre, and where it is already running, it will close at once. Whatever obstacles I encounter I shall smash to pieces. It's infuriating to think of being cheated out of one's own good name after spending a lifetime establishing it — seeing it misused to help others soar up from the depths and touch the sun, the moon and the stars that they could never have reached in their wildest dreams. *He presses the bell-button.*

MARJORY   What are you doing?

OBERON   Ringing the bell. Tobin will then appear and can summon a cab in which we shall seek out Wing.

MARJORY   Wing?

OBERON   A dead Wing or a living Wing. But if no living Wing is to be found, then we'll break open all the drawers and pigeon-holes and turn the bed upside down. We'll soon see where the manuscript is hidden. Then we take it to Moberly. And this demolition job will be the end of Fenwick, too. I'll show no mercy: I come first — then everyone else, a long way behind. I take precedence — I've earned it — and I won't descend to their level.

*Enter Tobin from rear.*

OBERON    We need a cab, Tobin. A good one. The driver must know London like the back of his hand and take the shortest route. We're in a hurry — perhaps we can catch the coward before he escapes, while he's still packing and we can — — What's the matter, Tobin?

TOBIN    *had been looking at the clock.* Forgive me. *He goes to the mantelpiece and adjusts the clock.* The time was wrong. I hadn't wound up the clock while you were away. I'll just put it right. It is exactly five o'clock.

*The clock strikes five.*

TOBIN *listening.*    That was the doorbell, too. *Starts to go off.*

OBERON *was transfixed. Now moves and calls out.*    Tobin!

TOBIN *turns.*

OBERON    We have a visitor. We're expecting him. Show him in. *To Marjory.* Should we be here? No, we're in the library — we'll come from there. *To Tobin.* Have him wait here. — Is there anything else, Tobin?

TOBIN    The cab?

OBERON    No longer needed, Tobin — now we have our visitor.

*Exit Tobin to rear.*

OBERON *already mounting the steps, left, with Marjory.*    I deliberately chose the library to appear from. *Stopping on the landing.* I shall look down on him and he shall look up to me. That establishes the correct relationship right away. *Exeunt into library.*

*Tobin opens the sliding door: enter Hunter and Wing, their gaze fixed on Tobin. Tobin gives a slight bow and closes the door again from outside.*

HUNTER *looks at Wing and exclaims.*    Brutus!

WING *in confirmation.*    From college!

HUNTER    To a T.

WING    As if he's just got down off his high horse.

HUNTER    And stopped tormenting himself with pupils who don't appreciate the finer points of poetic sublimity.

WING    If only he hadn't had that speech impediment, we wouldn't have laughed.

HUNTER    He got carried away.

WING    But he had a lisp.

HUNTER    Though he didn't hear it himself.

WING    Though we could.

HUNTER    We couldn't help it. That's why it's stamped on our memory. The speech in the Forum.

WING    Reciting that was your *pièce de résistance*.

HUNTER    I still can.

WING    Mark Anthony's lines?

HUNTER    A la Brutus.

WING    Incredible, Frank.

HUNTER    Listen, Fenton. *He takes up position with his back to the stairs, right, and declaims in a slight lisp.*

> Friends, Romans, countrymen, lend me your ears;
> I come to bury Caesar, not to praise him.
> The evil that men do lives after them,
> The good is oft interred with their bones;
> So let it be with Caesar. The noble Brutus
> Hath told you Caesar was ambitious;
> If it were so, it was a grievous fault,
> And grievously hath Caesar answer'd it.
> Here, under leave of Brutus and the rest, —
> For Brutus is an honourable man;
> So are they all, all honourable men, —
> Come I to speak in Caesar's funeral — to speak ——

*Breaking off.* What's the matter? You're looking more and more serious? The whole class used to laugh at that.

*Wing, facing Hunter and thus the stairs, has stopped smiling and is staring towards the landing, where Oberon and Marjory have appeared.*

HUNTER *turns and sees them. Somewhat embarrassed in the general silence.* Shakespeare — from *Julius Caesar* — Third Act — Scene Two ————

OBERON *nonplussed.* Yes, Shakespeare —— *To Marjory.* But why two?

HUNTER Because the first scene is the murder at the Capitol, so it stands to reason —

MARJORY Oh, do be quiet — no more Shakespeare!

HUNTER *shyly.* I forgot I was in the house of a great writer. *He steps aside.*

OBERON *to Marjory — indicating Hunter.* Is that — Wing?

MARJORY No, not that one.

OBERON The other one. — Let us go down. He hasn't come alone. Let's clarify the role of the companion first, whether we consent to that. *Pausing at some distance from Wing.* You are sufficiently well known to me — from my daughter's report. I didn't think you would turn up.

WING I didn't want to.

OBERON *bemused.* You didn't want to — yet you came. Why did you not want to?

WING I'd already said all I had to say this morning.

OBERON More of a denial than a confession — and it was only my daughter's perspicacity that saw through your behaviour. You did confess.

WING I acknowledged my part — and was only unsure whether I ought to reveal the other party. We hadn't anticipated the situation — and Frank was in the museum, looking out over the rooftops. — This is Frank. Frank Hunter. We're friends and we lodge together at Mrs Hittington's.

OBERON *somewhat disconcerted.* Where is this museum that writers use to —?

HUNTER *stepping forward.* Above our room. It's an annexe, a tower. A spiral staircase leads up to it. You can look out over the rooftops of London. All kinds of roofs: curved ones, pointed ones, dome-shaped ones, flat ones. With skylights — without skylights. Tall chimneys — low chimneys. There's nothing like it in all the world.

MARJORY Oh, do stop. Unfortunately I wasn't able to inspect them, nor do I feel any curiosity at present concerning — roofs. What was under your own roof was quite enough.

WING That was me. Not a pretty sight. I was so embarrassed. Everything seemed to be against me: as if I had presumptuously claimed to have written the play myself, without Frank.

*Oberon starts back. Marjory takes his arm.*

WING My head was spinning. Telling me that Potts was a relative of Mrs Hittington's — that Mrs Hittington had sent me scurrying to Potts with the parcel — *To Marjory.* You didn't let me draw enough breath to whistle — for then Frank would have heard me from the museum and come down and had his say. — *To Oberon.* And there would have been no need for this interview, which is only wasting your time. — If only Frank had come and said his bit. After all, I had already — testified. But Frank thought that would be best. He always knows best. He can even declaim Shakespeare — which I can't.

*Silence reigns.*

OBERON *to Marjory.* Two of them, Marjory —— *He leads her over to the fireplace and sits down in an armchair.*

MARJORY *stands upright behind him.*

OBERON *drops his eyes, shrugs — then looks at Hunter and Wing.* So let us negotiate. *Sarcastically.* What point is there in my resisting? You've already taken my name — so do take a seat — the chairs are worth much less. *He invites them to sit.*

*Hunter and Wing approach hesitantly and finally sit down.*

OBERON *beckoning Marjory to sit in the armchair beside him.*   There are two of us as well. Even if the fighting strength of an Amazon is less than that of a warrior —

MARJORY   Please don't treat me any differently.

OBERON   — the purer the steel, the sharper the sword! — I mention that lest anyone think for a moment that I might shrink — out of regard for myself —

MARJORY   Or for me!

OBERON   I am ready to make any and every sacrifice — to sacrifice myself — to ensure that the one who bears this name shall not be insulted! *He gazes at the portrait above the mantelpiece.*

MARJORY *follows his gaze — in a hushed voice.*   Abel Oberon!

*Hunter and Wing likewise look up at the portrait. All are moved to silence.*

OBERON *begins the negotiation.*   A play has been running nightly at Fenwick's — *The Gordian Egg.*

HUNTER *quickly.*   You don't like the title?

OBERON *nonplussed.*   Do I like the title —?

HUNTER   We reached an agreement on that. Wing proposed *The Egg of Columbus.* I thought that first-rate. I had suggested *The Gordian Knot.* Wing called that excellent. — But I declared his title was better — and he maintained mine was. Each of wanted to yield to the other. So we had to meet each other half-way, and called it *The Gordian Egg.*

WING   The egg alone would not have been enough, nor the knot. The plot we had contrived was a conflict that needed two strong men to resolve it — Columbus and Alexander the Great together. By logic *and* by force — for isn't that how men act?

HUNTER   So the fusing together has a deeper meaning as well.

OBERON *with great effort.*   The play that is running at Fenwick's — whatever it's called —

HUNTER   The title is immaterial, it's the production that counts. We saw the first night. It lived up to all our hopes. We were in the circle — and lucky to get in at all, for the house was immediately sold out — and all the seats at a huge premium. Your name exercises the most fabulous pull!

OBERON   Which you knew how to exploit very cleverly.

HUNTER   We had no cause to regret the choice. Only your name could have persuaded Fenwick to assemble such an outstanding team of actors. It spurred him on to produce the best that London has ever had to offer. We clapped like mad at the end.

WING   Till our hands were burning.

OBERON   And did you not wonder why I didn't appear to acknowledge your applause?

HUNTER   We really didn't think about you. We were simply happy to have seen a good play.

OBERON   And I can see you're quite pleased with yourselves.

HUNTER   But we didn't feel any entitlement to the applause.

OBERON   No — selfless in the extreme. Until it's time to settle accounts —

HUNTER *to Wing.*   Did that ever occur to you?

WING   What?

HUNTER   To make money from the applause.

WING   No more than it did to you.

HUNTER   In other words, never!

OBERON   So it's to be more of a practical sort of reckoning. In that case, I'm afraid you will be deeply disappointed. Fenwick's prowess, that you praise so highly —

HUNTER   Without justification? You mean, the performance is no longer up to scratch?

OBERON   I didn't see the première, so I couldn't compare —

HUNTER *to Wing.*   Fenton — we must go tonight. We must see for ourselves if Fenwick no longer meets expectations — if he has failed in the duty he owes to the name it bears. If we detect any kind of dereliction — even the most trivial is a crime — we shall report back here. *To Oberon.* We shall come straight from the theatre and call upon you to ban it. What they are doing is unworthy of your name. A scandal that cries out to heaven. You have the power to wipe it out. Do so!

OBERON *looks at Marjory.*

HUNTER   That would have happened already if we hadn't liked the first night. You were away, on your travels. It's in the paper today. But we would still have reached you. Through your publisher, Moberly — your butler would have told us where to cable you. Ban Fenwick, it would have said — and our signature. We would have acknowledged a flop — but not a triumph. That should be left to run unhindered.

*Tobin opens the sliding door: Eileen Moberly rushes in past him.*

EILEEN   Isn't Papa here yet? *Stopping short.* Ah — you've got visitors. Tobin didn't tell me. I didn't leave him time to.

*Tobin shrugs and closes the sliding door. Everyone has risen from their armchairs.*

EILEEN *to Marjory.*   Won't you introduce me —?

MARJORY *finally makes the introductions.*   Mr Hunter. Mr Wing. — Miss Eileen Moberly.

*Eileen sits — the others follow suit.*

EILEEN   Am I disturbing you? *To Hunter and Wing.* I'm always interrupting. Some people always come at the wrong time. I never know why. And I never ask. *To Oberon.* Didn't Papa ring to say he'd be late?

OBERON   I would have had to tell him to —

EILEEN   He's definitely coming. You couldn't have put him off. He only gave me hints — and I was to fetch him from Villa Oberon. At five. It's past five now.

MARJORY   Don't you know where you can reach him?

EILEEN   He's with Hubbard at the hotel. But he was going to leave after he spoke to me. He had to go somewhere else first — it was important — then he was going to come here.

OBERON   Perhaps this Hubbard detained him?

EILEEN   Papa is trying to escape from Hubbard. He's being pursued by him since last night. We should have had supper with him yesterday, that would have been the answer. Then he could have said what's on his mind. As it is, he rang Papa three times during the night. Said he couldn't sleep, and didn't want to sleep either — for thinking of the performance he'd seen at Fenwick's. How could anyone do it better? He said it was both a matter of principle and his ambition to put on better productions in America than he had seen done in Europe. But in this instance, there could be no improvement. It was sheer perfection — and even more miraculously, still unsurpassable after nearly a hundred and fifty performances. It made the same lasting impact as on the first night — faultless — leaving nothing to be desired. — Papa was quite exhausted at breakfast after that — though you can't blame someone who's fired up for not having the patience to wait until the next morning to get it off his chest. And he was already waiting for Papa at his office — and wouldn't let up — trying to think how to go one better than Fenwick. — In the evening Papa had to go with him to the theatre again to search for some possibility — but there isn't any. Papa is at his wit's end — why couldn't Fenwick have done Hubbard a favour and played just a little bit worse for once? But what good is despair? It's a huge deal he's making with Hubbard. He mentioned a sum — I didn't really understand. *To Oberon.* It surely can't be —?

MARJORY *quickly.*   Let's leave that to your father when he comes — *Making quick decisions.* Look, I can't give you my full attention right now — Could you take Mr Wing — Mr Wing like books — it's going to be his future profession — you could show him our library. *To Hunter.* I take it you can speak for your friend.

WING   What Frank says goes for me, too.

EILEEN *to Wing.*   I keep interrupting and people always find different ways of getting rid of me. You wanted to see the books.

WING   I do prefer looking at books than —

EILEEN   Than —?

WING   I didn't mean it that way.

EILEEN   I hope not! *Both go up the stairs, left, to the library. Exeunt.*

OBERON *to Hunter.*   It would seem it's no longer necessary for you to inspect Fenwick's spectacle. Sheer perfection — according to an expert.

HUNTER   One you can really trust?

OBERON   You can rest assured that business is booming — provided it's not halted in some other way.

HUNTER   What sort of danger could threaten Fenwick?

OBERON *flaring up.*   The danger that I —

MARJORY *placatory.*   Don't get angry.

OBERON *calmly.*   I'm simply astonished you're so sure you've achieved your object after playing what you think is an unbeatable trump card. I admit you had some right to feel confident. The scrupulous precautions you took — *Now addressing Marjory.* Here you have two young people — we now know there are two of them — one couldn't have mounted the attack by himself , not when everything had to be synchronized like clockwork. First: ascertain the most opportune moment. That turned out to be the moment I left on my travels. When I took up the Raja of Jodhpur's invitation — *He pauses to see what effect these last words have had. As none is forthcoming, he continues.* The coast was now clear in London. I was far away, reportedly diverting myself hunting tigers and riding elephants. No danger of me thwarting your plan. Cut off as I was in my Indian fairyland. Deaf and blind in a distant dreamworld. Time for action here, time for the first step. After personally making sure I had gone to the station and got on the train. One of the two was always following on my heels, like a shadow. *Turning abruptly to Hunter.* Am I right? Shall I continue?

HUNTER   Yes —

OBERON *to Marjory.*   The next day is the one they are waiting for. There's not a moment to be lost. Why wait any longer? What is there to think about? The result of their efforts is ready and waiting. With a name on the title page of someone oblivious to its misuse. They take it out of its folder — and this is the best bit —

they then take it to the rival theatre manager, who naturally swallows the bait of the big name on the front — after that you'd have had to pull his head off before he'd let go. They were good psychologists, those two — they knew all about the rivalry between Burbage and Fenwick. Otherwise why avoid Burbage, who would have taken a more critical look and bided his time. *As before, to Hunter.* Am I right? Shall I continue?

HUNTER   Yes. —

OBERON *to Marjory.*   But Fenwick was in a hurry to stage it. Purely out of self-interest. He would play his trump — at once and with a flourish. The best possible cast, signed up at once, expense no object. Inconceivable that it wouldn't work. And work it did — people in the street now imitate Fenwick's actors when they raise their hat — Fenwick takes out a lease on a second theatre — Mr Hubbard comes from New York and offers an unimaginable amount —— so they attain their objective: to enrich themselves without scruple, and then to threaten me — if I refuse to be bought off with what they offer me — for my sanction and my silence. *Again to Hunter.* Shall I continue?

HUNTER   Yes. —

OBERON *to Marjory.*   I'm an easy catch. As they worked out. The forgers also lay traps. How can I avoid their snare? One foot gets caught and you go lame. I can't escape unharmed. After all, I kept silent at first — why so long? Can I really have known nothing? People will inquire whether the Raja of Jodhpur takes a newspaper. He can't just hunt tigers. There must be a close season even for tigers. Would he not have read about it in the paper then? Maybe I wasn't at the Raja's after all. Then where was I? Where in the world does the news not get through to — and why exactly would I want to go there? *To Hunter.* Go on, say it, tell us if you know whether I was in Scotland or in India. There are two of you, after all — one will have been constantly eavesdropping on me — whether I'm about to return or still in hiding. You knew where I was hiding, didn't you?

HUNTER *in the same tone of astonishment.*   Yes. —

OBERON   Were you up on the cliffs?

MARJORY   In Scotland?!

HUNTER *as if coming to his senses.*   No —

OBERON   You said yes. You said yes to everything.

HUNTER    I wanted you to keep talking. It was so exciting. About being followed.

OBERON    But not by you?

HUNTER    By me?

OBERON    By one of the two of you.

HUNTER    You mean — Wing?

OBERON    I mean —

HUNTER *finally understanding.*    You think that we —

OBERON    I know it!

HUNTER *shaking his head — calmly.*    That's not how it was. It came about — *He drops his eyes, then looks up at Oberon.* Do you remember the first thing you wrote?

MARJORY *answering for Oberon.*    They were poems.

HUNTER    Poetry! — Like a spring bursting out of a rock, when the rock succumbs to its pressure — those subterranean urges striving towards the light — the writer's first, deep breath of pure air — poetry! A mystery to him — as he stammers, and gives it shape and form, and brings it to perfection. His supreme moment — perhaps he'll never know such creative happiness again, crystal-clear. For the spring has begun its course, it becomes a stream, babbling through woods with singing birds and rustling leaves. The stream becomes a river, with towns along its banks, polluting it and darkening its waters. It grows into a mighty waterway, embankments enclose it, constrain it, make it suitable for shipping and trade. Until it finally reaches the sea and it shakes off all its loads and shackles like an emancipated slave and pours out into the endless flux — only to be swallowed up in an infinity of salt water.

OBERON    Is that a mirror you are holding up to me?

HUNTER    It's meant to convey how we felt when we —

OBERON    Like the spring breaking through the rock, could do no other but follow its course.

HUNTER  We didn't really stop to think. Wing reads a lot of books — it's his profession. An awful lot of books. He reads words on the page like sheep eat grass. That's his pasture. Mine is entomology, that's how I earn my living — or will when I've finished my exams. I investigate the tiniest living creatures — I'm totally obsessed with it. Once, up the Amazon — I had to sign on as a porter — I discovered dragon-flies that celebrate their nuptial flight by — *Breaks off.* — Wing covers his ears when I get started, and reads out loud. So I let him read on while I prepare my insects. That way I find out what people are writing. The authors don't always bring it off as well as they'd like. Or they employ a great deal of ingenuity concealing what they had in mind. That's even more remarkable. Then I would draw Wing's attention to these conscious or unconscious omissions, and we'd get into the habit of filling in the gaps the authors had left. Finally, we found ourselves inventing our own gaps that we would then pad out. I would suggest something to Wing — Wing would suggest something back to me. That's how we got from filling in gaps to — the end product.

OBERON  And this end product, that you produced by padding out gaps — perhaps gaps in my work, too — you palmed off as mine.

HUNTER  There were various reasons for that. Naturally we had noticed that you weren't too particular any more about what you were offering the public. And we saw why. Fame demands total involvement. You can't be expected to indulge yourself by keeping up the output as well. When you're in the spotlight, as you are, you've other obligations to your fellow-men. And more than one light — a dazzling sea of lights — so you don't see where this one or that one is coming from, whether or not it's a lamp you lit with your own hand. Each spark of light is swallowed up like droplets in a cloud hanging over some soaring Olympian summit. Impossible to cast your eyes down and distinguish what's happening far below.

OBERON  I could distinguish very well. The first day I got back I instigated enquiries —

HUNTER *laughing.*  That was poor Wing. *To Marjory.* You really put him on the rack. He's the weaker partner. He reads too much. Insects keep you on your toes. I don't think I would have let you hurry off, only half in the picture, after you had climbed those four flights of stairs to reach us. But it was Wing who received you — I went up into the museum so as not to disturb his tryst. That's what I was sure it was — little did I know what was coming.

MARJORY  What was coming was the discovery you dreaded.

HUNTER   Just so. But weren't we right to dread that Mr Oberon would ban any further performances? *To Oberon.* But no ban appeared in the papers.

*Tobin opens the sliding door.*

TOBIN   Mr Moberly.

MARJORY *to Oberon, quickly making up her mind.*   I'll take Moberly into the conservatory. *Exit through lacquered door; Tobin shuts it behind her.*

*Oberon has risen and leans against the mantelpiece.*
*Hunter stands beside his armchair.*

OBERON   I may not have told the papers yet — but a call to Fenwick will suffice — which I've also put off — besides, my publisher Moberly can take care of that, now he's arrived.

HUNTER *horrified.*   You're going to let Mr Moberly in on it?

OBERON   The opportunity presents itself. Where's your courage now? Afraid of Moberly?

HUNTER   I was just reminded of the shock we had this morning, when we suspected Mrs Hittington knew all. We put the wrong construction on the cross she had marked in our newspaper. Afterwards she confessed that Potts was a relative of hers and had spotted Wing in her house. So then she had Wing down as your secretary, a badly paid one at that, while you were off travelling round the world. She held that against you. We could laugh again, the danger had passed. But now Moberly is to find out — Moberly, who will never understand, can never understand ——??

OBERON   It will have to be explained to him —

HUNTER *fervently.*   You're asking too much of him. He produces nice books, but he doesn't write them. I'm not underestimating that — I never would. It deserves respect. But you can't mix oil and water. When the oil has ignited, you mustn't put water on the flame. Don't put out the light. It burns bright every night at Fenwick's and dispels the darkness. Must it be snuffed out?

OBERON   And you expect me to —

HUNTER    Yes, send him away. He's chosen a bad moment to come. You are still undecided. It's all still too new. You haven't had time yet to reach a heartfelt decision. Time will tell. Give yourself time. Leave town — embark on a trip!

[...]

# MHRA New Translations

The guiding principle of this series is to publish new translations into English of important works that have been hitherto imperfectly translated or that are entirely untranslated. The work to be translated or re-translated should be aesthetically or intellectually important. The proposal should cover such issues as copyright and, where relevant, an account of the faults of the previous translation/s; it should be accompanied by independent statements from two experts in the field attesting to the significance of the original work (in cases where this is not obvious) and to the desirability of a new or renewed translation.

Translations should be accompanied by a fairly substantial introduction and other, briefer, apparatus: a note on the translation; a select bibliography; a chronology of the author's life and works; and notes to the text.

Titles will be selected by members of the Editorial Board and edited by leading academics.

Alison Finch
General Editor

## Editorial Board

Professor Malcolm Cook (French)
Professor Alison Finch (French)
Professor Ritchie Robertson (Germanic)
Dr Mark Davie (Italian)
Dr Stephen Parkinson (Portuguese)
Professor David Gillespie (Slavonic)
Dr Duncan Wheeler (Spanish)
Dr Jonathan Thacker (Spanish)

# For details of how to order please visit our website at:
www.translations.mhra.org.uk

Lightning Source UK Ltd.
Milton Keynes UK
UKOW06f0602070616

275768UK00003B/13/P